Margaret C. Moran
W. Frances Holder

AP* SUCCESS

Governmer
& Politic

3rd edition

THOMSON

PETERSON'S

Australia • Canada • Mexico • Singapore • Spain • United Kingdom • United States

THOMSON

PETERSON'S

Corporation and Peterson's

.2 billion, The Thomson Corporation (www.thomson.com) is a leading global provider of integrated
r business, education, and professional customers. Its Learning businesses and brands
.com) serve the needs of individuals, learning institutions, and corporations with products and
ional and distributed learning.

e Thomson Corporation, is one of the nation's most respected providers of lifelong learning online
eference guides, and books. The Education Supersite[SM] at www.petersons.com—the Internet's
education resource—has searchable databases and interactive tools for contacting U.S.-accredited
ams. In addition, Peterson's serves more than 105 million education consumers annually.

idi Sheehan.

gn, Inc.

n, contact Peterson's, 2000 Lenox Drive, Lawrenceville, NJ 08648;
d us on the World Wide Web at www.petersons.com/about.

5 4 3 2 1   05 04 03 02

CONTENTS

Quick Reference Guide.. v

Key Supreme Court Cases vii

Red Alert **1**
    10 Strategies for Acing the Test 1
    10 Facts about the AP U.S. Government & Politics Test 3
    Scoring High on the AP U.S. Government & Politics Test 7
    Practice Plan for Studying for the AP U.S. Government & Politics Test .. 11
    The Panic Plan 15
    Why Take the Diagnostic Test?...................................... 17

Diagnostic Test **19**
    Section I... 20
    Section II.. 33
    Answers and Explanations 34
    Suggestions for Free-Response Essay 1 48
    Suggestions for Free-Response Essay 2 49
    Suggestions for Free-Response Essay 3 50
    Suggestions for Free-Response Essay 4 51
    Self-Evaluation Rubric for the AP Essays 52

Chapter 1 Strategies for Multiple-Choice Questions.................. 55
    Practice Plan 55
    Basic Information about the Test.................................... 56
    Pacing 59
    Analyzing Questions... 60
    Educated Guessing 64
    Practice Set 1 65
    Answers and Explanations 67
    Practice Set 2 69
    Answers and Explanations 72
    Practice Set 3 75
    Answers and Explanations 77

Chapter 2 About Writing the Essays 79
    Practice Plan 79
    Basic Information about the Essay Section 80
    Some Practical Advice 81
    The Essay: A Quick Review 81
    Writing an Outstanding Essay....................................... 81
    What to Expect in the AP Essays 85
    Planning and Writing the Essays 88
    A Word of Caution... 90
    A Word of Encouragement 90
    Understanding the Directions....................................... 91
    Practice Essay 1 92
    Practice Essay 2 92
    Practice Essay 3 92
    Practice Essay 4 93
    Suggestions for Practice Essays..................................... 94
    Self-Evaluation Rubric for the AP Essays 103

CONTENTS

Chapter 3 Constitutional Foundation of the Federal Government ... **105**
Section 1. Theories of Government.................................. 105
Section 2. Adopting the Constitution 107
Fast Facts about the Constitution................................ 115
Section 3: Form of Government................................... 121

Chapter 4 Institutions of the Federal Government: Congress, the Presidency, the Bureaucracy, the Judiciary **129**
Section 1: Congress 131
Section 2: The Presidency.. 143
Section 3: The Federal Bureaucracy.............................. 149
Section 4: The Federal Judiciary................................. 153

Chapter 5 Political Behavior and Political Groups **159**
Section 1: Political Behavior, Public Opinion, and the
Mass Media 159
Section 2: Interest Groups, Political Parties, and Elections 163

Chapter 6 The Public Policy Agenda **169**
Section 1: Economic Policy....................................... 169
Section 2: Social and Domestic Policy............................ 173
Section 3: Foreign and Defense Policy 176

Chapter 7 Civil Liberties and Civil Rights........................ **179**
Section 1: Civil Liberties 179
Section 2: Civil Rights 184

Glossary of Terms................................. **195**

Practice Test 1 .... **211**
Section I 212
Section II... 224
Answers and Explanations 225
Suggestions for Free-Response Essay 1 240
Suggestions for Free-Response Essay 2 241
Suggestions for Free-Response Essay 3 242
Suggestions for Free-Response Essay 4 244
Self-Evaluation Rubric for the AP Essays 245

Practice Test 2 .... **247**
Section I 248
Section II... 261
Answers and Explanations 262
Suggestions for Free-Response Essay 1 277
Suggestions for Free-Response Essay 2 278
Suggestions for Free-Response Essay 3 279
Suggestions for Free-Response Essay 4 281
Self-Evaluation Rubric for the AP Essays 283

Practice Test 3 .... **285**
Section I 286
Section II... 299
Answers and Explanations 301
Suggestions for Free-Response Essay 1 319
Suggestions for Free-Response Essay 2 321
Suggestions for Free-Response Essay 3 323
Suggestions for Free-Response Essay 4 324
Self-Evaluation Rubric for the AP Essays 325

Answer Sheets................................. **327**

QUICK REFERENCE GUIDE

	PAGE
Analyzing Multiple-Choice Questions	60
Basic Information about the Test	56
Educated Guessing: A Helpful Technique	9
The Essay: A Quick Review	81
Fast Facts about the U.S. Constitution	115

Quick Guide to the Information Graphics

Establishing a New Nation	109
Articles of Confederation	111
Working Out Compromises	112
Provisions of the U.S. Constitution	116
Expansion of the Franchise	119
Dual Federalism: Parts 1 and 2	122
System of Checks and Balances	126
Comparison of the Branches of the Federal Government	130
How a Bill Becomes a Law	141
Iron Triangles (Subgovernments)	152
Federal Court System	154
Some Important Civil Rights Legislation	190

Scoring Overview	7
What to Expect in the AP Essays	85
Writing an Outstanding Essay	81

5 IMPORTANT STRATEGIES

1. Highlight the key words in the question so you will know what you are looking for in the answer choices.

2. With a *not/except* question, ask yourself if an answer choice is true about the subject of the question. If it IS true, cross it off and keep checking the remaining answer choices.

3. If you aren't sure about an answer but know something about the question, eliminate what you know is wrong and make an educated guess.

4. All parts of an answer choice must be correct for the answer to be correct.

5. For a tiered or multistep question, decide what the correct answer is and then determine which answer choice contains ONLY that answer.

Be sure to review all of the answers in the *Answers and Explanations* for the practice tests. They contain additional information about the principles and practices of U.S. government and politics.

	PAGE
Multiple-choice *Practice Sets* in Chapter 1	65
Practice Essays in Chapter 2	92
Diagnostic Test	19
Practice Test 1	211
Practice Test 2	247
Practice Test 3	285

KEY SUPREME COURT CASES

The following Supreme Court cases are discussed in some detail in the review chapters or in the *Answers and Explanations* for the *Diagnostic Test* and the *Practice Tests*. Knowing about these cases may help you answer essay questions if you need to use examples to illustrate your points.

Affirmative Action   PAGE
Regents of the University of California v. *Bakke* (1978) 46, 72, 186

Gender Discrimination
Reed v. *Reed* (1971) 36, 187

Line-Item Veto
Clinton v. *City of New York* (1998) 147

Nationalization of the Bill of Rights
Gitlow v. *New York* (freedom of speech, 1925) 179

Mapp v. *Ohio* (exclusionary rule, 1961) 182, 237

Gideon v. *Wainwright* (right to counsel, 1963) 182

Miranda v. *Arizona* (right to counsel and to remain silent, 1966) 183

Principle of Soverignty of the Federal Government/Interstate Commerce
Gibbons v. *Ogden* (1824) 135

Principle of Implied Powers
McCulloch v. *Maryland* (1819) 135

Principle of Judicial Review
Marbury v. *Madison* (1803) 156, 228

Redistricting/Racial Gerrymandering
Abrams v. *Johnson* (1997) 133

Baker v. *Carr* (1962) 132

Bush v. *Vera* (1996) 133

Easley v. *Cromartie* (2001) 133

Miller v. *Johnson* (1995) 133

Shaw v. *Reno* (1993) 133

Shaw v. *Hunt* (1997) 133

Wesberry v. *Sanders* (1964) 132, 225, 274

Right to Privacy
Griswold v. *Connecticut* (1965) 187

Roe v. *Wade* (1973) 188

Separate but Equal
Brown v. *Board of Education of Topeka, Kansas* (1954) 68, 184, 267

Plessy v. *Ferguson* (1896) 184, 262

10 STRATEGIES FOR ACING THE TEST

PREPARING FOR THE TEST

1. Read the *AP Course Description for U.S. Government & Politics* available from the College Board and the *10 Facts About the AP U.S. Government & Politics Test* on pages 3–6 in this book.

2. Choose your Practice Plan from pages 11–16 in this book.

3. Choose a place and time to study every day. Stick to your routine and your plan.

4. Even though they are time-consuming, complete the *Diagnostic* and *Practice Tests* in this book. They will give you just what they promise: practice—practice in reading and following the directions, practice in pacing yourself, practice in understanding and answering multiple-choice questions, and practice in writing timed essays.

5. Complete all your assignments for your regular AP U.S. Government class. Ask questions in class, talk about what you read and write, and enjoy what you are doing. The test is supposed to measure your development as an educated and analytical reader and writer.

THE NIGHT BEFORE THE TEST

6. Assemble what you will need for the test: your admission materials, four number 2 pencils, two pens, a watch (without an alarm), and a healthy snack for the break. Put these items in a place where you will not forget them in the morning.

7. Don't cram. Relax. Go to a movie, visit a friend—but not one who is taking the test with you. Get a good night's sleep.

THE DAY OF THE TEST

8. Wear comfortable clothes. If you have a lucky color or a lucky piece of clothing or jewelry, wear it—as long as you won't distract anyone else. Take along a lucky charm if you have one.

9. If you do not usually eat a big breakfast, this is not the morning to change your routine, but it is probably a good idea to eat something nutritious if you can.

10. If you feel yourself getting anxious, concentrate on taking a couple of deep breaths. Remember, you don't have to answer all the questions, you can use EDUCATED GUESSES, and you don't have to write four perfect essays.

10 FACTS ABOUT THE AP U.S. GOVERNMENT & POLITICS TEST

1. THE AP PROGRAM OFFERS HIGH SCHOOL STUDENTS AN OPPORTUNITY TO RECEIVE COLLEGE CREDIT FOR COURSES THEY TAKE IN HIGH SCHOOL.

The AP program is a collaborative effort of secondary schools, colleges and universities, and the College Board through which students like you who are enrolled in AP or honors courses in any one or more of nineteen subject areas may receive credit or advanced placement for college-level work completed in high school. While the College Board makes recommendations about course content, it does not prescribe content. The annual testing program ensures a degree of comparability among high school courses in the same subject.

2. MORE THAN 2,900 COLLEGES AND UNIVERSITIES PARTICIPATE.

Neither the College Board nor your high school awards AP credit. You need to find out from the colleges to which you are planning to apply whether they grant credit and/or use AP scores for placement. It is IMPORTANT that you obtain each school's policy IN WRITING so that when you actually choose one college and register, you will have proof of what you were told.

3. THE AP U.S. GOVERNMENT & POLITICS TEST MEASURES FACTUAL KNOWLEDGE AND A RANGE OF SKILLS.

In the course description for AP U.S. Government & Politics, the College Board lists five areas of skills and abilities that the test measures. The list covers

- factual knowledge: facts, concepts, and theories of U.S. government.

- comprehension of the typical patterns of political processes and behaviors and their effects.

- analysis and interpretation of governmental and political data and of relationships in government and politics.

- the ability to interpret in writing a variety of topics in U.S. government and politics.

- the ability to craft well-organized and specific essays.

4. THE AP U.S. GOVERNMENT & POLITICS TEST HAS TWO SECTIONS: MULTIPLE CHOICE AND A FOUR-PART ESSAY SECTION.

Study Strategy

See Chapter 1 for multiple-choice strategies and Chapter 2 for strategies to use in writing your essays.

The total test is 2 hours and 25 minutes. Section I: Multiple Choice has 60 questions and counts for 50 percent of your total score. You will have 45 minutes to complete it.

In Section II, you are given four essay topics to write about. Unlike the old government test or some of the other AP tests, you have no choice about which four essays you will respond to. This part of the test is 100 minutes (1 hour and 40 minutes) and counts for 50 percent of your total score.

5. THE AP U.S. GOVERNMENT & POLITICS TEST COVERS SIX AREAS OF AMERICAN GOVERNMENT AND POLITICS.

Study Strategy

See Chapters 3-7 for a brief review of U.S. government and politics.

In its course description for the AP U.S. Government & Politics test, the College Board lists six broad areas of study and twenty-three categories that are further broken down. The basic course outline looks like the following:

- Constitutional Basis of the Government

  - Influences on the Framers of the Constitution

  - Separation of powers/checks and balances

  - Concept of federalism

  - Theories of democratic government

- Political Beliefs and Behaviors of Individuals

  - Basic political beliefs that individuals hold

  - Ways people acquire political knowledge and attitudes

  - Factors that influence how and why people develop different political beliefs and behaviors

  - Methods of political participation, including voting

  - Public opinion

- Political Behavior of Groups: Functions, Activities, Sources of Power, Influences

  - Political parties

  - Interest groups, including PACs

  - The mass media

  - Elections

- National Government: Organization, Functions, Activities, Interrelationships

    - Presidency

    - Congress

    - Federal judiciary

    - Federal bureaucracy

    - Role of voters, nongovernmental groups, and public opinion

- Public Policy

    - How policy is made and by whom

    - How policy is implemented: the role of the bureaucracy and the courts

    - Influences: political parties, interest groups, voters, and public opinion

- Civil Rights and Civil Liberties

    - Constitutional guarantees

    - Role of judicial interpretation

    - Impact of the Fourteenth Amendment

In designing the test, the test writers allot a certain percentage of questions to each broad area. Note that one question may actually ask you about several areas because topics may overlap. For example, a question about civil rights might involve the role of the federal judiciary and the Constitution. The following list shows the range of questions that might appear on an AP U.S. Government & Politics test:

- Constitutional Basis of the Government—5 to 15 percent

- Political Beliefs and Behaviors of Individuals—10 to 20 percent

- Political Behavior of Groups: Functions, Activities, Sources of Power, Influences—10 to 20 percent

- National Government: Organization, Functions, Activities, Interrelationships—35 to 45 percent

- Public Policy—5 to 15 percent

- Civil Rights and Civil Liberties—5 to 15 percent

As you can see, the largest number of questions (between 21 and 27), will deal with the institutions of the national government.

6. THERE IS NO REQUIRED LENGTH FOR YOUR ESSAYS.

It is the quality, not the quantity, that counts. Realistically, a one-paragraph essay is not going to garner you a high score because you cannot develop a well-reasoned analysis and present it effectively in one paragraph. An essay of five paragraphs is a good goal. By following this model, you can set out your ideas with an interesting beginning, develop a reasoned middle, and provide a solid ending.

7. YOU WILL GET A COMPOSITE SCORE FOR YOUR TEST.

Test-Taking Strategy

See "Scoring High on the AP U.S. Government & Politics Test," pp. 7–8.

The College Board reports a single score from 1 to 5 for the two-part test, with 5 being the highest. By understanding how you can balance the number of questions you need to answer correctly against the essay score you need to receive in order to get at least a "3," you can relieve some of your anxiety about passing the test.

8. EDUCATED GUESSING CAN HELP.

No points are deducted for questions that go unanswered on the multiple-choice section, and don't expect to have time to answer them all. A quarter of a point is deducted for wrong answers. The College Board suggests guessing IF you know something about a question and can eliminate a couple of the answer choices. Call it "educated guessing." You'll read more about this on page 9.

9. THE TEST IS GIVEN IN MID-MAY.

Most likely the test will be given at your school, so you do not have to worry about finding a strange building in a strange city. You will be in familiar surroundings, which should reduce your anxiety a bit. If the test is given somewhere else, be sure to take identification with you.

10. STUDYING FOR THE TEST CAN MAKE A DIFFERENCE.

Study Strategy

Stop first at pp. 11–16 and read "Practice Plan for Studying for the AP U.S. Government & Politics Test."

The first step is to familiarize yourself with the format and directions for each part of the test. Then, you will not waste time on the day of the test trying to understand what you are supposed to do. The second step is to put those analytical skills you have been learning to work, dissecting and understanding the kinds of questions you will be asked; and the third step is to practice "writing on demand" for the essays. So turn the page, and let's get started.

SCORING HIGH ON THE AP U.S. GOVERNMENT & POLITICS TEST

Around early July, you and the colleges you designate will receive a single composite score from 1 to 5, with 5 being the highest, for your AP U.S. Government & Politics Test, and your high school will receive its report a little later. The multiple-choice section is graded by machine, and your essays are graded during a marathon reading session by high school and college teachers.

A different reader scores each of your essays. None of the readers know who you are (that's why you fill in identification information on your Section II booklet and then seal it) or how the others scored your other essays. The grading is done on a holistic system; that is, the overall essay is scored, not just the development of your ideas, your spelling, or your punctuation. For each essay, the College Board works out grading criteria for the readers to use, much as your teacher uses a rubric to evaluate your writing.

WHAT THE COMPOSITE SCORE MEANS

The College Board refers to the composite score as weighted because a factor of 1.0000 for the multiple-choice section and a factor of 3.1579 for the four free response essays are used to determine a raw score for each section of the test. That is, the actual score you get on the multiple-choice questions—say 48—is multiplied by 1.0000. The actual score you get on the four essays—say 30 out of a possible 36—is multiplied by 3.1579. This number and the weighted score from the multiple-choice section are added and the resulting composite score—somewhere between 0 and 180—is then equated to a number from 5 to 1.

WHAT DOES ALL THIS MEAN TO YOU?

Without going into a lot of math, it means that you can leave blank or answer incorrectly some combination of multiple-choice questions that give you 36 correct answers and write four reasonably good essays and get at least a 3. Remember that a majority of students fall into the 3 range, and a 3 is good enough at most colleges to get you college credit or advanced placement. A score of 4 certainly will. It takes work to raise your score a few points, but it is not impossible. Sometimes, the difference between a 3 and a 4 or a 4 and a 5 is only a couple of points.

The highest score you can receive on an essay is a 9, and all four essays are worth the same percentage (25 percent) of your total Section II score. It is possible to get a variety of scores on your essay—7, 5, 5, 6, for example, The chances are that you will not get a wide range of individual essay scores like 6, 2, 5, 3. Even if you did, you could still get at least a 3 and possibly a 4, depending on how many correct answers you have in the multiple-choice section balanced against how many wrong answer you have.

AP Grade	AP Qualifier	Composite Scores	Probability of Receiving Credit
5	Extremely Well Qualified	117–180	Yes
4	Well Qualified	96–116	Yes
3	Qualified	79–95	Probably
2	Possibly Qualified	51–78	Rarely
1	No Recommendation	0–50	No

According to the College Board, more than 60 percent of the 57,000 students who took the test in a recent year received at least a 3. The cut-off points for categories may change from year to year, but it remains in this range. (You should check with the college to which you plan to apply. At the time of printing, one college has changed its policy to require a score of at least a 4.) This chart shows the actual conversion scale in a recent year. What it means is that you neither have to answer all the questions, nor do you have to answer them all correctly, nor write four "9" essays to receive AP credit.

EDUCATED GUESSING: A HELPFUL TECHNIQUE

You may be concerned about guessing when you are not sure of the answer or when time is running out. We have more to say about pacing in Chapter 1, but even the College Board recommends guessing IF you know something about the question and can eliminate one or more of the answer choices. But we call it "educated guessing." Here are some suggestions for making an educated guess:

- Ignore answers that are obviously wrong.

- Discard choices in which part of the response is incorrect. Remember that a partially correct answer is a partially incorrect answer—and a quarter-point deduction.

- Reread the remaining answers to see which seems the most correct.

- Choose the answer that you feel is right. Trust yourself. Your subconscious usually will guide you to the correct choice. Do not argue with yourself. This works, though, only IF you know something about the content of the question to begin with.

You may still be concerned about the quarter-point deduction, known as the "guessing penalty," for an incorrect answer, and you are wondering if taking a chance is worth the possible point loss. We are not advocating guessing, but we are advocating making an educated guess. Recognize that if you use this technique, your chances of increasing your score are very good. You will have to answer four questions incorrectly to lose a single point, yet one correct educated guess will increase your score by 1 point. IF you know something about the question and can eliminate one or more answer choices, why not act on your idea?

Test-Taking Strategy

There is no penalty for unanswered questions, but an unanswered question won't get you any points either.

Some Reminders about the AP U.S. Government & Politics Test

Here are three important ideas to remember about taking the test:

Study Strategy

See Chapter 1 for strategies.

1. It is important to spend time practicing the kinds of questions that you will find in the multiple-choice section because 50 percent of your score comes from that section. You do not have to put all your emphasis on the essay questions.

Study Strategy

See Chapter 1 for more on pacing.

2. You can leave some questions unanswered and still do well. Even though you will be practicing how to pace yourself as you use this book, you may not be able to complete all 60 questions on the day of the test. If you come across a really difficult question, you can skip it and still feel that you are not doomed to receive a low score.

3. There is a guessing penalty. If you do not know anything about a question or the answer choices, do not take a chance. However, if you know something about the question and can eliminate one or more of the answer choices, then it is probably worth your while to choose one of the other answers. Use EDUCATED GUESSING. Even the College Board advises this strategy.

PRACTICE PLAN FOR STUDYING FOR THE AP U.S. GOVERNMENT & POLITICS TEST

The following plan is worked out for nine weeks. The best study plan is one that continues through a full semester. Then, you have time to think about ideas and to talk with your teacher and other students about what you are learning, and you will not feel rushed. Staying relaxed about the test is important. A full-semester study plan also means that you can apply what you are learning here to class work—your essay writing—and apply your class work—everything that you are reading—to test preparation. The plan is worked out so that you should spend 2 to 3 hours on each lesson.

Week 1

First: Take the *Diagnostic Test,* pp. 19–33, and complete the self-scoring process.

List the areas that you had difficulty with, such as timing, question types, or writing on demand.

Then: Reread pp. 3–8 about the basic facts of the test and its scoring.

Divide Chapters 3 and 4 into sections of about ten pages each. Read a section or a chapter each week for weeks 2–8.

Week 2

Lesson 1
- Read "Top 10 Strategies for Acing the Test," p. 1.
- Reread "Scoring High on the AP U.S. Government & Politics Test," pp. 7–8.
- Review the list you made after the Diagnostic Test to see what you need to learn in order to do well on the multiple-choice section.
- Read Chapter 1, "Strategies for the Multiple-Choice Questions," pp. 55–78.
- Do one set of practice questions at the end of the chapter, and review the explanation of the answers.

Lesson 2
- Review Chapter 1, "Strategies for Multiple-Choice Questions," pp. 55–78, and do another set of practice questions at the end of the chapter.
- Review the answers for these practice questions.
- Read half of Chapter 3, "Constitutional Foundation of the Federal Government," and find out more about any of the terms and concepts that are unfamiliar to you.

Week 3

Lesson 1
- Read "Top 10 Strategies for Acing the Test," p. 1.

- Reread "Scoring High on the AP U.S. Government & Politics Test," pp. 7–8.

- Review Chapter 1, "Answering the Multiple-Choice Questions," pp. 55–78.

- Review the list you made after the *Diagnostic Test* to see what you need to learn about the multiple-choice section.

- Do the last set of practice questions at the end of the chapter, and review the answers.

Lesson 2
- Finish reading Chapter 3, and find out more about any of the terms or concepts that are unfamiliar to you.

Week 4

Lesson 1
- Read Chapter 2, "About Writing the Essays," pp. 79–104.

- Answer the first *Practice Essay* at the end of the chapter.

- Complete the self-scoring process, and compare your score against your score on the *Diagnostic Test.*

- Ask a responsible friend, an AP classmate, or a teacher to evaluate your essay against the scoring guide. Where did you improve from the *Diagnostic Test*? What still needs improvement?

Lesson 2
- Read half of Chapter 4, "Institutions of the Federal Government: Congress, the Presidency, the Bureaucracy, the Judiciary." Find out more about any of the people, terms, or concepts that are unfamiliar to you.

Week 5

Lesson 1
- Reread Chapter 2, "About Writing the Essays," pp. 79–104.

- Write the second *Practice Essay.*

- Complete the self-scoring process, and compare the score with your score on the *Diagnostic Test* essays.

- Ask a responsible friend, an AP classmate, or a teacher to evaluate your essay against the scoring guide.

Lesson 2
- Finish reading Chapter 4 and find out more about any people, terms, or concepts that are unfamiliar to you.

Week 6

Lesson 1
- Answer the multiple-choice section of Practice Test 1 and complete the self-scoring process.

- Compare the score to your score on the *Diagnostic Test.* Which question types continue to be a concern?

- Reread Chapter 1, "Strategies for Multiple-Choice Questions," as needed.

- Read Chapter 5, "Political Behavior and Political Groups," and find out more about any people, terms, or concepts that are unfamiliar to you.

Lesson 2
- Complete the essays on *Practice Test 1,* and score your essay against the rubric.

- Again, ask a responsible friend, an AP classmate, or a teacher to evaluate your essay against the scoring guide.

- Compare your scores to the scores on the *Diagnostic Test.* Where did you improve? Where does your writing still need work?

Week 7

Lesson 1
- Write essays for *Practice Essays 3* and *4* in Chapter 2. Score your essays against the rubric.

- Ask a responsible friend, an AP classmate, or a teacher to evaluate your essays on the scoring guide as well. Compare these scores to your scores on the Diagnostic Test.

- Reread Chapter 2 as needed.

Lesson 2
- Read Chapter 6, "The Public Policy Agenda," and find out more about any people, terms, or concepts that are unfamiliar to you.

Week 8

Lesson 1
- Read Chapter 7, "Civil Liberties and Civil Rights," and find out more about any people, terms, or concepts that are unfamiliar to you.

- Answer the multiple-choice section of *Practice Test 2* and complete the self-scoring process.

- Compare the score to your score on the *Diagnostic Test.* Are there any question types that continue to be a concern?

- Reread Chapter 1, "Strategies for Multiple-Choice Questions," as needed.

Lesson 2
- Write the essays in *Practice Test 2,* and complete the self-scoring process.

- Compare the score to your scores for the two tests.

Week 9

Lesson 1
- Take *Practice Test 3* in one sitting and complete the self-scoring process. Check your results against the other three tests.

Lesson 2
- If you are still unsure about some areas, review those chapters and the practice activities.

- Read through the *Glossary* and the notes you made on the people, terms, and concepts you were not sure about.

- Reread "Scoring High on the AP U.S. History Test," pp. 7–8, and "Top 10 Strategies for Acing the Test," p. 1.

THE PANIC PLAN

Eighteen weeks, nine weeks, how about two weeks? If you are the kind of person who puts everything off until the last possible minute, here is a two-week Panic Plan. Its objectives are to make you familiar with the test format and directions, to help you get as many right answers as possible, and to write the best free-response essays you can.

Week 1
- Read "Top 10 Strategies for Acing the Test," p. 1, and "Scoring High on the AP U.S. Government & Politics Test," pp. 7–8.

- Take the *Diagnostic Test*. Read the directions carefully and use a timer for each section.

- Complete the self-scoring process. You can learn a lot about the types of questions in the multiple-choice section—and review important information about government—by working through the answers.

- Read Chapter 3, "Constitution Foundation of the Federal Government," pp. 105–128.

Multiple Choice
- Answer the multiple-choice section on *Practice Test 1*.

- Complete the self-scoring process, and see where you may still have problems with question types.

- Read all the answer explanations, including those you identified correctly.

- Now read Chapter 1, "Strategies for Multiple-Choice Questions," paying particular attention to any question types that were difficult for you to answer.

Essays
- Complete Section II on *Practice Test 1*.

- Score your essays using the rubric. List your weaknesses.

- Read Chapter 2, "About Writing the Essays."

- Write two *Practice Essays* from Chapter 2.

- Score your essays against the rubric, noting areas for improvement.

- Ask a responsible friend, an AP classmate, or a teacher to evaluate your essays on the scoring guide as well. Compare it to your score on the *Diagnostic Test*.

Week 2
- Reread "Top 10 Strategies for Acing the Test," p. 1, and "Scoring High on the AP U.S. Government & Politics Test," pp. 7–8.

- Complete *Practice Test 2* and score the multiple-choice and essay sections. Score the essays against the rubric.

- Compare your scores with those from the *Diagnostic Test* and *Practice Test 1*.

- Read Chapters 4, 5, 6, and 7.

Multiple Choice
- Work at least two practice sets of multiple-choice questions in Chapter 1, "Strategies for Multiple-Choice Questions."

- Complete the multiple-choice section of *Practice Test 3*. Read all the answer explanations to review more information about government.

Essays
- Write the last two *Practice Essays* in Chapter 2. Ask a responsible friend, an AP classmate, or a teacher to evaluate your essays.

- If you have time, write the essays in *Practice Test 3* and score those against the rubric.

WHY TAKE THE DIAGNOSTIC TEST?

What do you know about the format and questions on the AP U.S. Government & Politics Test? If you knew all you needed to know, you probably would not be reading this book. Taking a practice test is one way to learn about the test and what it will be like taking it on the real test day. It is a long test, and you will need to pace yourself in answering the multiple-choice questions and in planning and writing your essays. Taking the *Diagnostic Test* will help you learn how much time you can spend on each item.

Practice may not make perfect, but you can improve your score with practice. The more you learn about your strengths and weaknesses in test-taking abilities and in analytical skills, and the more you work on strengthening them, the better your score.

How should you take this test? Just as though it were the real test, so that means setting aside 2 hours and 25 minutes of uninterrupted, quiet time to take the test, plus the time to score your answers.

- Make a photocopy of an answer sheet at the back of this book.

- Assemble four number 2 pencils and two pens along with the answer sheet and eight pieces of paper on which to make notes and write your essays.

- Use a timer or a stopwatch to time each section of the test.

- Follow the directions for both sections of the test—multiple choice and essay. Set your timer for the allotted time for each section.

- When you have completed the test, check how many questions you were able to answer on the multiple-choice section and how far you got in completing the essays. This information will help you in pacing yourself for the other practice tests and for the real test.

- Then, check the multiple-choice questions against the *Quick-Score Answers,* page 34.

- Read the explanation for each answer, even if your answer was correct. You might learn something you didn't know about the content of the question.

- Score each of your essays against the rubrics. Be honest in your evaluation. Knowing your weaknesses is the only way to turn them into strengths.

- Turn to the *Practice Plan* and design your study plan from now until test day.

Diagnostic Test
AP GOVERNMENT AND POLITICS

On the front page of the test booklet, you will find some information about the test. Because you have studied this book, none of it should be new to you, and much of it is similar to other standardized tests that you have taken.

The page will tell you that the following exam will take 2 hours and 25 minutes—45 minutes for the multiple-choice portion, Section I, and 100 minutes for the essay part, Section II. There are two booklets for the exam, one for the multiple-choice section and one for the essays.

The page in your test booklet will also say that SECTION I

- is 45 minutes.

- has 60 questions.

- counts for 50 percent of your total score.

Then you will find a sentence in capital letters telling you not to open your exam booklet until the monitor tells you to open it.

Other instructions will tell you to be careful when you fill in the ovals on the answer sheet. Fill in each oval completely. If you erase an answer, erase it completely. If you skip a question, be sure to skip the answer oval for it. You will not receive any credit for work done in the test booklet, but you may use it for making notes.

You will also find a paragraph about the guessing penalty—a deduction of one-quarter point for every wrong answer—but also words of advice about guessing if you know something about the questions and can eliminate several of the answers.

The final paragraph will remind you to work effectively and to pace yourself. You are told that not everyone will be able to answer all the questions and it is preferable to skip questions that are difficult and come back to them if you have time.

SECTION I	TIME—45 MINUTES	60 QUESTIONS

Directions: Each question or incomplete sentence is followed by five suggested responses. Select the best answer and fill in the corresponding oval on the answer sheet.

1. All of the following were weaknesses of the Articles of Confederation EXCEPT

   (A) nine of the thirteen states had to approve all laws.
   (B) a national court system ruled on the constitutionality of laws.
   (C) Congress worked in committees without a chief executive.
   (D) all states were required to approve amendments.
   (E) Congress could raise money by borrowing or by asking states for money.

2. Which of the following affects the political socialization of American voters as they age?

   (A) Political allegiance of their parental family
   (B) Peers
   (C) Educational level
   (D) Economic issues
   (E) Mass media

3. The Pendleton Act established

   (A) the Federal Reserve System.
   (B) the civil service system for federal jobs.
   (C) the military draft.
   (D) citizenship for Native Americans.
   (E) direct primaries.

4. The primary qualification needed to gain a top-level position in a presidential administration is

   (A) to have prior government experience.
   (B) to be a political supporter of the president.
   (C) to be an expert in a particular field.
   (D) to be able to form alliances with the opposition party in Congress.
   (E) to be able to react well under stress.

5. A major criticism of independent regulatory agencies is that

   (A) they are separate from all three branches of government.
   (B) they have both quasi-judicial and quasi-legislative functions.
   (C) the amount of regulation the agencies enforce may add to the price that consumers pay for the goods or services of regulated industries.
   (D) they write rules and regulations that have the force of law and then enforce them.
   (E) commissioners often come from the very industries they are supposed to regulate.

6. The nation's policy agenda is set by

   (A) the House.
   (B) the Senate.
   (C) a joint conference committee.
   (D) the president.
   (E) the party in power.

Question 7 refers to the following table.

Turnover in Midterm Elections

Year	President's Party	Senate: Gain/Loss for President's Party	House: Gain/Loss for President's Party
1978	D	-3	-15
1982	R	+1	-26
1986	R	-8	-5
1990	R	-1	18
1994	D	-8	-52
1998	D	0	+5

7. The above table best supports which of the following statements about off-year elections?

   (A) In 1998, the American people, sick of the Lewinsky scandal, showed their support for the president by voting out Republicans and voting in Democrats.

   (B) The party of the president generally loses seats in the midterm election.

   (C) The shift in voting pattern between 1994 and 1998 shows the fickleness of the American voter.

   (D) The Democrats lost twice as many seats in Congress in 1994 as the Republicans did in 1982.

   (E) Campaigning on the Contract with America in 1994, Republicans turned over a record number of seats.

8. The Supreme Court uses which of the following standards in judging sex discrimination cases?

   (A) Probable cause

   (B) Due process

   (C) Reasonableness

   (D) Exclusionary rule

   (E) Suspect classification

9. What is the major cause for nonvoting?

   (A) Poll taxes

   (B) Red tape involved in registering to vote

   (C) Status as a legal alien

   (D) Lack of a sense of political efficacy

   (E) Lack of interest

10. "Soft money" in an election campaign is

   (A) money provided through the Federal Election Commission to presidential candidates.

   (B) money raised by state and local party organizations for activities related to building the party but not to electing a particular candidate.

   (C) contributions by Political Action Committees.

   (D) contributions by corporations and labor unions.

   (E) individual contributions to any one candidate up to a limit of $2,000 for a federal primary and for a federal general election.

11. The results of the Census are used by which arm of government to reapportion seats in the U.S. House of Representatives?

   (A) The Executive branch

   (B) The Judiciary

   (C) The House itself

   (D) The House and Senate

   (E) State legislatures

GO ON TO THE NEXT PAGE

12. All of the following were sources for the U.S. Constitution EXCEPT

    (A) John Locke's *Two Treatises of Government.*

    (B) the Articles of Confederation.

    (C) Jean-Jacques Rousseau's *Social Contract.*

    (D) William Blackstone's *Commentaries on the Laws of England.*

    (E) Alexis de Tocqueville's *Democracy in America.*

13. Most incumbents in Congress win reelection for all of the following reasons EXCEPT

    (A) incumbents find it easier than their challengers to raise money.

    (B) by reason of their position, incumbents are better known than their challengers.

    (C) many districts are drawn in such a way as to favor a particular political party, thus giving it a safe seat in the House.

    (D) voters feel more comfortable with the kind of continuity in policy that incumbents represent.

    (E) incumbents use their office to solve problems for their constituents, thus building loyalty.

14. Party unity in each house of Congress is maintained by

    (A) logrolling.

    (B) party votes.

    (C) committee assignments.

    (D) the whip system.

    (E) the pork barrel.

15. The Supreme Court has interpreted which of the following to extend to a right to privacy?

    I. Bill of Rights

    II. Tenth Amendment

    III. Fourteenth Amendment

    (A) I only

    (B) II only

    (C) II and III

    (D) I and III

    (E) I, II, and III

16. Which of the following has the biggest impact on short-term voting behavior?

    (A) Gender and age

    (B) Income and occupation

    (C) Region of the country and family

    (D) Party identification

    (E) Candidates and issues

17. All of the following are generally true about third parties in the United States EXCEPT

    (A) they have often been organized around a single issue.

    (B) a single strong personality has often dominated a party.

    (C) some economic discontent has often spurred the formation of third parties.

    (D) most of the important third parties have not split from the major political parties but have rallied the politically disenfranchised to join the new party.

    (E) third parties have often forced the major parties to deal with issues they would rather have continued to ignore.

18. Since the 1950s, the major business of Congress has centered on

(A) civil rights.
(B) the budget process.
(C) foreign policy issues.
(D) immigration issues.
(E) social policy.

19. Congress's purpose in passing the line-item veto was

(A) to enable the president to veto specific spending items in appropriations bills only.
(B) to enable the president to veto only a portion of any bill in the hope that an entire bill would not be vetoed.
(C) to delegate some of the legislative responsibility of Congress to the president in an attempt to speed the law-making process.
(D) to replace the use of the pocket veto.
(E) to satisfy campaign promises to conservatives.

20. All of the following are examples of the interdependence of government and the economy EXCEPT

(A) the Federal Reserve System.
(B) the Federal Housing Administration.
(C) the Savings and Loan bailout.
(D) Medicare.
(E) federal investments in research and development for the Internet.

GO ON TO THE NEXT PAGE

Questions 21 and 22 refer to the following graph.

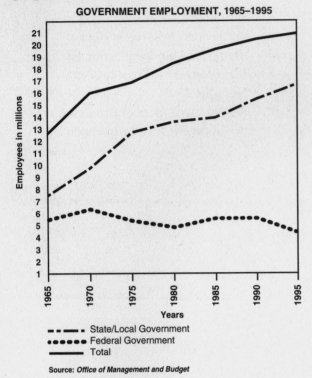

GOVERNMENT EMPLOYMENT, 1965–1995

Employees in millions

Years

- - - - State/Local Government
●●●●●● Federal Government
——— Total

Source: *Office of Management and Budget*

21. Which of the following conclusions is supported by the graph?

(A) While employment in the federal government leveled off in the 1980s, employment on the state and local levels continued to grow.

(B) The single largest growth period in the combined number of government employees—federal, state, and local—occurred between 1965 and 1970.

(C) The employment figures for the federal government in the years 1970, 1980, and 1990 include temporary employees hired to work for the Census Bureau.

(D) For the period shown on the graph, state and local government has grown consistently.

(E) There is a relationship between the growth or decline in the number of employees on the state and local level and on the federal government level.

22. Which of the following is the most likely explanation for the data on the graph?

(A) The size of the federal workforce has remained constant in relation to the size of the total civilian workforce.

(B) As more programs have been turned over to the states, state and local government workforces have grown.

(C) The federal workforce grows at a rate that keeps pace with the economy.

(D) Efforts have been made to control and even cut the size of the federal bureaucracy, but no similar efforts have been made at the state and local levels.

(E) The ratio of federal workers to state and local government workers is about 1 to 3.

23. A member of which of the following demographic groups would be least likely to support a Democratic candidate for president?

(A) African American
(B) Upper income
(C) Urban
(D) Northern Protestant
(E) Under 30 years of age

24. Which of the following is a key concept of federalism?

    (A) Federalism is based on a unitary form of government.
    (B) State constitutions may override the national constitution in certain matters.
    (C) The line between national and state powers is often unclear and flexible.
    (D) In the federal system, state governments cannot exercise any powers other than those delegated to them in the U.S. Constitution.
    (E) The treatment of states depends on the size of their population in relation to that of other states.

25. A major reason for rewriting the laws regarding presidential primaries was

    (A) to ensure the end of winner-take-all primaries.
    (B) to end the practice of "front loading" the primary schedule.
    (C) to transform the primaries into ineffective tools for selecting a party's presidential candidate in order to make it easier for the party's influential members to select their choice.
    (D) to end preference primaries.
    (E) to increase the participation of the average voter.

26. All of the following are true of the Supreme Court's rejection of a writ of certiorari EXCEPT

    (A) the Supreme Court agrees with the lower court's ruling.
    (B) the Supreme Court may not think the case involves an important enough issue.
    (C) the lower court's ruling will stand.
    (D) the Supreme Court may not wish to take up the subject.
    (E) the Supreme Court may not think the merits of the case are the best for addressing the issue.

27. A president's success in winning passage of legislation is directly related to

    (A) how close the next midterm elections are.
    (B) whether the president's party holds the majority in both houses of Congress.
    (C) whether the president is in the last year of a second four-year term.
    (D) how well received the annual State of the Union speech is by the American people.
    (E) whether the nation is involved in a military conflict abroad.

GO ON TO THE NEXT PAGE

28. The guarantees of the Bill of Rights were extended to protect citizens against actions of the states through

(A) passage of a series of civil rights acts in the nineteenth and twentieth centuries.

(B) ratification of the Thirteenth Amendment.

(C) ratification of the Fourteenth Amendment.

(D) ratification of the Fifteenth Amendment.

(E) a series of Supreme Court decisions.

29. All of the following are current tools of U.S. foreign policy EXCEPT

(A) containment.

(B) economic aid.

(C) the United Nations.

(D) collective security.

(E) mutual deterrence.

30. To call the formulation of public policy in the United States "government by public opinion" is inaccurate for all of the following reasons EXCEPT

(A) the form of government is a representative democracy.

(B) because the federal judiciary is appointed rather than elected, it hands down decisions without the pressure of having to please voters.

(C) the Constitution safeguards the civil rights and liberties of those who hold minority opinions as well as those who hold majority opinions.

(D) public policy is influenced by a number of factors in addition to public opinion, such as the workings of interest groups, PACs, and political parties.

(E) public opinion never shapes public policy, only reflects it.

31. The Twelfth Amendment is a direct result of which of the following?

(A) The reform efforts of progressives

(B) The election of Jefferson over Burr as president

(C) The suffrage movement

(D) The outcome of the election of 1824

(E) The temperance movement

32. The agenda for the Senate is controlled by

(A) the majority leader.

(B) the majority and minority leaders.

(C) the president pro tempore.

(D) the vice president of the United States.

(E) House caucus.

33. The most significant effect of iron triangles is

(A) the Whistleblower Act of 1989.

(B) the difficulty in changing entrenched agencies.

(C) the revolving door between agency employees and clientele organizations.

(D) the tendency for waste and duplication in the federal government.

(E) the difficulty in creating new agencies to take on additional work.

34. A significant reason for reforming the organizational structure and procedures of Congress in the 1970s was

(A) to establish the sunshine rule for hearings.

(B) to increase the number of subcommittees.

(C) to allow committee members who disagree with their committee chairs to present their opinions.

(D) to reduce the power of committee chairs.

(E) to end the use of secret ballots to pick committee chairs.

35. All of the following are constitutional protections for people accused of a crime EXCEPT

(A) writ of habeas corpus.
(B) freedom from unreasonable search and seizure.
(C) bill of attainder.
(D) right to confront witnesses.
(E) no double jeopardy.

36. Interpretations of which of the following clauses of the Constitution have been used to define the practice of federalism?

(A) Due process
(B) Nonenumerated rights
(C) Commerce
(D) Necessary and proper clause
(E) Supremacy

37. Among the common set of fundamental political beliefs and opinions that Americans hold is a belief

(A) in affirmative action.
(B) in freedom for the individual.
(C) in the value of government solutions over private sector solutions to national problems.
(D) in the status quo.
(E) in deregulation of industry.

38. According to *The Federalist,* No.10, which of the following would not have surprised Madison?

I. Proliferation of public interest groups
II. Political activism by labor unions
III. Establishment of PACs

(A) I only
(B) II only
(C) III only
(D) I and II only
(E) I, II, and III

GO ON TO THE NEXT PAGE

Question 39 refers to the following table.

Federal Government Revenue (in billions of dollars)

Year	Individual Income Tax	Corporate Income Tax	Social Insurance & Retirement	Excise Taxes	Other	Total
1940	0.9	1.2	1.8	2.0	0.7	6.5
1950	15.8	10.4	4.3	7.6	1.4	39.4
1960	40.7	21.5	14.7	11.7	3.9	92.5
1970	90.4	32.8	44.3	15.7	9.5	192.8
1980	244.1	64.6	157.8	24.3	26.3	517.1
1990	466.9	93.5	380.8	35.3	56.2	1,032.0
1999	868.9	182.2	608.8	68.1	78.3	1,806.3

Source: *Office of Management and Budget*

39. The data on the table support which of the following statements?

(A) Consistently since 1940, individual income taxes have been the largest revenue source for the federal government.
(B) The total receipts taken in by the federal government have grown threefold since 1940.
(C) The amount of money generated through social insurance and retirement receipts has grown at the same rate as individual income tax receipts.
(D) Among the receipts in the Other category are estate and gift taxes.
(E) The period between 1980 and 1999 saw the greatest increase in the amount of revenue generated by social insurance and retirement receipts.

40. Congress has limited the power of the president

(A) to appoint ambassadors.
(B) to issue executive orders.
(C) to negotiate treaties with other countries.
(D) to claim executive privilege.
(E) to commit troops to military action abroad.

41. The power of the Supreme Court to review and determine the constitutionality of state constitutional provisions and laws and state court decisions is based on

I. the principle of judicial review.
II. the supremacy clause of the U.S. Constitution.
III. the Judiciary Act of 1789.

(A) I only
(B) II only
(C) III only
(D) I and II
(E) II and III

42. The role of television in shaping public perceptions of events and politicians became important as a result of

(A) the televised Army-McCarthy hearings.
(B) television news coverage of the Korean War.
(C) the televised Kennedy-Nixon debates in 1960.
(D) television's coverage of the Vietnam War.
(E) television's coverage of the civil rights movement.

43. In order to enforce desegregation, all of the following had to be in place EXCEPT

(A) appropriate legislation.
(B) courts willing to hand down court orders to force school districts to desegregate.
(C) an extension of the interpretation of the due process clause to cover school desegregation.
(D) executive branch support on the department and agency levels to implement court decisions.
(E) political support.

44. Which of the following appears to be how the news media use election polls?

(A) To educate the public about the issues
(B) To decide which candidates are the most likely to win and then follow those candidates closely
(C) To report information as polling organizations release it
(D) To educate the public about the candidates
(E) To shape public opinion

45. Attempts to reform campaign finance laws have met with resistance because

(A) interest groups cannot agree on what the reforms should include.
(B) political campaigns have become so expensive that legislators are reluctant to vote for changes in the laws.
(C) no one will sponsor a reform bill in Congress.
(D) PACs provide access to the political process, and interest groups join to defend that access.
(E) many feel that money spent for issues advocacy by interest groups should be regulated also.

46. The power of the federal courts was enlarged in the 1960s and 1970s

(A) as a way to bring about policy changes.
(B) through a series of procedural changes.
(C) by establishing the right of groups to file class action suits.
(D) but reduced through a series of Supreme Court appointments by Presidents Reagan and Bush.
(E) as a result of decisions the Supreme Court handed down in civil rights cases.

47. All of the following control the flow of cases to be heard by the Supreme Court EXCEPT

(A) the justices themselves.
(B) the solicitor general.
(C) the justices' law clerks.
(D) the Federal Bureau of Investigation.
(E) the federal appeals courts.

48. All of the following are true about the pocket veto EXCEPT

(A) both the House and the Senate need two-thirds majorities to overturn it.
(B) the president receives a bill less than ten days before Congress will adjourn and does not act on it.
(C) it is a tool to make Congress modify the bill if both houses do not have the votes to override the veto.
(D) the president chooses not to go on record as opposing a particular bill.
(E) the president sends the bill back to Congress with a veto message.

GO ON TO THE NEXT PAGE

49. The conservative coalition in Congress refers to

(A) the members of the Religious Right.

(B) pro-life advocates and Christian fundamentalists.

(C) Dixiecrats.

(D) Republicans and Southern Democrats.

(E) Reagan Democrats and Republicans.

50. The managerial presidency is a direct outgrowth

(A) of an interest on the part of recent presidents to make use of scientific concepts of management.

(B) of the desire to control the growing bureaucracy of the executive branch.

(C) of reforms mandated by Congress.

(D) of Reagan's attempts to decentralize the executive branch.

(E) of Clinton's National Performance Review program.

51. Voters in elections at the state level are more likely to cast their ballots based on

(A) party loyalty.

(B) how personable the candidates are.

(C) specific issues.

(D) the economy at the state level.

(E) perceptions gained through media coverage of the candidates.

Question 52 refers to the following table.

Selected Federal Aid to State and Local Governments (in millions of dollars)

Budget Category	1970	1980	1990
Administration of Justice	42	529	473
Agriculture	604	569	1,382
Energy	25	499	438
Transportation	4,599	13,087	18,700
Community and Regional Development	1,780	6,486	5,128
Education, Worker Training, Social Services	6,417	21,682	22,833
Health	3,849	15,758	42,928
Income Security	5,795	18,495	35,403

Source: *Office of Management and Budget*

52. Which of the following statements is supported by the data in the above table?

(A) About 20 percent of state and local government revenue comes from the federal government as intergovernmental revenue.

(B) The number of federal regulatory mandates to state and local government has increased as federal funding has declined.

(C) The largest amount of federal funding goes to state and local governments to support health and human services programs.

(D) Federal funding of state and local governmental programs increased across the board between 1970 and 1990.

(E) In general, the impact of federal regulations on state and local governments increased more between 1970 and 1980 than between 1980 and 1990.

53. Which of the following is NOT true about education policy in the United States?

(A) The federal government is the single largest provider of funding for education.

(B) The federal government sets national education goals, but the states implement them as they see fit.

(C) The federal government provides student loans for higher education.

(D) The federal government establishes job training programs.

(E) The federal government established a tuition tax credit system for parents of students and for adult students.

54. The controversy over affirmative action has centered around

(A) the argument that ensuring diversity in a group is misguided social engineering.

(B) whether there is a compelling need to remedy past injustices when they are not currently present in specific instances.

(C) the use of quotas.

(D) whether the Constitution is color blind.

(E) how to eliminate discrimination and provide opportunities for all Americans.

55. An independent federal judiciary is the purpose of

(A) having federal judges elected every seven years.

(B) having the president appoint federal judges with the advice and consent of the Senate.

(C) using the impeachment process for alleged wrongdoing by a federal judge.

(D) lifetime tenure for almost all federal judges.

(E) congressional hearings into the fitness of a person to serve as a federal judge before his or her appointment.

56. Grants-in-aid programs are used by the federal government

(A) to provide aid to foreign nations.

(B) to ensure certain minimum standards for programs within the states.

(C) to finance the student loan program.

(D) to underwrite community policing programs.

(E) to replace categorical-formula grants.

57. At the committee stage, which of the following is most likely to influence the thinking and decision of a member of Congress?

(A) Constituents

(B) Party loyalty

(C) Lobbyists

(D) Fellow members of Congress

(E) The member's staff

GO ON TO THE NEXT PAGE

58. Which of the following behaviors illustrates the weakening of political parties since the 1960s?

   I.   Split-ticket voting
   II. Increase in the number of independents
   III. The growth of a gender gap among voters

   (A) I only
   (B) II only
   (C) III only
   (D) I and II
   (E) I and III

59. The most important result of the Voting Rights Act of 1965 was

   (A) the increase in registered voters among African Americans in the South
   (B) the increase in the number of African Americans who held public office
   (C) the influence that African Americans were able to wield in Southern politics
   (D) the increase in African-American officeholders in Northern states
   (E) the right of the federal government to step in and register African-American voters in districts where less than 50 percent of adult African Americans were registered

60. A major outcome of the New Deal in terms of public policy was

   (A) the dominance of the Democratic party on the national level for much of the twentieth century.
   (B) the shift made by African Americans from the Republican to the Democratic party.
   (C) the emergence of the farm vote.
   (D) the end of attempts to change the number of Supreme Court justices.
   (E) the delegation of policy-making power by Congress to the president.

STOP If you finish before time is called, you may check your work on this section only. Do not turn to any other section in the test.

SECTION II   TIME—100 MINUTES

Directions: You have 100 minutes to answer all four of the following questions. It is suggested that you take a few minutes to outline each answer. Spend approximately one fourth of your time (25 minutes) on each question. Support the ideas in your essay with substantive examples where appropriate. Make sure to number each of your responses with the number that corresponds to the question.

1. "Money is the mother's milk of politics."
   —Jesse Unruh, mid-twentieth century
                      California politician

   To what degree is Jesse Unruh's comment relevant today? Do you agree or disagree with his assessment of the relationship between money and politics?

2. A major issue that has carried over into the twenty-first century is the proper role of the judiciary. There are those who believe that the courts should have a role in making public policy and there are critics who disagree. With which view do you agree? Support your opinion with examples of policy making by the courts.

3. Many millions of people in the United States do not vote. Compare characteristics of voters and nonvoters. Include reasons why some people vote and others do not vote.

4. The Framers of the Constitution created a democracy for the new United States. Discuss the five aspects of democracy that form the basis of our government and identify the one Americans seem to value the most.

S T O P   If you finish before time is called, you may check your work on this section only. Do not turn to any other section in the test.

ANSWERS AND EXPLANATIONS

Quick-Score Answers					
1. B	11. C	21. B	31. B	41. E	51. A
2. D	12. E	22. B	32. B	42. C	52. C
3. B	13. D	23. B	33. D	43. C	53. A
4. B	14. D	24. C	34. D	44. B	54. C
5. E	15. D	25. E	35. C	45. D	55. D
6. D	16. E	26. A	36. D	46. B	56. B
7. B	17. D	27. B	37. B	47. E	57. C
8. C	18. B	28. C	38. E	48. E	58. D
9. E	19. A	29. A	39. A	49. D	59. C
10. B	20. D	30. E	40. E	50. B	60. E

DIAGNOSTIC TEST

1. **The correct answer is (B).** Under the Articles of Confederation, there was no national court system. Because there was no chief executive, choice (C), there was no unifying force for government policies. Because all thirteen states, rather than a majority, were required to ratify amendments, it was unlikely that small states and large states or Northern states and Southern states would agree on issues, choice (D). Although nine of the thirteen might agree on laws, it was difficult to get the representatives of any nine states to appear for sessions, choice (A). Congress was hampered in its duties because it could not levy taxes; it could only request money from the states or borrow it, which required approval, choice (E).

Test-Taking Strategy

Read the question and all the answer choices carefully. Be sure you understand the nuances of the question. On a quick reading, you might have selected choice (A) and wondered why the College Board was asking such an easy question.

2. **The correct answer is (D).** Four of the choices, (A), (B), (C), and (D), may seem correct. All have some influence on a person's choice of political loyalties, but only (D) is correct in this context. While the political affiliation of the parental family indicates the most likely political orientation of a person, choice (A), economic issues, choice (D), may intervene to change political loyalties as people age. Hence, Bill Clinton's emphasis on the economy in the 1992 election. Choice (E), mass media, is more likely to shape people's attitudes and opinions about specific issues.

3. **The correct answer is (B).** The Federal Reserve System, choice (A), was established by the Federal Reserve Act of 1913. The Selective Service Act reestablished the military draft, choice (C), in 1948. Although the draft was suspended in 1973 after the Vietnam War, men are still required to register for military service when they turn 18. Native Americans were given citizenship in 1924, choice (D). Direct primaries, choice (E), are regulated by state laws.

4. **The correct answer is (B).** Choices (A), (C), (D), and (E) are useful qualifications for one of the top jobs among the appointive positions in a presidential administration, but it helps more to know the person in charge. Top-level positions like cabinet secretaries and ambassadors go to presidential loyalists—often large contributors to the president's party, choice (B).

Test-Taking Strategy

Look for key words in questions. Here the key words are major criticism.

5. **The correct answer is (E).** All five choices tell you truthful facts about independent regulatory agencies. Choices (A), (B), and (D) are not raised by critics as problems, even though choices (A) and (D) may seem as though they might be. Choices (C) and (E) are criticisms, but choice (E) is the major criticism of the two. It is part of the "revolving door" critique: agency employees come from the industries they regulate and agency employees leave the government to work in the industries they regulated.

6. **The correct answer is (D).** Since Franklin Roosevelt sat in the White House, the nation's policy agenda more and more has been set by the president. As with Bill Clinton, that does not necessarily mean that the party in power, choice (E), agrees with all of what the president is asking for. Choice (C), a joint conference committee, meets to iron out differences in bills passed by the House and by the Senate. Choices (A) and (B) are illogical.

Test-Taking Strategy

Don't try to read too much into stimulus-based questions. Read the question carefully, be sure you know what it is asking, and read each answer before deciding on your choice.

7. **The correct answer is (B).** Choices (A), (C), and (E) may seem correct, but read the question again. It asks you to look for the statement that the data on the table best supports. There is no information on the table about the issues in the 1994 or 1998 elections, so choices (A), (C), and (E) cannot be correct. That leaves choices (B) and (D). The Democrats turned over 60 seats in 1994, whereas the Republicans turned over only 27 seats in 1982, so choice (D) is incorrect. On a first reading, choice (B) would be a good candidate for the answer because it is a generalization rather than a specific instance.

8. **The correct answer is (C).** In handing down its decision in *Reed* v. *Reed* (1971), the Supreme Court established the standard of reasonableness in judging the constitutionality of sex discrimination cases. Using sex as the basis for classification in law "must be reasonable, and not arbitrary, and must rest on some ground of difference." Choice (E), suspect classification, is the standard established by the Supreme Court for race discrimination cases. The Fourth Amendment states that no one can be searched or arrested without probable cause, choice (A). The Fifth Amendment guarantees that the government cannot move against a person or his or her property without following lawful procedures, choice (B). According to the exclusionary rule, choice (D), no illegally seized evidence may be used against a defendant in court; this was established first for the federal court system and then in the landmark case, *Mapp* v. *Ohio* (1961), for state courts.

9. **The correct answer is (E).** Sometimes the answers are as simple as they seem. Lack of political interest is the basic reason why people don't vote. Choice (D) may sound good, but analysis of voter behavior doesn't bear it out. Poll taxes, choice (A), were eliminated in state contests in 1966 by the Supreme Court on the basis of the equal protection clause of the Fourteenth Amendment and in federal elections by the Twenty-Fourth Amendment. Registering to vote, choice (B) is being made easier in many states, but nonetheless it is not the correct answer. Legal aliens may not vote, but they represent only a very small percentage of the population, so choice (C) is incorrect.

Study Strategy

Electoral laws and systems are new topics added to the test in recent years. Be sure you know about them, including campaign finance laws.

10. **The correct answer is (B).** Choice (A) is the opposite of unregulated money. Choices (C) and (D) may be contributors of soft money, but neither group defines the concept. Choice (E) is the amount of money that an individual or company may contribute directly to any one candidate. This amount is regulated by law.

11. **The correct answer is (C).** The answer is in Article I, Section 2, Clause 3 of the Constitution. Based on the Census, Congress establishes the number of representatives that each state has. Because the Constitution separates the executive and legislative branches of government, it would be illogical for the executive, choice (A), to reapportion congressional districts. This reasoning also makes choice (B) an illogical answer, although the courts could rule on cases brought before them that dealt with reapportionment issues, such as *Wesberry* v. *Sanders*. Don't be confused by choice (E). State legislatures redraw the actual district boundaries when states gain or lose representatives.

12. **The correct answer is (E).** De Tocqueville's work, choice (E), was written after the Constitution was signed. The word *democracy* in the title is a clue. A work talking about democracy in the United States would probably not have been written before the Constitution. Don't be confused by choice (B).While the Framers of the Constitution did away with the Articles, the Articles had a direct impact on what was included in the Constitution, both negatively and positively. Such weaknesses in the Constitution as the lack of a chief executive and the central government's lack of the power to tax were remedied, while elements of the Articles as well as language such as "full faith and credit shall be given in each State to the public acts, records, and judicial proceedings of every other state" were used and built on.

Test-Taking Strategy

Be sure you understand what the question is asking. Don't be confused by what is a cause and what is an effect of an action.

13. **The correct answer is (D).** Continuity in office means that there is less chance of changes in policy, which may be a good thing or a bad thing depending on one's viewpoint, but it is not a reason why incumbents are heavily favored to win reelection. Continuity of policies is a by-product of the continual reelection of incumbents, not a cause. Choices (A), (B), (C), and (E) are all true.

14. **The correct answer is (D).** The majority party and minority party whips and the assistant whips keep tabs on how party members are planning to vote on bills and will attempt to persuade members who are leaning toward voting against the party. Party votes, choice (B), is the outcome of the effective use of the whip system, not the cause of party unity. Two or more legislators agreeing to support each other's bills is called logrolling, choice (A). Pork-barrel legislation, choice (E), refers to legislation that supports federal funding for local projects; members of Congress support one another's pet projects in return for support for their own projects. Choice (C) does not relate to the question at all.

Test-Taking Strategy

For tiered questions like this, decide which point(s), I through III, is correct and then match that choice to the answer choices.

15. **The correct answer is (D).** While the Constitution does not mention a right to privacy, both the Bill of Rights (I) and the Fourteenth Amendment (III) guarantee private property rights. The Supreme Court has extended these rights to personal behavior. The Tenth Amendment is a good distracter because it deals with powers reserved to the people and the states, but it's the wrong choice. Once you have decided that only I and III are correct, look for the answer choice that has only those two items, choice (D).

16. **The correct answer is (E).** While party identification, choice (D), is the major long-term factor in how people vote, it is the candidates and the issues, choice (E), in any given election that influence how people vote. Choices (A), (B), and (D) are all factors in how people vote over time, but they are incorrect in the context of this question.

17. **The correct answer is (D).** Most of the important minor, or third, parties have been splinter parties, such as Theodore Roosevelt's Bull Moose Party and George Wallace's American Independent Party. While they—and other third parties—have attracted the politically disillusioned, their power bases have been built on defectors from the major parties. Choices (A), (B), (C), and (E) are all true about third parties and; therefore, in this *not/except* question they are the wrong answers.

18. **The correct answer is (B).** Since the 1950s, the budget-making process has increased in the amount of time Congress spends on it. Roughly half of all roll-call votes deal with appropriations, tax legislation, budget resolutions, reconciliation bills, and level of authorization for funding.

19. **The correct answer is (A).** Choice (A) was the purpose of the bill authorizing the line-item veto, but the Supreme Court ruled that it violated the Constitution by giving the president the power to change legislation—the budget—that Congress had passed. Choice (C) is incorrect because it states the Court's finding as the reason for passing the line-item veto. Choice (B) is incorrect because the line-item veto applied only to appropriations bills. Choices (D) and (E) are unrelated to the issue and incorrect.

20. **The correct answer is (D).** Through the Federal Reserve System, choice (A), the government sets monetary policy in an attempt to regulate the economy. In an effort to encourage home ownership, the government through the Federal Housing Authority, choice (B), provides insurance for home mortgages, thus reducing a bank's risk in offering mortgages to low- and middle-income families. The government provided the money to save faltering savings and loan corporations, choice (C), in an effort to stabilize the economy. One of the government's roles since the beginning of the nation has been to encourage commerce—business. Economic growth is the potential by-product of the government's investment in research and development for the Internet, choice (E).

21. **The correct answer is (B).** Don't be confused by the ascending lines for state and local government. While they were growing in any 5-year span, the number of federal employees—except for the period between 1965 and 1970—was declining or remaining steady at a lower rate. Between 1965 and 1970, the total government workforce grew by more than 6 million. Choice (A) has two elements: (1) employment in the federal government leveled off in the 1980s and (2) employment on the state and local levels grew. By reading the line graph, you can see that federal government employment in the 1980s rose between 1980 and 1985 and was somewhat steady between 1985 and 1990, making the first part of the answer choice incorrect. Choice (C) is correct, but that information is not presented on the graph. The dip in the state and local workforce around 1985 makes choice (D) incorrect. Choice (E) is false; no relationship is shown between growth and decline in the workforce in any period shown.

22. **The correct answer is (B).** The question is asking you for a cause to explain the effect illustrated by the graph. Choices (A), (B), (C), and (E) are all true statements, but choices (A), (C), and (E) do not explain why state and local government would increase while the federal government workforce would decrease. Only choice (B) provides an answer. Choice (D) is a good distracter, but beware of answers that are absolutes. How can you be sure that not one state or local government has attempted to cut back on the number of people it employs?

23. **The correct answer is (B).** Upper-income voters tend to be Republicans. The characteristics in choices (A), (B), (C), and (E) tend to describe Democrats.

24. **The correct answer is (C).** If the Constitution spelled out the lines of power between national and state governments explicitly, there would be no need for court cases to determine the boundaries. The Framers deliberately included the amendment process and the system of checks and balances to give the new government flexibility and stability. By definition, choice (A) cannot be correct. A federal system must have more than one part. The Constitution and Supreme Court interpretations make choice (B) incorrect. The Tenth Amendment states that those powers not delegated to the federal government "nor prohibited to the states, are reserved to the states respectively, or to the people," making choice (D) incorrect. Choice (E) is incorrect. The federal system guarantees equal treatment of the states; political influence may depend on a state's size and wealth—for example, Delaware's influence in comparison with California's.

25. **The correct answer is (E).** Although internal party rules have ended the practice of winner-take-all primaries for Democrats, a few states still allow these primaries and the Republican Party runs winner-take-all primaries in those states. Choice (A) then is incorrect. The new primary laws have worsened the problem of the front-loaded primary schedule; more states are now having their presidential primaries earlier, making choice (B) incorrect. Choice (C) is incorrect. Choice (D) is incorrect because more than half the states hold preference primaries with delegates to the national conventions being chosen at state party conventions.

Test-Taking Strategy

For not/except *questions, ask yourself if the answer is true for the context of the question. If it is, cross it off and go on to the next answer.*

26. **The correct answer is (A).** A writ of certiorari is an order from the Supreme Court to a lower court to send up the records on a case on the basis of a petition by either side in the case. Refusing to issue a writ does not necessarily mean that the Supreme Court agrees with the lower court's ruling, so choice (A) is incorrect and is, therefore, the correct answer in this *not/except* question. Choices (B), (D), and (E) are all reasons that may affect the Court's decision about whether to hear a case, and choice (C) is the outcome if the cert is rejected.

27. **The correct answer is (B).** While choices (A), (C), (D), and (E) may seem like good choices, history shows that choice (B) is the best indicator of whether a president will win passage of legislation.

28. **The correct answer is (C).** The Fourteenth Amendment states:

> . . . No state shall make or enforce any law which shall abridge the privileges or immunities of citizens of the United States; nor shall any State deprive any person of life, liberty, or property, without due process of law; nor deny to any person within its jurisdiction the equal protection of the laws.

Choices (A) and (E) might be confusing because the civil rights laws of the late nineteenth and the twentieth centuries as well as a series of Supreme Court decisions put teeth into the amendment. Choice (B), the Thirteenth Amendment, abolished slavery. The Fifteenth Amendment, choice (D), guaranteed the vote to former enslaved African Americans.

29. **The correct answer is (A).** Containment was a policy of the cold war begun under Dwight Eisenhower and his secretary of state, John Foster Dulles, to control the spread of communism. Choice (D), collective security, is a policy of entering into mutual security agreements such as the North Atlantic Treaty Organization by which all signatories agree that an attack against one member is an attack against all members; the policy began after World War II and is still a tool of U.S. foreign policy. Mutual deterrence, choice (E), also began after World War II and continues as a way to discourage attack by developing and maintaining military strength.

30. **The correct answer is (E).** Public opinion may shape public policy, making choice (E) incorrect. Choices (A), (B), (C), and (D) are all true statements and, therefore, incorrect answer choices. Although choice (B) is true, federal judges are recommended by and appointed by elected or appointed officials themselves and may not be without party ideologies and loyalties.

31. **The correct answer is (B).** The Twelfth Amendment set up separate ballots for president and vice president as a direct result of the confusion in the election of 1800. The House decided the outcome because both Aaron Burr and Thomas Jefferson had the same number of electoral votes. Although Burr had run for the vice presidency, he wanted to be president, but because there was no separate election, there was no way to distinguish votes. The election of 1824, choice (D), was also decided in the House, but the issue was different. No candidate had a majority of electoral votes. The direct election of senators, the Seventeenth Amendment, was a result of the reform efforts of progressives, choice (A). The Nineteenth Amendment gave women the right to vote, choice (C). The Eighteenth Amendment was a victory for the temperance movement, choice (E).

32. **The correct answer is (B).** Together, the majority and minority party leaders in the Senate control the body's calendar, which is the same as its legislative agenda. Choice (A) is a distracter because the two leaders need to work together to move bills along and determine when to call for votes. The president pro tempore, choice (C), who serves in the absence of the vice president, is a largely ceremonial position, usually held by a well-known member of the majority party. Choice (D), the vice president, holds the title of president of the Senate but may not speak in support of or against a bill. He does vote to break a tie. Choice (E) is illogical.

33. **The correct answer is (D).** Because of the difficulty in getting agencies to change, choice (B), the government finds itself creating new agencies to take on new work, resulting in waste and duplication. This explanation also shows that choice (E) is incorrect. Choice (A) is a result of the difficulties involved in dealing with iron triangles, but it is a very specific outcome, whereas choice (D) represents a generalization or a more inclusive response. Choice (C) may be a true statement but is an incorrect response to the question.

34. **The correct answer is (D).** This question is similar to question 33. Choices (A), (B), (C), and (D) are true about the congressional reforms of the 1970s, but choice (D) is the broadest, most inclusive answer. The other three choices were steps taken to either directly or indirectly limit the committee chair's power. Choice (E) is the opposite of rule changes in the Senate.

35. **The correct answer is (C).** A bill of attainder is legislation that inflicts punishment without a trial and is outlawed in Article I, Sections 9 and 10 of the Constitution. The same Section 9 guarantees the writ of habeas corpus against the federal government, choice (A). The Fourth Amendment guarantees choice (B). The Fifth Amendment covers choices (D) and (E).

36. **The correct answer is (D).** The necessary and proper clause (Article I, Section 8, Clause 18), also called the elastic clause, is the basis for the implied powers of the federal government. Due process, choice (A), relates to the right of every citizen to a fair hearing and to limits on what the law can do, that is, the law may not act in an arbitrary manner. Choice (B) refers to the Ninth Amendment and the non- or unenumerated rights, those powers that although not specifically listed belong to the people. Choice (C) refers to Article 1, Section 8, Clause 8. Choice (E) refers to Article VI, Section 2, which states that the Constitution, federal law, and treaties made by the national government supersede any state constitutions or state laws.

37. **The correct answer is (B).** A fundamental belief of the American people is freedom of the individual; other fundamental values are equality and democracy. Choice (A) is a policy and not a core value, although it flows from the belief in equality. In many sectors of the population, affirmative action is highly controversial. Choice (C) is the opposite of how people feel about government solutions to problems. Choice (D) is illogical. Choice (E) is not a fundamental belief, although many people share the idea that there are too many government regulations.

38. **The correct answer is (E).** In *The Federalist,* No. 10, Madison said that "liberty is to faction what air is to fire." Reading through the answer choices, all relate to "factions" in Madison's sense of the word—groups of like-minded people who lobby for their interests. You may think that III, PACs, would have surprised Madison, but they are interest groups like the other two answer choices. Therefore, only choice (E), which includes all three items, is correct.

39. **The correct answer is (A).** This is a fact you should know independent of the table. The table shows that choice (B) is incorrect because revenues by 1999 were slightly more than twice what they were in 1940. Choice (C) is incorrect because there is no relation between the rate of income tax receipts and social insurance and retirement receipts. The rates are independent of each other and are governed by laws that change independently of each other. Choice (E) is illogical; because of a growing economy as well as inflation, it is illogical to think that tax receipts would not grow continually.

40. **The correct answer is (E).** The War Powers Act of 1973, passed over President Richard Nixon's veto, limited the ability of the president to send troops abroad without congressional approval. The act was passed in reaction to the use of troops in Vietnam by Presidents Lyndon Johnson and Nixon. Choices (A) and (B) are powers reserved in the Constitution for the executive branch but are exercised with the advice and consent of the Senate. Choice (D) is illogical.

Test-Taking Strategy

In a tiered question, decide which item(s) is correct and then find the answer choice that corresponds.

41. **The correct answer is (E).** The Constitution does not specifically state that the Supreme Court has the authority to review and overturn state laws or actions, but the supremacy clause, which states that the Constitution is the supreme law of the land, appears to support the view of the Supreme Court as the logical arbiter. In addition, the Judiciary Act of 1789 gave the Supreme Court the right to overturn state constitutions and state laws that it believes conflict with the Constitution, federal law, or treaties. Therefore, items II and III are correct, and only choice (E) contains both items. Item I is a distracter; the principle of judicial review was established in *Marbury* v. *Madison* as based on the Judiciary Act of 1789.

42. **The correct answer is (C).** While those who listened to the Kennedy-Nixon debates on the radio thought that Nixon had won them, those who watched the debates on television favored Kennedy, who was more telegenic and at ease than Nixon. National television news was still in its infancy during the Korean War, choice (B), and few Americans had TV sets. The same is true for the time period, the early 1950s, of the Army-McCarthy hearings, choice (A), although they were televised. The Kennedy-Nixon debates predated both choices (D) and (E), so these answers are incorrect, although television did shape American public opinion to a degree in each case.

43. **The correct answer is (C).** The Court had to extend the interpretation of the equal protection under the law clause of the Fourteenth Amendment, not the due process clause. Choices (A), (B), (D), and (E) are all true and show how the various branches of the federal government depend on one another in order to make and implement policy.

44. **The correct answer is (B).** Choices (A) and (D) are similar but incorrect. Choice (C) is a partially correct statement in that the news media do report the results of polling organizations' surveys, but often the media choose which items and what part of a voter survey to report. Choice (E) may be an indirect result of choice (B), but it does not state how the news media use voter surveys.

45. **The correct answer is (D).** While choice (B) has merit, the main reason for lack of reform is choice (D). Without the power of money, organized labor and big business as well as liberal and conservative groups believe they would lose leverage on Capital Hill and have less chance of gaining policy decisions that support their interests. Choice (A) is incorrect because interest groups are spending their time fighting reforms rather than trying to agree on what the reforms should be. Choice (C) is incorrect because, for example, Senators John McCain, Russell Feingold, and Fred Thompson sponsored a campaign finance reform bill in 1996 that was defeated. Senators McCain and Feingold again sponsored campaign finance reform in 2001. Choice (E) is illogical and not an issue.

46. **The correct answer is (B).** Judicial policy changes occurred because the Supreme Court chose to rule on a series of cases that revolved around issues such as civil rights and abortion. This change was brought about by the justices' decisions related to the cases they chose to hear and the interpretations of the laws they made, thus choice (A) is incorrect, as is choice (E). Policy changes increased the policy-making powers, not the other way around. The Supreme Court made changes in procedural matters, choice (B), increasing the types of cases that could be brought and easing some of the regulations related to filing court cases. Choice (C) is an example of one such procedural change. Although Presidents Ronald Reagan and George H. W. Bush sought to reduce the policy-making decisions of the Supreme Court through the appointment of supposedly conservative justices, choice (D), the Supreme Court continued for the most part to hand down decisions considered to lean on the side of loose constructivism.

47. **The correct answer is (E).** Choice (E) is illogical because if an appeals court has ruled in a case, it has no reason to send its own decision on appeal to the Supreme Court. Choices (A), (B), (C), and (D) all have some say in the flow of cases that the Supreme Court accepts to hear. Next to the justices themselves, the most important influence is wielded by the solicitor general. This post represents the federal government in any case before an appellate court in which the government has a stake.

Test-Taking Strategy

In not/except *questions, ask yourself if the answer is true in the context of the question. If it is, cross it off and go on to the next question.*

48. **The correct answer is (E).** The president must receive a bill less than ten days before Congress adjourns in order to be able to "pocket" it, that is, not act on it, so choice (E) is an incorrect statement but the correct answer for this *not/except* question.

49. **The correct answer is (D).** The conservative coalition in Congress is made up of Republicans and Southern Democrats. This was true for much of the twentieth century and seems to be true into the twenty-first century. If you were eliminating answers to make an educated guess, choices (A) and (C) would be two you could cross off immediately; each answer has only one component, and the phrase in the question says "coalition."

50. **The correct answer is (B).** While choice (A) may seem like a good reason and is, therefore, a good distracter, choice (B) is the correct answer. In fact, the increasing powers of the president as a chief executive go back to the presidency of Wilson while Franklin Roosevelt made extraordinary use of his presidential powers. Choice (C) is incorrect because of the separation of powers. Both choices (D) and (E) are examples of the managerial president in action, not the cause.

51. **The correct answer is (A).** At the state level, choices (B) and (C) are less important because fewer people know about them. This is when party identification, choice (A), becomes the important factor in a voter's choosing a candidate for whom to vote. Choice (D) is an example of choice (C) and, therefore, is incorrect. Choice (E) is an element of choice (B) and, therefore, is incorrect.

Test-Taking Strategy

Read the information on the graphic. Don't choose an answer that is not supported by the data.

52. **The correct answer is (C).** Choice (C) is the only answer that relates to the data on the table. Although choice (A) is correct, the table does not deal with the total receipts of state and local governments. Choice (B) is also correct but is not dealt with on the table. Choice (D) is not true because the table shows that several line items decreased during this period. Choice (E) is both an incorrect statement and one that is not related to any data on the table.

53. **The correct answer is (A).** The majority of funding for public education in the United States comes from local government. Choices (B), (C), (D), and (E) are all aspects of recent federal education policy, and some elements go back to the 1950s.

54. **The correct answer is (C).** Choices (B), (C), (D), and (E) are all parts of the arguments for and against affirmative action, but choice (C) has been at the heart of the controversy and was the basis of the Supreme Court's decision in *Regents of the University of California* v. *Bakke*. Choice (A) is incorrect.

Test-Taking Strategy

In eliminating answers, look for the most inclusive answer and see if that makes sense in the context of the question.

55. **The correct answer is (D).** Choices (B) and (D) are true in this case, but choice (D) is the more inclusive answer and, therefore, the better response. Only a few federal judgeships are appointed for specified terms. Choice (A) is incorrect. Since federal judges cannot be voted out of office, choice (C) is the only way to remove a sitting judge, but it is not the purpose of having an independent judiciary. Choice (E) is a safeguard against appointing someone who is not intellectually suited to the job or who is dishonest.

56. **The correct answer is (B).** Choices (A) and (C) are incorrect. Choice (D) may be one of the uses that a grant-in-aid finances. Choice (E) is illogical because a categorical-formula grant is a type of grant-in-aid.

57. **The correct answer is (C).** At the floor stage, choices (A), (B), and (D) are more influential in the decisions that members of Congress make. At the committee stage, where less outside attention is paid to what goes on, lobbyists and interest groups have more influence, choice (C).

58. **The correct answer is (D).** Split-ticket voting (I) and an increase in independents (II) are both examples of the weakening of political parties. Item III, the gender gap, is not related to party identification. Only choice (D) has both items I and II.

Test-Taking Strategy

Look for the key words in questions. Here they are most important result.

59. **The correct answer is (C).** Let's look at this answer as a process of elimination. Choices (A), (B), and (C) all relate to effects that the Voting Rights Act of 1965 might have had in the South. Choice (D) relates to African Americans in the North, and although this statement is true, the Voting Rights Act was targeted at the South, so choice (D) can be crossed off. Choice (E) was a provision of the law and not an effect, so it can be eliminated. This takes us back to choices (A), (B), and (C). The first two choices are very specific, whereas choice (C) is the most inclusive answer, a generalization, and the correct response.

60. **The correct answer is (E).** Choices (A), (B), and (E) are true statements, but choice (E) is the most significant in terms of the shaping of the national policy agenda. This delegation is in sharp contrast to the limited policy-making duties of nineteenth-century presidents. Choice (C) is incorrect, and choice (D) may be as much coincidental as causal.

SUGGESTIONS FOR FREE-RESPONSE ESSAY 1

Study Strategy

Revise your essay using points from this list that will strengthen it.

You might have chosen the following points about politics and money for your essay evaluating Unruh's statement. Consider these points as you complete your self-evaluation.

- Politics cannot survive without money.

- Funding is a key ingredient of successful campaigns. Money is needed for:

    - television time/commercials.

    - print advertisement.

    - travel, housing, food.

    - salaries for campaign staffers.

    - banners, buttons, bumper stickers, etc.

- A correlation exists between the amount of money raised and spent and who wins.

- Campaign spending has increased exponentially over time.

	1952	1996
Total Spent on Election	$14,000,000	$160,000,000
Winning Presidential Campaign	Eisenhower: $5,000,000	Clinton: $46,000,000

- Restrictions on donations exist, but there are "soft money" loopholes.

	Candidate	National Party	Political Committee	Total per Calendar Year
Individual	$1,000	$20,000	$5,000	$25,000
PAC	$5,000	$15,000	$5,000	no limit
Non-PAC Committee	$1,000	$20,000	$5,000	no limit

- Efforts to reform campaign finance laws have met with stiff resistance from interest groups.

- Secret groups must disclose who is paying for campaign-style TV ads, radio spots, and phone calls.

- "Hard money" versus "soft money," "party-building" loophole

- Federal Election Committee as watchdog

SUGGESTIONS FOR FREE-RESPONSE ESSAY 2

Study Strategy

Be sure to complete the "Self-Evaluation Rubric" for each essay.

You might have chosen the following points about the courts and their role in setting public policy. Consider these points as you complete your self-evaluation.

Areas of Public Policy
- Set public policy in areas of slavery, civil rights, rights of the accused, right to privacy

Test-Taking Strategy

Use your opening paragraph to state what areas you will be limiting your essay to and then stick to these areas. It will help you focus your ideas and your writing.

Supporting Policy Role for Courts
- *Brown* v. *Board of Education*—declared segregated schools unconstitutional
- *Miranda* v. *Arizona*, *Mapp* v. *Ohio*, and *Gideon* v. *Wainwright*—extended constitutional protections to criminal defendants
- *Baker* v. *Carr*—"one man, one vote"
- *Roe* v. *Wade*—right to privacy, upheld abortion rights
- Because not beholden to the electorate, judges resistant to changing meaning of the Constitution to suit changing views of electorate
- Courts level the playing field; all groups can have day in court
- Courts as safety against potential tyranny of the majority
- Legislative action—amendment process to the Constitution—can reverse judicial decisions

Opposing Policy Role for Courts
- Justices swayed by political or social considerations
- *Scott* v. *Sanford*—Missouri Compromise unconstitutional
- *Plessy* v. *Ferguson*—established separate but equal
- *Regents of the University of California* v. *Bakke*, *Hopwood* v. *State of Texas*—affirmative action
- Decisions in school prayer cases rankle conservatives
- Supreme Court justices chosen for ideological compatibility with the president and the president's party
- Lower court justices also chosen for ideological compatibility with party in power
- Impartiality of judges not true
- Federal judges not beholden to the electorate; appointed for life for most positions

SUGGESTIONS FOR FREE-RESPONSE ESSAY 3

Test-Taking Strategy

Creating a table listing the characteristics of the groups you need to compare and contrast is a good way to use your planning time to answer a question like this.

You might have chosen the following points about voters and nonvoters for your essay contrasting their characteristics. Consider these points as you evaluate your essay.

Groups of people who tend to vote have the following characteristics in common:

- higher levels of income and education
- strong party identification
- active community involvement
- belief that voting is important
- homeowners
- white

Groups of people who tend not to vote have the following characteristics in common:

- lower levels of income and education
- weak party identification
- not active community members, isolated
- belief that voting makes little difference
- renters
- nonwhite

A few factors are so important that they influence voter turnout regardless of income, education, race, or party identification.

- A high sense of political efficacy on the part of the individual
- The degree of two-party competition in a race
- The combined effect of several factors rather than the force of one factor alone

SUGGESTIONS FOR FREE-RESPONSE ESSAY 4

Test-Taking Strategy

Don't be reluctant to state your opinion, but be sure to support it well with facts and evidence.

You might have chosen the following points about democracy for your essay analyzing democracy and the element of it that Americans seems to value most. Consider these points as you evaluate your essay.

Five Basic Concepts of Democracy

- Fundamental worth of each individual

  - each person's worth and dignity respected; sanctity of the individual

- Respect for the equality of all persons

  - Equality of opportunity

  - Equality before the law

- Majority rule/minority rights

  - Public policy comes from public will

  - Majority rule restrained by minority rights

- Compromise

  - Reach position acceptable to largest number

  - Give and take required

- Widest possible individual freedom

  - Balance individual rights with society's rights

  - liberty versus authority

Most Highly Valued Concept: Freedom

- Personal freedom

- Right to privacy

- Free exchange of ideas

- Freedom of expression, of thought, of speech, of religion, of assembly, of petition; Bill of Rights

SELF-EVALUATION RUBRIC FOR THE ADVANCED PLACEMENT ESSAYS

	8–9	5–7	2–4	0–1
Overall Impression	Demonstrates excellent understanding of U.S. government and legal system; outstanding writing; thorough and effective; incisive	Demonstrates good understanding of U.S. government and legal system; good writing competence	Reveals simplistic thinking and/or immature understanding of U.S. government and legal system; fails to respond adequately to the question; little or no analysis	Very little or no understanding of U.S. government and legal system; unacceptably brief; fails to respond to the question; little clarity
Understanding of the U.S. Government	Scholarly; excellent understanding of the question; effective and incisive; in-depth critical analysis; includes apt, specific references; acknowledges other views	Mostly accurate use of information about U.S. government and legal system; good understanding of the question; often perceptive and clear; includes specific references and critical analysis	Some inaccuracies in information regarding U.S. government; superficial understanding and treatment of the question; lack of adequate knowledge about U.S. government; overgeneralized	Serious errors in presenting information about U.S. government and legal system; extensive misreading of the question and little supporting evidence; completely off the topic
Development	Original, unique, and/or intriguing thesis; excellent use of fundamentals and principles of U.S. government; thoroughly developed; conclusion shows applicability of thesis to other situations	Adequate thesis; satisfactory use of knowledge of U.S. government; competent development; acceptable conclusion	Inadequate, irrelevant, or illogical thesis; little use of knowledge of government; some development; unsatisfactory, inapplicable, or nonexistent conclusion	Lacking both thesis and conclusion; little or no evidence of knowledge of U.S. government
Conventions of English	Meticulously and thoroughly organized; coherent and unified; virtually error free	Reasonably organized; mostly coherent and unified; few or some errors	Somewhat organized; some incoherence and lack of unity; some major errors	Little or no organization; incoherent and void of unity; extremely flawed

Rate yourself in each of the categories below. Enter the numbers on the lines below. Be as honest as possible so you will know what areas need work. Then calculate the average of the four numbers to determine your final score. It is difficult to score yourself objectively, so you may wish to ask a respected friend or teacher to assess your essays for a more accurate reflection of their strengths and weaknesses. On the AP test itself, a reader will rate your essays on a scale of 0 to 9, with 9 being the highest.

Each category is rated 9 (high) to 0 (incompetent).

ESSAY 1
SELF-EVALUATION
Overall Impression _____
Understanding of U.S. Government _____
Development _____
Conventions of English _____

TOTAL _____
    Divide by 4 for final score. _____

ESSAY 1
OBJECTIVE EVALUATION
Overall Impression _____
Understanding of U.S. Government _____
Development _____
Conventions of English _____

TOTAL _____
    Divide by 4 for final score. _____

ESSAY 2
SELF-EVALUATION
Overall Impression _____
Understanding of U.S. Government _____
Development _____
Conventions of English _____

TOTAL _____
    Divide by 4 for final score. _____

ESSAY 2
OBJECTIVE EVALUATION
Overall Impression _____
Understanding of U.S. Government _____
Development _____
Conventions of English _____

TOTAL _____
    Divide by 4 for final score. _____

ESSAY 3
SELF-EVALUATION
Overall Impression _____
Understanding of U.S. Government _____
Development _____
Conventions of English _____

TOTAL _____
    Divide by 4 for final score. _____

ESSAY 3
OBJECTIVE EVALUATION
Overall Impression _____
Understanding of U.S. Government _____
Development _____
Conventions of English _____

TOTAL _____
    Divide by 4 for final score. _____

ESSAY 4
SELF-EVALUATION
Overall Impression _____
Understanding of U.S. Government _____
Development _____
Conventions of English _____

TOTAL _____
    Divide by 4 for final score. _____

ESSAY 4
OBJECTIVE EVALUATION
Overall Impression _____
Understanding of U.S. Government _____
Development _____
Conventions of English _____

TOTAL _____
    Divide by 4 for final score. _____

Chapter 1

STRATEGIES FOR MULTIPLE-CHOICE QUESTIONS

This chapter provides some basic information about the AP U.S. Government & Politics Test as well as strategies for answering the different types of questions that you will find on it. During your time in school, you have answered hundreds, probably thousands, of multiple-choice items. This AP test is not that different, and like other tests, if you have studied and know some test-taking techniques, you can do well.

PRACTICE PLAN

Use the *Diagnostic Test* as a tool to improve your objective test-taking skills. Use the techniques explained in this chapter to practice answering the questions. Then correct your responses with the *Quick-Score Answers* provided for each *Practice Test*. If you do not understand why an answer is correct, refer to the explanations given after the *Quick-Score Answers*. It is a good idea to read the answer explanations to all of the questions anyway, because you may find ideas or tips that will help you better analyze the answer choices to questions on the next *Practice Test* you take and on the real test. The answer explanations often have additional information about the topic that could come in handy in answering other questions.

Study Strategy

Check the "Practice Plan for Studying for the AP U.S. Government and Politics Test," pp. 11–16.

After you have finished reviewing all the answers, ask yourself what your weak areas are and what you can do to improve your test-taking techniques and your knowledge of the underlying principles of American government. Are there some concepts that you need to spend time brushing up on? Or are you having trouble with the operations of the various branches of government? Review the strategies in this chapter and then study Chapters 3 through 7, which offer a brief review of U.S. government and politics. Then try taking *Practice Test 1*.

BASIC INFORMATION ABOUT THE TEST

1. Section I consists of 60 questions. There are five possible answer choices for each question.

2. You will have 45 minutes to answer the questions in Section I.

3. You will receive 1 point for each correct answer. Points are not deducted for questions that you leave blank. If you answer incorrectly, a quarter of a point is subtracted. This is the guessing penalty.

4. Section I counts for 50 percent of your score.

5. Of the five areas of skills and abilities that the College Board says this AP test measures, three relate directly to the multiple-choice section:

   - Factual knowledge: facts, concepts, and theories of U.S. government

   - Comprehension of the typical patterns of political processes and behaviors and their effects

   - Analysis and interpretation of governmental and political data and of relationships in government and politics

6. Both the essay questions and the multiple-choice questions are based on content from the following six areas of study dealing with U.S. government and politics:

   - Constitutional Basis of the Government

     - Influences on the Framers of the Constitution
     - Separation of powers and checks and balances
     - Concept of federalism
     - Theories of democratic government

   - Political Beliefs and Behaviors of Individuals

     - Basic political beliefs that individuals hold
     - Ways people acquire political knowledge and attitudes
     - Factors that influence how and why people develop different political beliefs and behaviors
     - Methods of political participation including voting
     - Public opinion

- Political Behavior of Groups: Functions, Activities, Sources of Power, Influences

  - Political parties
  - Interest groups, including PACs
  - The mass media
  - Elections

- National Government: Organization, Functions, Activities, Interrelationships

  - Presidency
  - Congress
  - Federal judiciary
  - Federal bureaucracy
  - Role of voters, nongovernmental groups, and public opinion

- Public Policy

  - How policy is made and by whom
  - How policy is implemented: the role of the bureaucracy and the courts
  - Influences: political parties, interest groups, voters, and public opinion

- Civil Rights and Civil Liberties

  - Constitutional guarantees
  - Role of judicial interpretation
  - Impact of the Fourteenth Amendment

7. The College Board breaks down the categories to show approximate percentages of questions in each broad area of study. The following list shows the range of questions that might appear on an AP U.S. Government & Politics test. The largest number of questions—between 21 and 27—deal with the national government, so spending time studying the four institutions of the national government would be time well spent.

   - Constitutional Basis of the Government—5 to 15 percent

   - Political Beliefs and Behaviors of Individuals—10 to 20 percent

   - Political Behavior of Groups: Functions, Activities, Sources of Power, Influences—10 to 20 percent

- National Government: Organization, Functions, Activities, Interrelationships—35 to 45 percent

- Public Policy—5 to 15 percent

- Civil Rights and Civil Liberties—5 to 15 percent

8. The majority of questions are statements to complete or questions to answer. Some questions are based on visuals, such as cartoons or tables, or on brief quotations and are known as stimulus-response questions. The graphics questions are usually straightforward read-and-interpret questions. Occasionally, you may find an additional question related to the visual that asks for an answer requiring knowledge other than what is shown on the graphic.

9. Generally, the questions in the beginning of the test tend to be easier, and questions become more difficult as you progress through the test.

Test-Taking Strategy

In skipping questions, be sure to skip their answer ovals on the answer sheet.

10. You can answer some combination of answers correctly, leave some questions blank, and write four acceptable essays and still get a score of 3. The more multiple-choice questions you answer correctly, the greater your chance of a higher score and the less pressure on you for writing exceptional essays.

These last two facts mean that you should try to answer as many of the questions at the beginning of the test as possible and that you do not have to answer all of the questions.

PACING

Test-Taking Strategy

Working out a plan to pace yourself is important.

Answering 60 questions in 45 minutes may seem like running a marathon in record time. It is important to remember that you may not be able to answer all the questions, even with educated guessing. But you should pace yourself so you can read all of the questions, answer the easier ones, and leave the harder ones to return to later.

Because the questions at the beginning of the test tend to be easier, you might plan to spend more time on those questions and less time on the final questions. For example, rather than allotting yourself 45 seconds to read and answer each question, think about dividing your 45 minutes into 15-minute segments. Then divide up the questions so that you tackle more in the first 15 minutes, when you are fresh, than in the last 15 minutes, when you are tired and the questions are more difficult. Or, if you start slowly, surge in the middle, and lag at the end, you might try to pace yourself to answer more questions in the middle of the test. One of the benefits of taking the *Diagnostic Test* and *Practice Tests* in this book is that you can devise a pacing schedule that best fits how you work.

In developing your plan, however, understand that when we say you may be working on 15 questions in the final 15 minutes, we do not necessarily mean that you are doing the last 15 questions on the test in those final 15 minutes. We mean that the last questions you work on should be the ones that are the most difficult for you to answer. You should skip truly difficult questions on your first pass through the test rather than spend time trying to figure them out. Even the College Board suggests this.

Here are some other suggestions to help you pace yourself:

* Don't spend too much time on a difficult question.

Test-Taking Strategy

Don't make marks on the answer sheet except to fill in answer ovals. Stray marks confuse the machine that scores the tests.

* If you read a question and the content and answer choices don't seem familiar, skip the question. Put an "X" next to it in the test booklet and be sure you skip the answer oval.

* If you read a question and don't know the answer immediately but at least one of the answer choices seems wrong, try the steps listed on page 9 for making an educated guess. If you can't immediately eliminate any other answer choices, don't spend any more time. Put a check (✔) next to the question and move on, skipping the answer oval for the question.

* When you have read through the entire test and have answered what you can immediately or with a few seconds' thought, go back first to the questions marked with a check and try those again. If you still have time, try the questions you marked with an X.

One word of advice: Don't worry if a question at the beginning of the test seems too difficult for you. Although we say the earlier questions tend to be easier, all things are relative. What may be a snap question for some students because the subject was their teacher's favorite may be a blank to other students because they only spent one class period on it.

ANALYZING QUESTIONS

As you have just read, the test assesses three types of skills and abilities and uses several question types to do this. The following examples illustrate how the test writers mix and match question types and content to assess what you know and can do.

QUESTIONS AND SENTENCE COMPLETIONS

Some questions simply ask for straight recall of information. They want to know what facts, terms, concepts, and generalizations you know. These questions may be in the form of a straightforward question or a sentence completion, such as

Marbury v. *Madison* established

(A) the scope of presidential war powers.
(B) the principle of judicial review.
(C) the principle of implied powers in the Constitution.
(D) Congress's right to regulate interstate commerce.
(E) the principle of separate but equal.

The correct answer is (B). If you did not know the answer immediately, you could eliminate at least one possible answer, choice (E). Madison served both as secretary of state and president before cases began to come to the Supreme Court about the rights of African Americans, the most logical topic for a "separate but equal" court case.

A question may also use a qualifier such as NOT, LEAST, or EXCEPT, such as

All of the following were provisions of the Constitution as originally ratified EXCEPT

(A) indirect election of senators.
(B) the counting of three fifths of slaves for purposes of determining representation in the House.
(C) abolition of the internal slave trade.
(D) enumerated powers.
(E) the elastic clause.

The correct answer is (C). The Constitution forbade the importation of slaves after 1808 but said nothing about the internal slave trade, which grew dramatically in the following decades with the spread of cotton agriculture.

Both of these questions ask you to recall certain information that you have learned. The second question has a twist. It wants the wrong answer—that is, it wants you to select the choice that was not a part of the Constitution as it was originally ratified. To answer questions that ask you to find the answer choice that does not belong, read each answer and ask yourself if the answer choice is correct in relation to the content. If it is, cross it off and try the next response. Keep going until you find a response that is not true in relation to the content of the question. Similar questions may use key words such as NOT and LEAST.

Key Words

Although most questions follow the questioning format or the sentence completion format, not all ask for straightforward recall. Some require analysis and interpretation.

- Look for words that signal cause-and-effect relationships, such as *because of, direct result of, consequence of, primary reason,* and *primary purpose.*

- Look for words that ask you to analyze or interpret, such as *most significant, significance of, most characteristic of, most accurately describes, best describes, best known for, primarily,* and *most influential.*

A word like *significant* means you should be looking for why something is important in the larger context of U.S. government and politics, possibly an underlying concept or a generalization. Words such as *best describes* or *least likely* are asking you to analyze the information and come up with an opinion based on facts. In both instances, one or more of the answer choices may be correct; you need to look for the one that is most inclusive, giving the broadest view of the subject.

TWO-STEP QUESTIONS

Two-step or tiered questions require you to decide which point or points are correct and then to determine which answer choice corresponds to your determination.

Medicaid is

  I. a federally funded program.
 II. a private insurance program.
III. a state-funded program.

(A) I and II
(B) I, II, and III
(C) I and III
(D) II and III
(E) I only

To answer this question, you first need to read each point and decide whether Medicaid is a federally funded program (I), a private insurance program (II), and/or a state-funded program (III). Medicaid, which pays for medical assistance for the poor—those who are under 65 and are eligible for welfare as well as poor children, poor pregnant women, and the elderly who are not eligible for welfare—is financed by both the federal government and state governments, so points I and III are correct. Then you need to determine which answer choice matches your response. Only choice (C) includes points I and III.

This question format is often used to ask you to put events in sequential order, such as how a bill becomes a law or what the steps are in the appeals process.

STIMULUS-RESPONSE QUESTIONS

Stimulus-response questions are based on visuals or on short quotations. Most often the visuals are political cartoons, tables, and graphs. The quotations may be taken from court decisions, from the Constitution, or from the writings of famous people. You cannot read and know every word in the Constitution or in relevant court cases, but when taking the test you can remember to

- read the quotation and highlight the key words in it.

- restate the quotation to be sure you understand it.

- read the question and highlight the key words in it.

- relate the question to the quotation.

- keep this restatement in mind as you read the answer choices.

Questions based on visuals usually ask you to choose the answer that is best supported by the data.

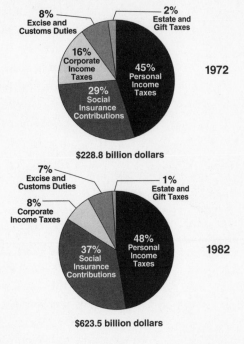

$228.8 billion dollars

$623.5 billion dollars

Department of Commerce

According to the two pie charts, the fastest-growing source of government revenue between 1972 and 1982 was

(A) Personal Income Taxes.
(B) Social Insurance Contributions.
(C) Corporate Income Taxes.
(D) Excise and Customs Duties.
(E) Estate and Gift Taxes.

The correct answer is (B). In this question, as in most questions on the test, the relationship is usually clear. The problem comes when you try to read too much into the data and choose an answer that may be true but which the given data does not support. When confronted with a question based on a table or graph, follow these helpful hints:

• Read the question stem first and highlight key words.

• Read the title of the graphic.

• Read the categories on the x and y axes of line graphs or bar graphs.

• Read all the labels identifying the data.

• Look for trends in the data.

• Read the question again and then read the answer choices.

In the end, knowing the type of question you are being asked is less important than paying attention to what the question is asking you. Circle, underline, or bracket the key words in the question. Use them to guide you to the correct answer.

EDUCATED GUESSING

Remember what we said about educated guessing in *Scoring High* on page 9. As you practice taking the tests in this book, use the strategies for making educated guesses when you know something about a question but are not sure of the answer. Once you see how educated guessing can help raise your score, you will feel more confident using the strategies during the real test.

PRACTICING

Study Strategy

Once you have finished a Practice Set, *read all the* explanations. *The reasoning involved and the additional information may help with questions on the real test.*

Read and answer *Practice Set 1* on the next page. Jot down your answers to the questions in the margin or on a separate sheet of paper. If you do not understand a question, you may check the explanation immediately. You may refer to the answers question by question, or you may wish to score the entire set at one time. Either is acceptable.

Follow the same procedure with *Practice Sets 2* and *3*. You might want to complete *Practice Set 2* and correct the answers before you try *Practice Set 3*. That way you will have another chance to work on any specific areas of weakness in your test-taking skills.

PRACTICE SET 1

Directions: Each question or incomplete sentence is followed by five suggested responses. Select the best answer and fill in the corresponding oval on the answer sheet.

1. Social Insurance Contributions (FICA) include

   I. Old Age, Survivors, and Disability insurance.
   II. Medicare.
   III. Worker's Compensation.

   (A) I
   (B) II
   (C) III
   (D) I and II
   (E) II and III

2. Which of the following was adopted to resolve the issue of representation in the House and Senate?

   (A) Three-Fifths Compromise
   (B) New Jersey Plan
   (C) Direct election of senators
   (D) Great Compromise
   (E) Virginia Plan

3. Why was the presidential election of 1980 of major significance?

   (A) It demonstrated the importance of the economy in presidential elections.
   (B) It signaled a shift among voters to conservatism.
   (C) It reawakened interest in party politics.
   (D) It was the first time a movie star was elected president.
   (E) It showed a weariness with Jimmy Carter's leadership style.

Questions 4 and 5 refer to the following amendment from the Constitution.

All persons born or naturalized in the United States, and subject to the jurisdiction thereof, are citizens of the United States and of the State wherein they reside. No state shall make or enforce any law which shall abridge the privileges or immunities of citizens of the United States; nor shall any State deprive any person of life, liberty, or property, without due process of law; nor deny to any person within its jurisdiction the equal protection of the laws.

4. All of the following types of cases are prosecuted under this amendment EXCEPT

   (A) sexual harassment.
   (B) blocking access to public places.
   (C) obstructing the right to vote.
   (D) burning the U.S. flag.
   (E) refusing college admission to students based on race.

5. Which of the following Supreme Court decisions was based on this amendment?

   (A) *Gideon* v. *Wainwright*
   (B) *Wesberry* v. *Sanders*
   (C) *Brown* v. *Board of Education of Topeka*
   (D) *Schechter Poultry* v. *the United States*
   (E) *Mapp* v. *Ohio*

6. An iron triangle refers to the cooperative relationship found

   (A) among the three levels of the federal judiciary.
   (B) in the separation of powers.
   (C) between a congressional committee, a government agency, and their client interest groups.
   (D) in the system of checks and balances.
   (E) between a federal department, a regulatory agency, and a congressional committee.

7. The bully pulpit is a tool for shaping public opinion used by

   (A) the media.
   (B) the president.
   (C) the Speaker of the House.
   (D) interest groups.
   (E) the Senate majority leader.

8. The Miranda rule is an example of

   (A) procedural due process.
   (B) equal protection under the law.
   (C) police power.
   (D) substantive due process.
   (E) habeas corpus.

ANSWERS AND EXPLANATIONS

Quick-Score Answers			
1. D	3. B	5. C	7. B
2. D	4. D	6. C	8. A

PRACTICE SET 1

Test-Taking Strategy

For two-step questions, determine which point(s) is correct and then find the answer choice that corresponds to that point(s).

1. **The correct answer is (D).** After you read the question stem, read through the points and decide which ones complete the sentence correctly. FICA includes Old Age, Survivors, and Disability Insurance (I) and Medicare (II), but not Worker's Compensation (III). Then check which of the five answer choices include points I and II. Only choice (D) has both and is, therefore, the correct answer.

2. **The correct answer is (D).** According to the Great or Connecticut Compromise, there would be two legislative houses. In the lower house, each state would have representation based on population, whereas in the upper house each state would have two representatives. Choice (A) refers to the compromise about counting slaves as part of the population, and choice (B) refers to a plan for allotting the same number of representatives for each state. Choice (E) was a plan to base representation on state population.

Test-Taking Strategy

The key words here are major significance.

3. **The correct answer is (B).** Choices (A), (D), and (E) were all factors in the election of 1980, but the election's significance lay in the turn of many voters toward more limited government. Ronald Reagan was the first conservative president elected since Calvin Coolidge. Reagan campaigned on a platform of lower taxes, reduced government spending, and a strengthened military. Choice (C) is incorrect.

4. **The correct answer is (D).** The amendment quoted is the Fourteenth Amendment, which is used to prosecute cases that violate a person's civil rights or civil liberties. Choices (A), (B), (C), and (E) all relate to these areas of the law. Choice (D) relates to the First Amendment's guarantee of freedom of speech. Do not be confused by choice (E). While the Fifth Circuit Court of Appeals ruled in *Hopwood* v. *State of Texas* that a state college or university cannot use race as a factor in granting admissions or scholarships, a person still cannot be denied admission because of his or her race. (The *Hopwood* decision relates only to the jurisdiction of the Fifth Circuit—Texas, Mississippi, and Louisiana.)

5. **The correct answer is (C).** The decision in choice (C), *Brown v. Board of Education of Topeka,* was based on the equal protection clause of the Fourteenth Amendment. The decision in choice (A), *Gideon* v. *Wainwright,* continued the nationalization of the guarantees of the Bill of Rights, in this instance, the Sixth Amendment's guarantee of the right of the poor to an attorney in felony cases. The Supreme Court decision in choice (B), *Wesberry* v. *Sanders,* cited Article I, Section 2 of the Constitution as the basis for overturning the case, one in the series of "one man, one vote" cases the Court has heard. The law that authorized the National Recovery Administration (NRA) was overturned in *Schechter Poultry* v. *United States,* choice (D), on the basis that it violated the commerce clause of Article I. The Supreme Court ruled in choice (E), *Mapp* v. *Ohio,* that evidence obtained through unreasonable search and seizure violated the Fourth Amendment and could not be used in a trial.

Test-Taking Strategy

This is a disguised definitional question, asking you to define a term by giving an example.

6. **The correct answer is (C).** Although there are three levels of the federal judiciary, choice (A), this answer is incorrect. Choices (B) and (D) are good distracters but are the wrong answers. Choice (E) is illogical because a regulatory agency is part of the federal bureaucracy.

7. **The correct answer is (B).** The term *bully pulpit* was coined by President Theodore Roosevelt and refers to the use of the president's position to rally public support for issues. By virtue of his office, the president's words and actions are newsworthy. No other public official has the same ability to focus national attention, thus making choices (C), (D), and (E) incorrect. Choice (A) is illogical since the media are the tools the president uses.

Test-Taking Strategy

This is another definitional question. These types of questions are asking you to recall information and then apply it to a situation.

8. **The correct answer is (A).** Procedural due process, choice (A), means that the police may not violate a person's rights in the enforcement of the law. Reading a suspect his or her rights under the Miranda decision is an example of procedural due process. Substantive due process, choice (D), refers to the finding of the courts that a law is unreasonable. Choices (B), (C), and (E) are incorrect. Choice (E) refers to the order to bring an accused person before a court of law to determine whether he or she is being held lawfully.

PRACTICE SET 2

Directions: Each question or incomplete sentence is followed by five suggested responses. Select the best answer and fill in the corresponding oval on the answer sheet.

1. The case against John Peter Zenger is considered a landmark case in the development of which freedom?

   (A) Speech
   (B) Religion
   (C) The press
   (D) The right to bear arms
   (E) The right to assemble

2. The major significance of the delegated powers listed in the Constitution is

   (A) that the powers correct areas of weakness in the Articles of Confederation.
   (B) that Congress is given the power to levy and collect taxes.
   (C) that the delegated powers relate to matters of common concern across the states.
   (D) that the states reserve some powers to themselves.
   (E) that the Tenth Amendment asserts that powers not given to the states reside with the federal government.

3. In *Regents of the University of California v. Bakke*, the Supreme Court ruled

   (A) that affirmative action programs were unconstitutional.
   (B) that President Johnson had erred in issuing his executive order requiring those who received federal money to hire and promote members of minorities.
   (C) that while strict racial quotas were unconstitutional in determining admissions, race could be taken into consideration.
   (D) that bilingual education was not mandatory.
   (E) that the Civil Rights Act of 1964, which prohibited discrimination in hiring and firing, wages, and promotion based on sex, race, religion, or place of birth, was constitutional.

4. All of the following are examples of the concept that third parties often develop out of some radical approach to a problem EXCEPT the

   (A) Populists.
   (B) Progressives.
   (C) Know-Nothings.
   (D) Democrats (Andrew Jackson era).
   (E) Republicans (founded in 1854).

5. The most significant fact about the 1960 presidential election was

(A) that the primaries pitted two branches of the Democratic Party against each other.

(B) that an incumbent vice president lost his bid for the presidency.

(C) the role television played in determining the outcome of the election.

(D) the fact that voters elected the first Roman Catholic president.

(E) that in an attempt to balance the ticket, the Democrats chose a Southerner as the vice presidential nominee.

6. In the mid-twentieth century, which of the following issues would most likely have resulted in a vote along sectional lines in Congress?

(A) Gay rights legislation

(B) Civil rights legislation

(C) Aid to education

(D) Equal Rights Amendment

(E) Social Security increases

7. Which of the following are provisions of the Immigration Reform and Control Act of 1986?

I. Knowingly hiring an undocumented alien is a crime.

II. For one year, undocumented aliens could take advantage of an amnesty program to become legal residents of the United States.

III. Undocumented aliens are prohibited from receiving social security benefits.

IV. Undocumented aliens are prohibited from public housing.

(A) I only

(B) II only

(C) I and II

(D) III and IV

(E) I, III, and IV

Question 8 refers to the following pie charts and tables.

ELECTION OF 1860

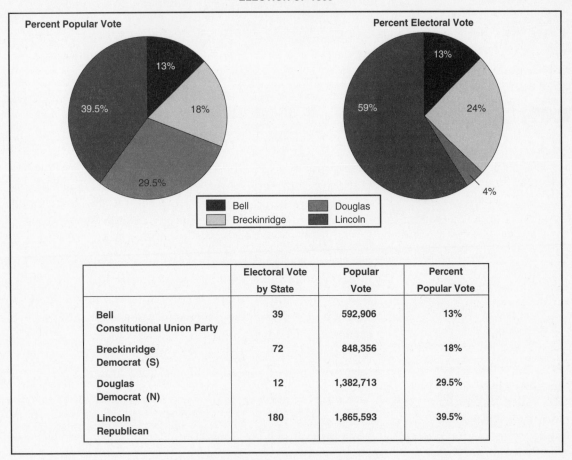

	Electoral Vote by State	Popular Vote	Percent Popular Vote
Bell Constitutional Union Party	39	592,906	13%
Breckinridge Democrat (S)	72	848,356	18%
Douglas Democrat (N)	12	1,382,713	29.5%
Lincoln Republican	180	1,865,593	39.5%

8. The information on these pie charts and table illustrates what problem that can occur with the emergence of third parties in presidential elections?

(A) Most splinter parties break off from the Democratic Party.

(B) A strong showing by third-party candidates can throw a presidential election into the House.

(C) A strong showing by a third-party candidate can give that candidate leverage in bargaining with the front-runner.

(D) A strong showing by third-party candidates can result in a president elected by less than a majority of the voters.

(E) To win, a candidate must win the states with the largest populations.

ANSWERS AND EXPLANATIONS

Quick-Score Answers			
1. C	3. C	5. C	7. C
2. C	4. D	6. B	8. D

PRACTICE SET 2

1. **The correct answer is (C).** Zenger published articles in his newspaper accusing the colonial governor of New York of election fraud, misappropriating public funds, and bribery. According to British libel law, it did not matter if the accusations were true, but Zenger's lawyer argued that the truth did matter and won Zenger's acquittal. Although British libel laws did not change, this case emboldened colonial newspapers to express opinions unpopular with the government and laid the foundation for freedom of the press as guaranteed in the U.S. Constitution. The First Amendment guarantees choice (C) as well as choice (A), freedom of speech; choice (B), freedom of religion; and choice (E), the right to assemble. Choice (D), the right to bear arms, is guaranteed by the Second Amendment.

Test-Taking Strategy

The key words are major significance.

2. **The correct answer is (C).** Choices (A), (B), (C), and (D) are true statements, but choice (D) does not relate to the delegated powers, so it can be eliminated. Of the other three choices, choices (A) and (B) are very specific. Choice (C) is a general view of delegated powers and thus a better answer. Choice (E) is the opposite of what the Tenth Amendment states. All powers not specifically delegated to the federal government reside with the states.

3. **The correct answer is (C).** The *Bakke* decision had a limited application and was not applied to all affirmative action programs, so choice (A) is incorrect. Choice (B) is incorrect; the decision did not overrule Johnson's executive order. Choice (D) is incorrect and does not relate to affirmative action. Choice (E) is incorrect; the constitutionality of the law was not questioned.

Test-Taking Strategy

For not/except questions, if an answer is correct in the context of the question, cross it off and go to the next answer.

4. **The correct answer is (D).** The Democrats who formed to support Andrew Jackson were something of an anomaly in the history of American third parties. Their purpose was to elect Jackson; there was no particular single driving social, political, or economic issue they wished to solve. The Populists, choice (A), were interested in reforms aimed at helping farmers, such as coinage of silver. Choice (B) advocated a number of reforms at all levels of society: government, business, social mores, and politics. Choice (C) formed to limit immigration and to keep Catholics and naturalized citizens out of government. Choice (E) formed from the Whig and Free-Soil Parties and abolitionists.

Test-Taking Strategy

The key words are most significant. *This question and answer also highlight an important concept about the role of television in shaping public opinion.*

5. **The correct answer is (C).** In a series of televised debates between Vice President Richard Nixon, the Republican nominee, and John F. Kennedy, the Democratic nominee, Kennedy showed that he had the experience and ability to handle himself that Nixon claimed Kennedy lacked. The television camera was also more flattering to Kennedy, who was more handsome and more at ease than the heavy-jowled and perspiring Nixon. Choices (A), (B), (D), and (E) are all true statements about the election of 1960 but are not particularly significant in terms of contributing principles or generalizations to the study of U.S. government and politics. The 1960 election, however, marked the arrival of television as an important medium for the communication—and manipulation—of political messages.

Test-Taking Strategy

The key words are most likely.

6. **The correct answer is (B).** In the mid-twentieth century, civil rights legislation still caused Southerners to vote as a bloc in Congress. Choice (A), gay rights legislation, was not an acknowledged political issue at mid-century. Choices (C), (D), and (E) are incorrect.

7. **The correct answer is (C).** The Immigration and Reform Act of 1986 established a one-year amnesty program that allowed undocumented aliens in certain circumstances to become legal residents (II). Conversely, the law also punished those who knowingly hired undocumented aliens (I). Points III and IV are part of the 1996 Illegal Immigration Restrictions Act and are, therefore, incorrect responses to the question. Only choice (C) includes both points I and II.

8. **The correct answer is (D).** The only answer supported by the data is choice (D). When more than two candidates are in a presidential election, the person who wins the presidency may be elected by less than a majority of the voters. Choice (A) is not related to the data. Choices (B), (C), and (E) are true statements but are not related to the data. The number of electors each state has is the sum of its senators and members of the House; states with larger populations have more members of the House.

PRACTICE SET 3

Directions: Each question or incomplete sentence is followed by five suggested responses. Select the best answer and fill in the corresponding oval on the answer sheet.

1. In the elections of 1932 and 1936, which of the following groups was new to the Democratic coalition?

    (A) Northern political machines
    (B) Southern whites who were small farmers
    (C) African Americans
    (D) Southern political machines
    (E) First- and second-generation immigrants

2. The Twelfth Amendment deals with

    (A) presidential disability.
    (B) the election of the president and vice president.
    (C) the direct election of senators.
    (D) the inauguration of the president and vice president.
    (E) limits on presidential terms of office.

3. The two-party political system in the United States was primarily the result of

    I.   the fight over ratification of the Constitution waged by the Federalists and the Anti-Federalists.
    II. conflicts in Congress over Hamilton's financial proposals.
    III. conflicts within Washington's Cabinet over Hamilton's financial proposals.

    (A) I only
    (B) II only
    (C) III only
    (D) I and II
    (E) II and III

4. The right to privacy was expanded in

    (A) *Heart of Atlanta* v. *United States.*
    (B) *Roe* v. *Wade.*
    (C) the Fourteenth Amendment.
    (D) the Civil Rights Act of 1964.
    (E) the Fair Credit Reporting Act of 1970.

5. All of the following are true of Congressional oversight EXCEPT

    (A) by law, legislative oversight is the responsibility of congressional committees and subcommittees.
    (B) in reality, legislative oversight is not done systematically.
    (C) legislative oversight involves reviewing how well the executive branch is carrying out the programs and laws passed by Congress.
    (D) because members of congressional committees work so closely with members of federal agencies, oversight is easy to do.
    (E) oversight is often reserved for those programs or situations that will garner publicity for the congressional committee.

6. PACs most often support

    (A) controversial issues.
    (B) federal judges.
    (C) organized labor.
    (D) officeholders seeking reelection.
    (E) corporate clients.

7. A New Democrat is more likely to favor all of the following EXCEPT

    (A) gun control.
    (B) abortion rights.
    (C) welfare reform.
    (D) tax cuts.
    (E) protection of Social Security.

8. Federal personal income taxes are

    (A) proportional.
    (B) regressive.
    (C) progressive.
    (D) proportional and regressive.
    (E) progressive and proportional.

ANSWERS AND EXPLANATIONS

Quick-Score Answers			
1. C	3. E	5. D	7. D
2. B	4. B	6. D	8. C

PRACTICE SET 3

1. **The correct answer is (C).** From Reconstruction until Roosevelt, African Americans had traditionally voted the Republican ticket, the party of Lincoln. Southern small farmers, choice (B), had voted for Hoover in 1928 but returned to the Democratic Party under Roosevelt. Southern political machines were also Democratic, choice (D). Since the late 1800s, immigrants, choice (E), had traditionally voted for the Democrats who ran the Northern big city political machines, choice (A).

2. **The correct answer is (B).** The Twenty-Fifth Amendment deals with presidential disability, choice (A). The direct election of senators, choice (C), is stated in the Seventeenth Amendment. The Twentieth Amendment, referred to as the "lame duck" amendment, details the beginning of terms of office of the president and vice president, choice (D). The Twenty-Second Amendment limits the number of years a person may hold office as president, choice (E).

Test-Taking Strategy

Be sure all parts of an answer are correct. A partially correct answer is a partially incorrect answer— and a quarter-point deduction.

3. **The correct answer is (E).** Although people began to group themselves as Federalists and Anti-Federalists during the campaign to ratify the Constitution (I), real party lines were not drawn until the government was inaugurated (II and III). Choices (A) and (D) are incorrect because they both include point I. Choices (B) and (C) are incorrect because they contain only half the correct answer.

4. **The correct answer is (B).** Choice (A) upheld Congress's use of the commerce clause as the basis for civil rights legislation. Choice (C) defines the rights of citizens. Choice (D) prohibits discrimination in employment and created the Equal Employment Opportunity Commission. Choice (E) regulates the collection and dissemination of information about people's credit history, but it does not relate to the question.

5. **The correct answer is (D).** Choice (D) is the opposite of what happens. The friendly relationship between the committees and the agencies whose actions they are supposed to oversee is a reason why it is difficult to provide meaningful oversight. Choices (A), (B), (C), and (E) are all true about legislative oversight.

6. **The correct answer is (D).** Choice (A) is incorrect because PACs support the whole spectrum of political interests. Choice (B) is illogical because federal judges are appointed, not elected. Choices (C) and (E) are illogical because there are PACs that lobby for the interests of labor and PACs that support the interests of business; the question stem uses the phrase *most often.* Typically, PACs support incumbents in reelection campaigns.

7. **The correct answer is (D).** The New Democrat or Centrist position supports all of the choices except choice (D), tax cuts. Moneys lost in tax cuts could be used to shore up Social Security.

8. **The correct answer is (C).** Federal personal income taxes take a larger share of higher incomes than lower ones. Federal corporate income taxes are also progressive. Choice (A) takes the same percentage of all incomes. State or local sales taxes are regressive, choice (B), in that they take a larger proportion of lower incomes than higher ones. FICA is both proportional, because it takes the same percentage of tax out of everyone's income up to a maximum wage, and regressive, because it takes a larger percentage out of smaller incomes. Choice (E) is incorrect.

Chapter 2

ABOUT WRITING THE ESSAYS

Section II of the AP U.S. Government & Politics exam consists of four essay questions. You will have 100 minutes to answer all questions. There are no optional questions in this test; all four questions are mandatory. Together, these essays make up 50 percent of your score. Of course you want to earn a 9 on each of the essays, but you don't need to score that high to earn a 5 for your composite score. To perform well on the essay portion, you need to plan and to practice now so that on the day of the test, you will have the self-confidence to excel, not panic.

PRACTICE PLAN

Study Strategy

Check the "Practice Plan for Studying for the AP U.S. Government & Politics Test," pp. 11–16.

This chapter will help you to understand what the data-based and the free-response questions require and how to answer each type of question. You will have an opportunity to review the specifics of good essay writing and to learn some helpful techniques to use when you take the test. You will also practice writing sample essays and then use the rubric, or scoring guide, to pinpoint your weaknesses and to improve your writing skills as you tackle each new practice essay.

Use the *Diagnostic Test* and *Practice Tests* as tools to improve your writing, too. Apply the techniques described in this chapter to plan and write each essay within 25 minutes, the approximate time allowed per question on the actual Advanced Placement exam. When you have completed the essays, turn to the *Explanation of Answers* section following each test. First, score your essay with the *Self-Evaluation Rubric.* Then compare your work against the list of suggested points that you might have discussed in your essay. Look for your weak points and ask yourself how you can improve. Take several of the points from the list and rework your essay using those points to strengthen ineffective areas.

Reevaluate your essay. Again compare the points you made with the ones we suggest. Were you better able to dissect the question and discern what was required to answer it more effectively? By using our suggestions, did you improve your response by writing a more focused and more clearly developed answer? Ask yourself how much your work improved. Determine any remaining weak points and concentrate on improving them in subsequent essays.

Don't continue to revise your essay. You will not have the opportunity to polish your work to perfection on the test, and the evaluators know that you cannot write a perfect essay in 25 minutes. The purpose of reworking a practice essay is to help you pinpoint what the question is really asking and how you can best answer it with a clear, coherent, and unified essay. Keep in mind what you learned on your first attempt at the essay. Then go to the next essay question and repeat the process, building confidence as you go in your analytical skills and your ability to develop effective essays.

BASIC INFORMATION ABOUT THE ESSAY SECTION

Study Strategy

Use a watch to pace yourself as you write the practice essays. That way you will become comfortable with the time limit of the test.

1. Section II contains four essay questions, all of which you must answer.

2. You have 100 minutes to write your responses, so you should allow about 25 minutes for each question.

3. Most essays ask you to analyze, assess, or evaluate an aspect of government or politics.

4. Essay questions may be based on

   - a formal thesis.

   - an introductory statement that lists the tasks you must answer.

   - data (charts, graphs, tables, quotations, political cartoons).

5. Each essay is scored from 1 to 9, with 9 being the highest.

6. The readers, using a scoring guide developed by the College Board, evaluate each of the essays holistically.

7. The essays together account for 50 percent of your final composite score.

8. The essays will not have a single correct answer. Your answers will come from what you have learned in class. In addition, the essays often ask for your point of view, which you must support with evidence.

SOME PRACTICAL ADVICE

Red Alert

If you answer more than half the multiple-choice questions correctly and score in the middle or higher on the essays, you will receive at least a 3.

Test-Taking Strategy

While neatness and legible handwriting do not count, they do matter. If graders have difficulty reading your responses, they may tend to undervalue your essay.

If you consider these facts, you will realize that you need to do some planning and practicing. Since you have 100 minutes to write four essays, you cannot spend half the time on one essay and leave only 50 minutes for the remaining three. When you write the practice essays in this book, take 3 to 4 minutes to read the question and any data carefully and then plan what you will say. Use the remaining 20 minutes to write your essay and the final minute for a quick revision.

Although you must answer all four questions, begin with the essay that seems easiest. It will build your confidence. Because your four essays will be read by four different people, you do not have to worry that one weak essay will pull down the scores for the other three essays. Instead, you can be confident that your clear, coherent, unified—and neatly written—essays will stand out.

THE ESSAY: A QUICK REVIEW

You will recall that an essay is a group of paragraphs that work together to present a main point, or thesis. An essay contains an introductory paragraph, separate paragraphs that develop the thesis, and a concluding paragraph. You can see the parts of a five-paragraph essay—the beginning, called the introduction; the middle, called the body; and the ending, called the conclusion—on the next page.

Not all of your AP essays may require five paragraphs and one or two of your essays may have more than three body paragraphs. However, keeping this structure in mind will give you direction and help you organize your essay.

WRITING AN OUTSTANDING ESSAY

Test-Taking Strategy

Spend a little more time on your opening paragraph and your conclusion. You want to make a good first and last impression on your reader.

As obvious as it seems, you accomplish the results you want—a good score—not only by demonstrating your knowledge of U.S. government and politics but also by communicating your expertise in a well-constructed essay. You may have to plan and write your essays in a short period of time, but the characteristics of these essays are no different from those of any good writing: unity, coherence, and adequate development. First, you must determine your audience. Second, you need to establish your purpose. Third, you have to choose the appropriate tone. You can determine these three elements with a great deal of certainty even before you see the questions.

INTRODUCTION

Interesting Material and Background Information On Topic

Thesis Statement

*The introduction should catch the reader's attention,
establish the purpose and tone, and
present the thesis statement,
or the main idea.*

Body Paragraph 1

Supporting Information

*Each paragraph within the body of the essay should develop a subtopic
of the main point by providing strong supporting information.*

Body Paragraph 2

Supporting Information

*Each paragraph within the body of the essay should develop a subtopic
of the main point by providing strong supporting information.*

Body Paragraph 3

Supporting Information

*Each paragraph within the body of the essay should develop a subtopic
of the main point by providing strong supporting information.*

CONCLUSION

Reminder of Thesis Statement

Summary or Final Remarks

*The conclusion of an essay should bring the essay
to a satisfactory close and remind the reader of the main point.*

AUDIENCE

You have an audience of one—a College Board-trained reader who teaches high school or college U.S. government and who will be reading hundreds of papers similar to yours. She or he will have a scoring guide, or rubric, to aid in evaluating your paper. He or she will score your essay holistically—that is, there is no single score for things like content, grammar, and punctuation. The reader will consider every aspect of your writing for its contribution to the overall impression your essay makes.

PURPOSE

Your purpose is to get a score of 5 or better. To do that, you need to write a unified, coherent, and consistent essay that answers the question. A well-written essay that misses the point of the question will not get you a good score. That is why you need to read this chapter.

TONE

Your tone is the reflection of your attitude toward the subject of the essay. A writer's tone, for example, may be lighthearted, brusque, or serious. The safest tone to adopt is formal and persuasive, since you are often asked to take a position and support it. You do not want to be stuffy and pretentious by using phrases such as "one understands" or "we can surmise." On the other hand, do not be too casual either by writing things like "you know what I mean." Most students, however, err on the side of "faux" erudition, using big words and convoluted constructions. When in doubt, write what you mean simply and directly.

STYLE

Remember, you can determine your tone even before you walk into the testing venue. Perhaps you are wondering how to create that proper tone. You achieve the tone you want through style. Your style should be your own natural style that you use for school essays. That means

- using proper grammar and punctuation.
- choosing words that convey your meaning in an interesting rather than a pedestrian or vague way: "The outcome hinges on the Whip's ability to corral enough votes from the party's mavericks" versus "The Whip must try to convince the recalcitrant members of her party."

- avoiding the use of several words when one will do: "There were a number of factors involved that added to the problem. . ." versus "The four factors most responsible for the problem were . . ."

- avoiding hackneyed phrases and clichés such as "The candidate was on cloud nine as she accepted her party's nomination" versus "The candidate was smiling and waving at the delegates."

Your style adds interest to the paper. Fresh words and phrasing as much as a unique point of view about a subject can make a paper interesting to read.

UNITY AND COHERENCE

Unity is extremely important to ensure that you communicate effectively. Unity is another word for clarity. A unified paper is one that is clearly developed. Each paragraph has a topic sentence, and every sentence in the paragraph relates to every other and adds to the development of the topic sentence.

In the same way, each paragraph relates to every other, and every paragraph supports the overall thesis. This means, of course, that you need a thesis to develop. This chapter will help you with developing thesis statements that answer the essay questions.

Remember that your thesis statement contains the central argument that you have developed from brainstorming ideas to answer the essay question. As the Harbrace College Handbook, that venerable college English manual, states: "[Your thesis statement] is basically a claim statement; that is, it indicates what you claim to be true, interesting, or valuable about your subject."

Although you can place your thesis statement anywhere in your essay, it is probably safest to put it in the first paragraph, so you can refer to it as you write to be sure that everything you are writing develops and supports it. Putting the thesis first also gets you started writing.

ADEQUATE DEVELOPMENT

What is adequate development? You have a limited time to read and plan and then develop your ideas—neatly. The five-paragraph structure presented earlier will give you a format to work with: a one-paragraph introduction, a three-paragraph middle, and a one-paragraph ending. In the body of the essay, develop only one idea for each paragraph, and be sure to include information from your own experience and reading where relevant. You may need more than three paragraphs in the body of the essay to make your points, but this format provides a framework to begin.

You may be wondering why we include all this information about writing when the test is about U.S. government. Remember that you must show the evaluators you can work at a college level. Knowledge about the workings of government is not enough. You must communicate to your readers what you know and understand. Graders are not mind readers. If you cannot write the information in a comprehensible manner, you cannot demonstrate your expertise. A well-written essay that clearly communicates your knowledge and the position you are supporting will impress the evaluators and earn you a high score.

WHAT TO EXPECT IN THE AP ESSAYS

The essay questions you will have to answer will probably remind you of ones you have worked with in your AP class. You must discuss major issues in U.S. government and politics, and most essay questions will ask you to evaluate, assess, or analyze. Many questions relate to the formulation and implementation of public policy and the issues surrounding that process. Recent exams have included essay questions on a number of topics:

- The balance of powers at the federal level
- Implementation of public policy by the federal bureaucracy in relation to lobbies and special interest groups; how special interest groups accomplish their goals through electoral process and lobbying
- Differences between the Democratic and Republican Parties, especially in relation to public policy
- The relationship of voter characteristics to political party; socioeconomic, ethnic, age, and gender base of the electorate for each party
- Recent trend of women's involvement in politics
- Impact of increasing political participation by ethnic groups on economic policy, politics, and social policy
- Civil liberties; legislation and Supreme Court decisions as well as social and political factors countering efforts to end discrimination
- Balancing the budget versus actual budget policies
- Changes in the importance and influence of the party system
- Iron triangles or subgovernments
- Supreme Court decisions and their relationship to public policy
- Your view of political parties since the 1960 elections

In addition to knowing likely topics that you may encounter in the essay questions, it is useful to know key phrases that you are likely to find.

SOME KEY TERMS USED IN THE ESSAY QUESTIONS

KEY PHRASES FOR ESSAY QUESTIONS		
Phrase	**Task**	**Example**
To what extent	explain relationship and role	To what extent have special interest groups influenced the development and implementation of federal policies?
Evaluate the claim	determine the validity	Evaluate the statement that an individual's vote is no longer important in the governmental process.
Assess the accuracy	determine the truth of the statement	Assess the accuracy of the statement that the media, not platforms, determine elections.
Critically evaluate evidence that both supports and refutes	give examples that agree and disagree	Critically evaluate evidence that both supports and refutes the statement that the Supreme Court has infringed upon the powers of the legislative branch of government through its decisions.
Define and evaluate the contention	give a definition and analyze the point of view	Define the term *iron triangles* and evaluate the thesis that the impact of iron triangles is more negative than positive.
Analyze the effects	evaluate the impact	Analyze the effects of the aging population on public policy.
Compare the strengths and the weaknesses	show differences	Compare the strengths and weaknesses of third parties in presidential elections.
Explain	offer meaning, cause, effect, influence	Explain the impact of public opinion on policy implementation related to health care and social security.
Discuss	give examples that illustrate	Discuss the nature of federalism and the impact of its changing nature on unfounded mandates.

SPECIFICALLY ABOUT DATA-BASED ESSAY QUESTIONS

As we have mentioned, you are likely to find a data-based essay on the exam. These questions use statistical data in various formats, political cartoons, and perhaps a quotation as the basis for your writing. The data you may be asked to write about may be in the form of

- a chart, graph, or table of government data or public opinion survey results.

- a diagram.

- a drawing.

- a historical or contemporary political cartoon.

- a quotation or short excerpt.

- a flowchart.

- political campaign material.

Test-Taking Strategy

While a data-based essay may not require a formal thesis statement, it is a good idea to write one.

No matter what kind of stimulus is used, you must analyze, interpret, and often evaluate the material while incorporating it into a discussion of U.S. government and politics. Using your analytical skills, you must draw conclusions relating the data to the question and fitting the data into its governmental or political context.

Some of the phrases you might encounter in a data-based question:

- Identify trends

- Explain

- Using the data, identify/describe/explain

- Give similarities and differences

- Give an argument supporting or refuting a position

- Identify/explain/describe the point of view of the writer/artist/ cartoonist

In planning and writing your data-based response, follow the suggestions in this chapter. The format and techniques for the data-based essay are the same as for the other free-response essays. The major difference is that you need to be sure to include evidence from the data to support your contentions when you write your data-based essay.

PLANNING AND WRITING THE ESSAYS

You have reviewed the elements of a good essay, learned what topics you are likely to find, and discovered what form the questions may take. Here are specific techniques to help you ace Section II. The following advice works both for essay prompts that use a visual or data as the stimulus and those that present you with a statement or situation to analyze or evaluate.

PLANNING YOUR ESSAY

- Read the question carefully. If it is a data-based question, examine the cartoon, graph, chart, or quotation.

- Determine if you are required to give an opinion.

- Underline what the question is asking you to do (compare, contrast, analyze, assess, and so on). Circle any terms, events, and people that the question mentions.

- For a data-based question, also underline significant points in the data, including the title and any parameters given (span of years, type of data such as revenue, labels for x and y axes, and so on).

- Restate to yourself what the question is asking. Look at your underlining to verify that you understand what you are to do.

Test-Taking Strategy

Use the test booklet to jot down your quick list.

- Do not take time to write a formal outline, but make a list by brainstorming all the ideas and supporting evidence as well as counterarguments that come to mind as you read.

- If the question asks you to compare and contrast data or argue pros and cons, create a table to list the information.

- Be sure to include relevant outside information, especially for any data-based questions.

Test-Taking Strategy

One way to write a thesis statement is to restate the question as a definitive statement.

- Create a thesis statement from the ideas you generated.

- Turn this brainstorm into an informal working plan by numbering the items that you want to include in your essay in the order in which you want to include them. Do not be afraid to cross out some that no longer apply now that you have a thesis.

WRITING YOUR ESSAY

- Begin writing your first paragraph by stating the thesis clearly. Take a minute or two to be sure that you are writing a clearly stated and interesting introduction.

- Once you have written the first paragraph, read it to be sure that your ideas follow one another logically and that they support the thesis.

- Write a transition into the second paragraph. Check your list of ideas.

Review Strategy

Transitions are words or phrases that connect sentences and paragraphs; for example, words such as second, in the third place, in addition, moreover, however, more importantly, next.

- Use the vocabulary of political science, but do not overdo it or use words with definitions you are not sure of. Using the terminology of the subject lets your reader know that you are comfortable and familiar with the subject.

- Define your terms as you use them and any terms that have several denotations or connotations.

- Use transitions.

- Write one paragraph for each major idea or concept. Include examples to substantiate the points you make in the paragraph.

Test-Taking Strategy

If you think of additional ideas as you write, quickly jot them down in the margin or by your quick list. That way you will not lose your train of thought. Then, you can include the new ideas where appropriate.

- Keep writing until you have used all the RELEVANT ideas on your list. Check how well you are doing at incorporating supporting evidence and refuting counterarguments.

- Allow time to write a solid concluding paragraph. There are several ways to approach the conclusion: rephrasing the thesis, answering the questions by summarizing the main points of your argument, referring in some way back to your opening paragraph, or using an appropriate quotation.

REVISING AND PROOFREADING

Test-Taking Strategy

Take a watch on testing day to ensure you keep within the time frame.

- Pace yourself so that you have at least 1 or 2 minutes to reread your essay for proofreading and revision. Cross out any irrelevant ideas or words and make any additions—neatly. If you have been following your plan to develop your thesis, this time should be spent making sure your grammar and mechanics are correct and your handwriting is legible.

Your final product should include the following:

- A solid introductory statement: formal thesis, explanation of what is asked of you, references to the data

- Adequate support

- Specific examples as support

- A response that answers the question completely and accurately

- Satisfactory concluding remarks

A WORD OF CAUTION

You have now read extensively about what to do when writing the free-response essays. The following are some suggestions about what not to do:

- Do not write an improbable or vague or unrelated thesis.

- Do not be wordy in an effort to appear knowledgeable and impress the readers. They won't be.

- Do not make unsupported statements.

- Do not include irrelevant data, no matter how interesting.

- Do not use incorrect information. If you are not sure of some of your facts, leave them out.

- Do not use your opinions, thoughts, and feelings as fact. Express your opinion only when asked, and then support it with evidence.

A WORD OF ENCOURAGEMENT

Test-Taking Strategy

Don't panic. Everyone will be as nervous as you. If you draw a blank, take a deep breath, think about the topic, and jot down anything that comes to mind about the subject. That will help get you over your nervousness.

Your readers know that the writing time is limited, so you cannot produce four perfect, insightful, groundbreaking, definitive essays. They are looking for responses that show you have the ability and knowledge to produce college-level work. If you

- address the question

- define your terms

- thoroughly explain the issues

- express yourself clearly and logically

- support your position with evidence

- recognize other points of view

you will do well on your free-response essays.

Test-Taking Strategy

Express your personal opinion where appropriate, but be sure to support it with evidence.

UNDERSTANDING THE DIRECTIONS

You now know what to expect and how to write impressive essays within the 100 minutes allowed for Section II. It is time to put what you have studied into practice. First, examine the directions you will be given. The directions for Section II will read something like this:

> **Directions:** You have 100 minutes to answer all four of the following questions. It is suggested that you take a few minutes to outline each answer. Spend approximately one fourth of your time (25 minutes) on each question. Support the ideas in your essays with substantive examples where appropriate. Make sure to number each of your responses with the number corresponding to the question.

Test-Taking Strategy

Outlining need not be formal. Just numbering your ideas and ordering supporting evidence are enough because your time is limited.

Nothing in the directions should surprise you since you have already familiarized yourself with Section II's requirements by reading this chapter. However, by examining the instructions you will discover what the College Board finds important. The fact that the instructions mention outlining indicates how vital the College Board considers planning.

Note that the directions suggest spending about 25 minutes on each essay. Why? All four essays are equally important. If you manage your time as suggested, you will not lose points for an incomplete answer on your fourth response. Finally, the directions tell you to support your ideas with evidence. Without support, even the most insightful comments will be given minimal credit.

PRACTICE

Using what you have studied in your AP class and what you have learned in this chapter, practice writing the following four essays. Do one at a time. Evaluate each one using the *Self-Evaluation Rubric* at the end of the chapter. Then review the suggestions we provide and revise your essay once using points from our list to strengthen your position.

PRACTICE ESSAY 1

Since *Marbury* v. *Madison,* the Supreme Court has often embraced the principle of judicial activism. Define "judicial activism" and use one of the following cases to analyze the effect of judicial activism on public policy.

Virginia v. *United States* (1995)
Shaw v. *Hunter* (1995)
Reno v. *American Civil Liberties Union* (1996)
Printz v. *United States* (1997)

PRACTICE ESSAY 2

In recent years, critics have suggested that the United States adopt a parliamentary structure in order to be a better, more responsive government. Evaluate that contention by comparing the strengths and weaknesses of the governmental systems of democratic republics, such as the United States and France, and parliamentary democracies, such as Japan and Great Britain.

PRACTICE ESSAY 3

Answer the following question based on these statistics.

Nations Possessing Nuclear Weapons	Nations that May Have Nuclear Weapons
*United States**	Israel
*Russia**	North Korea
Great Britain	Iraq
*France**	Iran
*China**	
Belarus	
*Kazakhstan**	
*Ukraine**	
India	
Pakistan	

Italics identify nations that ratified the nuclear nonproliferation treaty. The asterisk (*) identifies nations with 500 or more nuclear warheads.

Based on the data presented in this table, interpret the proliferation and probable proliferation of nuclear weapons and analyze the implications for the foreign policy of the United States.

PRACTICE ESSAY 4

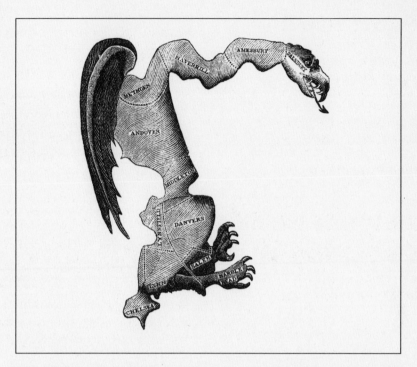

This cartoon was drawn in 1812. However, many people might feel that it still applies today. Analyze the cartoonist's point of view about gerrymandering, and discuss its relevance to the present.

SUGGESTIONS FOR PRACTICE ESSAYS

PRACTICE ESSAY 1

Steps to the Answer

1. Note that this question asks you to offer meaning, cause, effect, or influence as well as to define a term.

2. Think about what you know about judicial activism. Beginning with John Marshall's tenure, the Supreme Court has had a significant impact on public policy and has served an important role in the public arena. This is true of the court system in general.

3. Using the ideas you developed in your planning, create a thesis to serve as the core of your essay. Then select the three court cases that you know most thoroughly and that best support your thesis. Write about each one in a separate paragraph.

4. Write a thorough definition of judicial activism. Refer to earlier cases or include a brief history to add to your definition.

5. Write your essay using the organizing and writing suggestions contained in this chapter. Use transitional words and phrases to make your essay cohesive.

You might have chosen the following points to write about judicial activism and three of the cases listed. Consider them as you complete your self-evaluation.

Defining Judicial Activism

- The courts should play an active, creative role in shaping public policy.

- The courts should protect the long-range interests of the people against the short-range wishes of the government and, through them, the voters.

- The Constitution should be applied to important problems of social and political life.

Court Cases

Virginia **v.** *United States* **(1995)**

  - Sex-discrimination case

  - Virginia Military Institute (VMI), an all-male school

  - A separate school for women existed

  - Decision: VMI must admit women

Shaw v. *Hunter* (1995)

- First case to deal with minority gerrymandering

- Decision: Minority-majority gerrymandered districts declared unconstitutional

Reno v. *American Civil Liberties Union* (1996)

- First case to deal with the Internet

- Decision: Part of the Communications Decency Act held unconstitutional

- Guarantees of First Amendment extend to Internet

Printz v. *United States* (1997)

- According to the Brady Handgun Violence Protection Act, state and local law enforcement authorities were required to perform background checks on people purchasing handguns.

- Decision: That part of Brady Bill declared unconstitutional

- State and local officials could not be required by Congress to carry out a federal law.

Practice Essay 2

There are two ways to organize this kind of answer. Point-by-point organization involves taking one aspect of the discussion and comparing and contrasting both sides. Block style presents all aspects of one side and then all aspects of the other.

Steps to the Answer

1. Note that your answer must compare and contrast forms of government.

2. You are asked to discuss the aspects of republican democracy and parliamentary democracy and offer your own ideas about their strengths and weaknesses.

3. Using the ideas you developed in the planning stage, create a thesis expressing your opinion as the core of your essay. Key words here are *responsive* and *better*. You must consider whether a parliamentary system is more responsive and if it would make the government of the United States better.

4. To describe how the government would be more responsive and better, you need to define for yourself and then your reader what those two terms mean to you.

5. Since you will be writing an essay that compares and contrasts, determine if you will organize your response point-by-point or block style.

6. Interpret the data you present. Do not simply list them and explain them. Be sure to acknowledge the strengths of the opposing point of view. Consider doing so in the introductory paragraph or in the conclusion.

You might have chosen the following points about a republican democracy and a parliamentary democracy to compare and contrast. Consider them as you complete your self-evaluation.

GREAT BRITIAN

Constitution

Only partially written; written parts called the laws of the constitution; unwritten parts called the conventions of the constitution; flexible, open to change

Head of State/Government

Hereditary ruler; a constitutional monarch, head of state, living symbol of Great Britain; prime minister as head of government

Legislative Branch

Bicameral; House of Lords, little power; House of Commons, popularly elected from districts; elections five years apart at the most

Executive Branch

Fused with the legislative branch; prime minister leader of majority party; selects cabinet

Elections

No fixed time; no more than five years apart; held when prime minister's party's chances of holding power are good or when government faces a loss of confidence

Other

Nine law lords serve as final court of appeals; do not possess power of judicial review

FRANCE

Constitution

Written constitution, its sixteenth

Head of State/Government

President true chief executive; chooses premier

Legislative Branch

Bicameral parliament; parliamentary power limited; some matters, such as defense, outside its jurisdiction; laws must be passed by both houses and signed by president

Executive Branch

Runs foreign affairs and commands the military; can call for a referendum on national issues; can use dictatorial authority in emergency; presides over cabinet meetings; can dissolve parliament and call for general elections; control over legislation in hands of the government

Elections

The Senate chosen by electoral college for nine-year terms; limited power to propose legislation; the National Assembly directly elected for five-year terms unless parliament is dissolved

JAPAN

Constitution
Written; extensive list of basic freedoms; antimilitary clause

Head of State/Government
Emperor head of state with no real power; prime minister head of government

Legislative Branch
Bicameral national Diet; upper house, called House of Councilors, serves an advisory role; lower house, called House of Representatives, has greater power; no-confidence vote forces prime minister to resign or dissolve government; can make treaties, raise and appropriate funds

Executive Branch
Prime minister must be member of Diet; prime minister and cabinet perform executive function; prime minister represents the majority party, appoints cabinet, can dissolve House of Representatives

Elections
House of Councilors serves six-year terms; three-fifths elected from districts, two-fifths from nation as a whole; House of Representatives serves terms of four years or less, elected by districts

Other
Bureaucracy wields great power, plays key role in economy; Japan practices consensus politics, politicians seek broad agreement on issues

THE UNITED STATES

Constitution
Written constitution

Head of State/Government
President head of state and head of government

Legislative Branch
Bicameral: Senate and House of Representatives

Executive Branch
President, cabinet, and bureaucracy

Elections
Representatives every two years by districts; senators every six years by statewide election; president every four years by electoral college reflecting a popular vote

Other
Judicial branch separate; can review and overturn federal laws

PRACTICE ESSAY 3

Test-Taking Strategy

Remember to define any specialized terms and to write out any acronyms like START (Strategic Arms Reduction Treaty).

Steps to the Answer

1. Note that the question requires you to interpret, analyze, and evaluate the data on the chart.

2. Before you can present your thinking about how nations with nuclear weapons might affect U.S. foreign policy, you must describe and discuss what the data on the chart presents.

3. Then, you must discuss the implications of the chart for U.S. foreign policy, so you need to formulate your own point of view. Next, gather evidence from the chart and from your education, reading, and experience to offer as support for your opinions. Using the ideas you developed in the planning stage, create a thesis expressing your opinion as the core of your essay.

4. Since you will be writing an essay in which you present and support an opinion, your most effective organization is to discuss your ideas in the order of their importance, beginning with an explanation of the data and ending with your strongest argument. Then, write the essay.

5. Address the question again in your conclusion and consider including a policy solution or recommendation.

You might have chosen the following points about the implications of the nuclear powers chart on U.S. foreign policy. Consider them as you complete your self-evaluation.

- Many nations have signed the nuclear nonproliferation treaty, but the threat of nuclear disaster continues.

- At least five nations possessing nuclear weapons are not signatories, so their weapons are not inspected.

- Those that do not admit to having weapons are also a danger.

- Several nations with nuclear capacity have antipathy toward the United States and/or each other.

- Even signatories possess large numbers of nuclear weapons.

- The United States is allied with several nations that are capable of firing nuclear weapons, which means there is the potential for U.S. involvement in nuclear conflict is strong.

- The potential for terrorist organizations gaining nuclear weapons is a danger.

- Nations such as Israel, India, and Pakistan refuse to sign the nonproliferation extension.

- The development of nuclear deterrents, mothballing, and aiding other nations in deactivating weapons all raise budget concerns—"guns versus butter" argument.

- Foreign policy questions arise from dealing with nations that refuse to follow the letter or spirit of nonproliferation treaty.

- Selling U.S. nuclear technology raises economic and foreign policy issues.

PRACTICE ESSAY 4

Steps to the Answer

1. Note that the question requires you to identify and explain the cartoonist's point of view and then discuss its relevance to the contemporary period.

2. Remember to define terms, especially gerrymandering.

3. Although the question does not specifically ask, consider a brief recitation of the history of gerrymandering.

4. Using the ideas you developed in the planning stage, create a thesis as the core of your essay.

5. Since you will be writing an essay in which you define and explain a historical aspect of U.S. government, a chronological presentation is your most effective organization. In other words, after your introductory paragraph, begin with a historical overview and then relate that to the present. Develop your quick list with this organization in mind. Then, write your essay.

You might have chosen the following points about gerrymandering to use in your essay. Consider them as you complete your self-evaluation.

- Fierceness of the salamander indicates the cartoonist's disapproval of gerrymandering.

- Gerrymandering means electoral districts are drawn to the advantage of the dominant party or faction in the legislature

    - to concentrate the opposition's vote in a few districts.

    - to spread opposition so thinly among districts that it cannot carry an election.

- In 1842, state legislatures were made responsible for drawing congressional districts of contiguous territory.

- In 1872, Congress required districts to have approximately the same number of inhabitants.

- In 1901, districts were required to be compact.

- Reapportionment Acts of 1929 and 1932 left some requirements out, and the Supreme Court held that they were repealed.

- Gerrymandering, along with poll taxes and white primaries, were used to prevent African Americans from voting in the South.

- In 1960, *Gomillion* v. *Lightfoot* outlawed gerrymandering for the purpose of racial discrimination as a violation of the Fourteenth Amendment.

- In 1962, the decision in *Baker* v. *Carr* caused reapportionment of almost all federal, state, and local districts.

- In 1964, the decision in *Wesberry* v. *Sanders* held that population differences in Georgia's congressional districts were so great as to violate the "one person, one vote" principle.

- Also in 1964, in *Reynolds* v. *Sims* the Supreme Court held that both houses of a state legislature must be apportioned on the basis of population.

- In spite of decisions, gerrymandering continued, but it was now used to create districts to ensure the election of minority representatives.

- In 1993, in *Shaw* v. *Reno* the Supreme Court struck down North Carolina's creation of a district created to elect an African American. The district was found to violate the rights of white voters under the Fourteenth Amendment.

- In 1996, in *Shaw* v. *Hunt* the Supreme Court struck down North Carolina's creation of two gerrymandered districts drawn to elect African Americans. Using race as the determining factor in drawing the districts violated the Voting Rights Act.

- In 1996, in *Bush* v. *Vera* Texas districting to ensure the election of minority representatives was also struck down.

- In 1999 in *Hunt* v. *Cromartie* the federal district court of appeals for North Carolina invalidated on summary judgment the districts that had first been at issue in *Shaw* v. *Reno* and the *Shaw* v. *Hunt*. (Each time they had been redrawn and were the subject of new challenges.) The Supreme Court sent the case back to the appeals court for a full trial.

- In 2001, the Supreme Court in *Easley* v. *Cromartie* (formerly *Hunt* v. *Cromartie*) found that race could be a factor in drawing district boundaries so long as it was not the controlling factor.

SELF-EVALUATION RUBRIC FOR THE ADVANCED PLACEMENT ESSAYS

	8–9	5–7	2–4	0–1
Overall Impression	Demonstrates excellent understanding of U.S. government and legal system; outstanding writing; thorough and effective; incisive	Demonstrates good understanding of U.S. government and legal system; good writing competence	Reveals simplistic thinking and/or immature understanding of U.S. government and legal system; fails to respond adequately to the question; little or no analysis	Very little or no understanding of U.S. government and legal system; unacceptably brief; fails to respond to the question; little clarity
Understanding of the U.S. Government	Scholarly; excellent understanding of the question; effective and incisive; in-depth critical analysis; includes apt, specific references; acknowledges other views	Mostly accurate use of information about U.S. government and legal system; good understanding of the question; often perceptive and clear; includes specific references and critical analysis	Some inaccuracies in information regarding U.S. government; superficial understanding and treatment of the question; lack of adequate knowledge about U.S. government; overgeneralized	Serious errors in presenting information about U.S. government and legal system; extensive misreading of the question and little supporting evidence; completely off the topic
Development	Original, unique, and/or intriguing thesis; excellent use of fundamentals and principles of U.S. government; thoroughly developed; conclusion shows applicability of thesis to other situations	Adequate thesis; satisfactory use of knowledge of U.S. government; competent development; acceptable conclusion	Inadequate, irrelevant, or illogical thesis; little use of knowledge of government; some development; unsatisfactory, inapplicable, or nonexistent conclusion	Lacking both thesis and conclusion; little or no evidence of knowledge of U.S. government
Conventions of English	Meticulously and thoroughly organized; coherent and unified; virtually error free	Reasonably organized; mostly coherent and unified; few or some errors	Somewhat organized; some incoherence and lack of unity; some major errors	Little or no organization; incoherent and void of unity; extremely flawed

Rate yourself in each of the categories below. Enter the numbers on the lines below. Be as honest as possible so you will know what areas need work. Then calculate the average of the four numbers to determine your final score. It is difficult to score yourself objectively, so you may wish to ask a respected friend or teacher to assess your essays for a more accurate reflection of their strengths and weaknesses. On the AP test itself, a reader will rate your essays on a scale of 0 to 9, with 9 being the highest.

Each category is rated 9 (high) to 0 (incompetent).

ESSAY 1
SELF-EVALUATION
Overall Impression _____
Understanding of U.S. Government _____
Development _____
Conventions of English _____

TOTAL _____
Divide by 4 for final score. _____

ESSAY 1
OBJECTIVE EVALUATION
Overall Impression _____
Understanding of U.S. Government _____
Development _____
Conventions of English _____

TOTAL _____
Divide by 4 for final score. _____

ESSAY 2
SELF-EVALUATION
Overall Impression _____
Understanding of U.S. Government _____
Development _____
Conventions of English _____

TOTAL _____
Divide by 4 for final score. _____

ESSAY 2
OBJECTIVE EVALUATION
Overall Impression _____
Understanding of U.S. Government _____
Development _____
Conventions of English _____

TOTAL _____
Divide by 4 for final score. _____

ESSAY 3
SELF-EVALUATION
Overall Impression _____
Understanding of U.S. Government _____
Development _____
Conventions of English _____

TOTAL _____
Divide by 4 for final score. _____

ESSAY 3
OBJECTIVE EVALUATION
Overall Impression _____
Understanding of U.S. Government _____
Development _____
Conventions of English _____

TOTAL _____
Divide by 4 for final score. _____

ESSAY 4
SELF-EVALUATION
Overall Impression _____
Understanding of U.S. Government _____
Development _____
Conventions of English _____

TOTAL _____
Divide by 4 for final score. _____

ESSAY 4
OBJECTIVE EVALUATION
Overall Impression _____
Understanding of U.S. Government _____
Development _____
Conventions of English _____

TOTAL _____
Divide by 4 for final score. _____

Peterson's AP Success: Government & Politics

Chapter 3

CONSTITUTIONAL FOUNDATION OF THE FEDERAL GOVERNMENT

There are various definitions of **government**. Some are very broad: Government is the way that "a territory and its people are ruled," or government is the way that "a society makes and enforces its public policies." Other definitions may go into detail, describing government as the way a political entity (1) maintains order, (2) provides public services, (3) protects the nation's security, (4) socializes the young, (5) collects taxes, and (6) enforces policy decisions. However one may choose to define the term, over the centuries people have chosen to live under some form of government. This chapter will describe various theories of government, how the fledgling United States chose the federal system, the main provisions of the Constitution, and some important Supreme Court cases that dealt with major provisions of the Constitution.

SECTION 1. THEORIES OF GOVERNMENT

People choose the form, or structure, of the government under which they live based on their experiences and how they think their needs will be satisfied.

FAST FACTS
Democracy

- In a **democracy,** power rests with the people. In a **pure** or **direct democracy,** citizens vote on public questions. New England town meetings of the colonial era are an example of direct democracy. However, once a population began to increase greatly, direct democracy became unwieldy. Today, the common form of democracy is **representative democracy.** The larger populace elects a small group of men and women to represent their interests in the day-to-day workings of the government, which includes the making of public policy. If the representatives are not responsive to the electorate, they may be replaced during periodic elections.

- A **republican** form of government is similar to a democracy. The people elect representatives to manage the government, and those representatives are responsible to the electorate. The terms *democracy, representative democracy, republic,* and *republican form of government* are synonymous today.

- Both a democracy and a republic are forms of **limited government.** Their authority rests on what rights the people choose to cede.

- Political scientists list a number of **values** as characteristics of democracy. Among the most commonly listed are (1) individual liberty or freedom; (2) majority rule with minority rights; (3) belief in/respect for the worth of the individual; (4) equality of and for all persons, including equal opportunity; and (5) the necessity for compromise when values conflict.

- **Political processes** that need to be in place in a democracy include (1) free elections on the basis of equal representation; (2) the existence of competing political parties; (3) freedom of expression, including a free press; (4) freedom of assembly and protest; and (5) the extension of rights, including citizenship to all those who live within its borders.

- Certain conditions are required for democracy to flourish. Among those listed by political scientists are (1) a favorable economy, (2) widespread literacy, and (3) social consensus.

Who Really Governs in the United States?

- While representative democracy is the general principle upon which American government is built, political scientists have developed competing theories about who really governs—that is, who sets the public policy agenda.

- Those who put forward the **pluralist theory** believe that the government is influenced in its decision making by groups of people with shared interests who organize to put forward their agendas. Because of the number of interests that compete for attention on any given subject, no one group can dictate policy. Groups must compromise, and, therefore, many groups achieve some part of their agendas.

- **Hyperpluralism,** a variant of the pluralist theory, states that there are so many groups competing for attention that no meaningful compromises can be reached and no meaningful policies can be passed. Government becomes paralyzed in an effort to placate competing interests.

- Proponents of the **elite theory** of government believe that the upper class—the very wealthy—dominates the policy agenda. These are the CEO's of multinational corporations, the contributors of vast sums of money to political campaigns, the shapers of the economy. While there are many groups trying to capture the policy agenda, it is the elite's business agenda that dominates in Washington.

KEY WORDS AND TERMS

Review Strategy

See if you can relate these terms and ideas to their correct context in the "Fast Facts" section.

- **Aristotle's** *Politics*
- **constitutional government**
- **Plato's** *Republic*
- **the State: population, territory, sovereignty, government**

SECTION 2. ADOPTING THE CONSTITUTION

Although American colonists in growing numbers had opposed the various taxation policies of Great Britain over the years, the number of opponents had never been very large. Those who railed at the British government were mostly from the merchant and upper classes. However, as the taxation policies became broader in scope and more widely enforced, the discontent began to spread among the colonists until mob violence erupted when new laws were passed. Tax collectors were tarred and feathered, shops of suspected British sympathizers were ransacked, British revenue ships were set afire, people who bought British goods were intimidated, and British soldiers were harassed. It was against this backdrop that the Intolerable Acts were passed and the First Continental Congress met.

FAST FACTS
Colonial Governments

Review Strategy

You probably will not be asked any questions about the colonial or Revolutionary periods, but reviewing this information will provide a context to help you understand the development of the government system of the United States. You might also be able to use the information to support an argument in an essay.

- **Representative government** is the cornerstone of government at all levels in the United States. The **House of Burgesses** established by the Virginia Colony in 1619 was the first representative government in an English colony. Male colonists elected burgesses, or representatives, to consult with the governor's council in making laws for the colony. Prior to 1670, colonists did not have to own property in order to vote. In that year, the franchise was limited to free male property owners. In 1624, James I made the colony a royal colony but allowed the House of Burgesses to continue.

- In 1620, Pilgrims, who were fleeing persecution in England, drafted and signed the **Mayflower Compact.** This was the first document in the English colonies to establish self-government.

- The Puritans, seeking religious freedom like the Pilgrims, received a charter and established the Massachusetts Bay Colony. In the beginning, laws were passed by the **General Court,** which was made up of freemen, those few male colonists who owned stock in the Massachusetts Bay Colony. The other colonists rebelled, and in 1631 the leaders admitted any Puritan male in good standing to the General Court. As the colony continued to grow, the number of freemen became unwieldy. The law was changed so that freemen in each town in the colony elected two **representatives** to the General Court. Like Jamestown, Massachusetts Bay had a **representative form of government,** although it was limited in scope.

Review Strategy

Be sure you know what the phrase power of the purse means. It played a role in the duties that were assigned to the new Congress when the Constitution was drawn up.

- Except for Pennsylvania, which had a **unicameral legislature**, the colonies had **bicameral legislatures** modeled on the upper and lower houses of Parliament. The upper chambers were made up of the governor, his advisers, and councillors appointed at the suggestion of the governor by the monarch or proprietor, depending on the type of colony. In Rhode Island and Connecticut, the upper house was elected by the colonists, and in Massachusetts, the upper house was elected by the lower house. The lower houses were elected by the colonists every two years; but some governors, such as Berkeley in Virginia, refused to call elections for years. This is why the **power of the purse** became important. The legislatures had developed the right to levy taxes and pay the salaries of governors. By threatening to withhold his salary, the legislature could pass laws over a governor's objections.

- **Voting requirements** changed as the colonies grew. Originally, only Puritans could vote in Massachusetts Bay, and in royal colonies, only Anglicans. Catholics, Jews, Baptists, and Quakers were restricted from voting in certain colonies, and no colony allowed women, Native Americans, or slaves to vote. In all colonies, white males had to own land in order to vote. Over time, this changed so that men could own property other than land or could pay a tax to be eligible to vote.

Review Strategy

What was the significance of the English Bill of Rights to the colonists? Connect the bill to the later development of the Constitution and the U.S. Bill of Rights.

- In 1688, when the English deposed James II in the Glorious Revolution and installed William and Mary of Orange as monarchs, they also drafted an **English Bill of Rights.** This document guaranteed certain rights to every citizen, including the right to representative government.

Establishing a New Nation

TIME LINE TO CONSTITUTIONAL GOVERNMENT	
YEAR	EVENT
1699–1750	Passage of initial mercantile laws
1754–1763	French and Indian War Proclamation of 1763
1764	Sugar Act Currency Act
1765	Quartering Act Stamp Act Stamp Act Congress
1766	Declaratory Act
1767	Townshend Acts
1770s	Committees of Correspondence
1773	Tea Act

1774	Intolerable Acts
	    (also known as the Coercive Acts)
	Quebec Act
	    First Continental Congress

1775–1776	Second Continental Congress Declaration of Independence
1781	Articles of Confederation in Effect
1783	Treaty of Paris
1786	Annapolis Convention
1787	Constitutional Convention
1788	Ratification of U.S. Constitution by Ninth State
1789	Inauguration of First Presidential Administration
1790	Ratification by Thirteenth State

- Between 1775 and 1781, the **Second Continental Congress** transformed itself from an advisory body to the governing body of the new nation. Its original charge was to attempt to make peace with Great Britain; however, it (1) authorized and signed the **Declaration of Independence,** (2) adopted the **Articles of Confederation,** and (3) acted as the national government of the thirteen former British colonies.

- The **Declaration of Independence** has four major sections: (1) the **Preamble,** which describes why the colonists are seeking their independence, (2) the Declaration of Rights, (3) the List of Grievances, and (4) the formal Declaration of Independence. Thomas Jefferson drew on **Enlightenment** philosophers, such as **John Locke,** in his appeal to **self-evidence** and the **natural order (natural law).** Jefferson invoked Locke's idea of a **social contract** between the ruled **(consent of the governed)** and their ruler. If the ruler abuses the contract **(absolute despotism),** then the ruled have the right to overthrow the ruler.

Articles of Confederation

- From 1781 until 1788, when the U.S. Constitution was ratified by the ninth state, the new nation was governed under the **Articles of Confederation.** Because the former colonies were fighting against strong external control of their affairs, their leaders shaped a document that allowed each state a great deal of freedom at the cost of a **weak central government.** For example, the colonists who drafted the Articles of Confederation did not want a strong executive, so they established a government with no executive at all.

- State governments were similar to the colonial governments in that they divided power among a governor, a legislature, and a judiciary, with most power reserved to the legislature. Although each state constitution included a bill of rights, political power rested with the wealthy. Voting was restricted to propertied white men, and although Northern states had for the most part banned slavery, the Southern economy continued to depend on it.

- The weaknesses of the Articles were soon apparent. Although the new government could, among other powers, establish post offices, borrow and coin money, declare war, ask states for recruits to build an army, and build and equip a navy, these powers meant little in reality. Each member of the Confederation Congress was paid by his (no women allowed) state and voted according to his state legislature's instructions. Most importantly to the new nation ravaged by war, the Confederation Congress did not have the power to deal with the economic depression that hit the nation after the war—or with the growing sectional differences.

ARTICLES OF CONFEDERATION

WEAKNESSES	CONSEQUENCES
No chief executive; the Congress worked through committees	No coordination of committees and no uniform domestic or foreign policy
Required nine of thirteen states to approve laws (each state had one vote)	Rarely delegates from all thirteen states in Congress at once; often voted as blocs of smaller states (5) versus larger states (8)
Required all states to approve amendments	Never get agreement of all thirteen states, so Articles never amended
No power to levy or collect taxes; Congress could raise money only by borrowing or asking states for money	No reason for states to agree to requests; Congress always in need of money to fight the war
No power to regulate **interstate commerce**	Led to disputes between states and inability to regulate trade with foreign nations to protect American business
No power to enforce treaties	No power to force British to abide by the Peace/Treaty of Paris of 1783
No power to enforce its own laws	Only advise and request states to abide by national laws
No national court system; state courts interpreted national laws	Difficult to get states to abide by state court decisions

Drafting the Constitution

- At the **Annapolis Convention,** which was called to discuss the economic problems facing the nation, such as a growing **unfavorable balance of trade,** the delegates recommended a convention to amend the Articles. Meeting in Philadelphia in 1787, the new convention soon saw that a new document—a new government— was needed. Competing interests put forth different plans; the major areas of compromise appear on the next page.

- Other compromises included in the Constitution are (1) the **Three-Fifths Compromise** for counting slaves in determining taxes and representation for the House, (2) prohibition on importation of slaves after 1808, (3) the right of Congress to regulate **interstate commerce** and foreign trade but not to levy export taxes, (4) a four-year term for the president, and (5) election of the president by an electoral college.

WORKING OUT COMPROMISES			
	VIRGINIA PLAN	**NEW JERSEY PLAN**	**FINAL U.S. CONSTITUTION**
Representation	Based on wealth or population	Equal representation for each state	**Senate:** two representatives per state **House:** based on population
Executive	National executive chosen by Congress	Executive Committee chosen by Congress	**President** chosen by **electors,** in turn elected by the people
Judicial	National judiciary chosen by Congress	National judiciary appointed by Executive Committee	**Supreme Court** appointed by the president with Senate confirmation; lower courts established by Congress
Legislative	Two houses: upper elected by the people with lower elected by the upper house	One house: appointed by state legislators	Two houses: upper chosen by state legislatures (changed to direct election by Seventeenth Amendment); lower elected by the people

Ideological and Philosophical Background to the Constitution

- In addition to the obvious experiences of the colonists that were woven into the provisions of the Constitution (such as the right not to house troops), the Framers were also aware of the writings of the Enlightenment. The work of men like **John Locke** influenced not only Thomas Jefferson, who drafted the Declaration, but also the men who were responsible for crafting the Constitution. The French *philosophes*—**Jean-Jacques Rousseau, Montesquieu, Denis Diderot,** and **Voltaire**—were also known to the educated residents of the former colonies.

- In addition to political and social treatises, the former colonists were also familiar with three important English documents: (1) the **Magna Carta,** which limited the power of the monarchy and listed various rights that belonged to all English people by virtue of birth; (2) the **Petition of Right,** which also listed various rights that belonged to the people and established the principle that the monarch was not above the law; and (3) the **Bill of Rights**, which listed additional rights. Among these three documents, the English—and the former colonists—were used to such rights as (1) trial by jury, (2) due process, (3) no imposition of martial law by the monarch during times of peace, (4) no forced quartering of troops by civilians, and (5) freedom from cruel and unusual punishment.

Ratification

- Advocates and opponents soon squared off over **ratification** of the Constitution. **Federalists** favored ratification because they claimed that without a strong federal government, the nation would be unable to protect itself from external enemies or to solve internal problems. Initially, they argued that a **Bill of Rights** was unnecessary but agreed to its addition to gain support.

- **Anti-Federalists,** mainly farmers and others from the inland areas, claimed that (1) the Constitution was extralegal because the convention had not been authorized to create a new document, (2) that it took important rights away from the states, and (3) that the Constitution needed a Bill of Rights to guarantee individual liberties.

- By June 1788, nine states had ratified the Constitution, but without Virginia and New York, the union would have little chance of success. The fight in New York enlisted **Alexander Hamilton, James Madison,** and **John Jay** to write a series of essays called *The Federalist* in defense of the Constitution.

Defense of the Constitution

- Two of the most famous essays in *The Federalist,* No. 10 and No. 51, are by James Madison. In **No. 10,** Madison argues for a federal form of government over a pure democracy. He also discusses the "mischief of factions," which, he believes, are sown in the "nature of man."

- **No. 51** discusses Madison's belief that a major role of the Constitution is to protect minorities from "the tyranny of the majority." The Anti-Federalists, on the other hand, feared the growth of an aristocracy—not of nobility, but of power.

- To counteract the concern over majority rule, the Federalists built into the Constitution a number of provisions to check the power of majorities: (1) the division of powers between the national and state governments, (2) the separation of powers within the federal government, (3) the indirect election of senators, (4) the indirect election of the president, and (5) appointment of federal judges rather than their election. All of these provisions remain in effect more than 200 years later with the exception of the indirect election of senators, which was changed by the Seventeenth Amendment.

- Another famous essay is **No. 78** written by Alexander Hamilton in which he outlines the concept of judicial review as a basic principle of the Constitution.

KEY PEOPLE

- **Brutus, Anti-Federalist spokesman; Richard Henry Lee**
- **John Peter Zenger, trial for seditious libel, freedom of the press**

KEY WORDS AND TERMS

- **Albany Plan of Union**
- **Connecticut Compromise, Great Compromise, Roger Sherman**
- **Iroquois Confederacy**
- **New England Confederation**
- **Shays's Rebellion, impact of**
- **Virginia's Bill of Rights**
- **virtual representation versus direct or actual representation**

FAST FACTS ABOUT THE CONSTITUTION

Review Strategy

For information about how the Constitution has been changed and expanded through judicial interpretation, see "Some Key Supreme Court Decisions" on pp. vii–viii as well as individual chapters.

- The U.S. Constitution consists of a **Preamble, seven Articles,** and **twenty-seven Amendments.**

- The Constitution sets out the structure and powers of government, but it does not try to provide for every possibility. Knowing that they would not be able to provide solutions to all the circumstances that the nation would face in the future, the Framers developed the amendment process to allow later generations to change the government as situations arose.

- The **amendment process** and the **system of checks and balances** enables the government to be both flexible and stable.

- The U.S. Constitution is based on six principles of government:

    1. **Popular sovereignty:** The people are the only source of governmental power.

    2. **Federalism:** Government power is divided between a national government and state governments.

    3. **Separation of powers:** Executive, legislative, and judicial powers are divided among three separate and coequal branches of government.

    4. **Checks and balances:** The three branches of government have some overlapping powers that allow each to check— that is, restrain or balance—the power of the other two branches.

    5. **Judicial review:** The courts have the power to declare unconstitutional the actions of the legislative and executive branches of government.

    6. **Limited government:** The Constitution lists the powers granted to the federal government, reserved to the states, or shared concurrently.

- The first ten amendments to the Constitution are known as the **Bill of Rights** and were added to satisfy the **Anti-Federalists,** who opposed ratification because the proposed Constitution did not spell out the rights of the people.

- The **Thirteenth, Fourteenth,** and **Fifteenth Amendments** were passed after the Civil War to ensure the rights of newly freed slaves. These amendments figure prominently in the history of Reconstruction. Beginning in the 1960s, the Supreme Court used the Fourteenth Amendment as the basis for many **civil rights** decisions.

PROVISIONS OF THE UNITED STATES CONSTITUTION

ARTICLES	
Article I	Establishes the Legislative Branch Make up of the House of Representatives and the Senate, elections and meetings, organization and rules, passing of laws, powers of Congress, powers denied to the federal government, powers denied to the states; Three-Fifths Compromise for apportionment was repealed by the Fifteenth Amendment; **"necessary and proper clause"; "commerce clause"**
Article II	Establishes the Executive Branch Term, election, qualifications of the president and vice president; powers of the president; duties of the president; impeachment
Article III	Establishes the Judicial Branch Federal courts, jurisdiction of federal courts; defines treason
Article IV	Relations among the states, **"full faith and credit"** Honoring official acts of other states; mutual duties of states; new states and territories; federal protection for states
Article V	The amendment process
Article VI	Public debts, supremacy of national law, oaths of office; **"supremacy clause"**
Article VII	Ratification process
AMENDMENTS	
First Amendment	Freedoms of religion, speech, press, assembly, and petition
Second Amendment	Right to bear arms
Third Amendment	Restrictions on quartering of troops
Fourth Amendment	Protection against unlawful search and seizure
Fifth Amendment	Rights of the accused in criminal proceedings, **due process**
Sixth Amendment	Right to a speedy and fair trial
Seventh Amendment	Rights involved in a civil suit
Eighth Amendment	Punishment for crimes **(cruel and unusual punishment)**
Ninth Amendment	Powers reserved to the people **(nonenumerated rights)**
Tenth Amendment	Powers reserved to the states

PROVISIONS OF THE UNITED STATES CONSTITUTION—*continued*

AMENDMENTS—*continued*

Eleventh Amendment	Suits against states by a resident or by another state must be heard in state courts, not federal courts: repealed part of Article III
Twelfth Amendment	Election of president and vice president
Thirteenth Amendment	Ratified as a result of the Civil War; abolishes slavery
Fourteenth Amendment	Ratified after the Civil War; defines the rights of citizens; replaces part of Article I by requiring that African Americans be fully counted in determining apportionment; sets out punishment for leaders of the Confederacy; promises payment for federal debt as a result of the Civil War but not for debts of the Confederacy. This amendment's **"equal protection under the law"** provision figures prominently in later civil rights decisions by the Supreme Court.
Fifteenth Amendment	Ratified after the Civil War; grants the right to vote regardless of race, color, or previous servitude. Southern states defied the amendment until the 1960s when Congress passed various voting rights acts.
Sixteenth Amendment	Grants federal government the ability to tax income
Seventeenth Amendment	Provides for direct election of senators; replaces Article I, Section 3, paragraphs 2 and 3
Eighteenth Amendment **Twenty-first Amendment**	Prohibits manufacture, sale, or transportation of alcohol Repealed Eighteenth Amendment
Nineteenth Amendment	Grants women the right to vote
Twentieth Amendment	Modified sections of Article I and the Twelfth Amendment relating to when the terms of office begin for members of Congress and the president and vice president; known as the **"Lame Duck" Amendment** because it shortened the time that a defeated legislator/official served between the election and the new term of office
Twenty-second Amendment	Limits presidential term to two terms if elected on his/her own and to one term if serving out the term of a predecessor for more than two years
Twenty-third Amendment	Provides three presidential electors for the District of Columbia
Twenty-fourth Amendment	Abolishes the poll tax for federal elections; part of the civil rights legislation of the 1960s
Twenty-fifth Amendment	Provides for presidential disability and succession if the president is unable to perform his or her duties
Twenty-sixth Amendment	Expands the right to vote to include 18-year-old citizens
Twenty-seventh Amendment	Limits the ability of Congress to raise its own salary

Analyzing the Amendments

There are a number of ways to look at the Constitution and its amendments and how the rights and duties of citizens and the federal government have evolved.

- The **Bill of Rights** was proposed and ratified in response to the former colonists' experiences with the British government. By guaranteeing certain freedoms to the people or the states, these first ten amendments placed certain limits on each branch of the federal government and on the federal government in general. For example, by guaranteeing people the right to practice religion—or not to practice—the First Amendment forbade Congress from establishing a state religion similar to Anglicanism in England and in the royal colony of Georgia. (1) **Amendment I** limited the laws that Congress could pass. (2) **Amendments II, III,** and **IV** restricted the executive from infringing on certain rights of individuals as well. (3) **Amendments V, VI, VII,** and **VIII** further defined the actions of the federal courts in relation to the rights of individuals. (4) **Amendments IX** and **X** set boundaries for the federal government. All rights not listed in the Constitution as belonging to the federal or state governments or to the people are **reserved** to the states and to the people.

Review Strategy

See Chapter 7 for more information about the nationalization of the Bill of Rights, also known as selective incorporation.

- Additional limits were placed on the power of the federal government by the (1) **Eleventh Amendment,** which restricted the type of cases between states that the federal courts would hear, and the (2) **Twenty-seventh Amendment,** which prohibited from putting into effect any raise in salary for Congress until after the next Congressional election.

- Two amendments limited the power of the states—(1) the **Thirteenth Amendment,** which abolished slavery, and (2) the **Fourteenth Amendment,** which extended **due process** to state actions.

- One amendment, the **Sixteenth,** expanded the federal government's role by establishing the power of the government to tax personal and corporate incomes.

- The **Fourteenth Amendment** defined citizenship for the nation, and five of the amendments expanded the pool of eligible voters.

Amendment	Expansion of the Franchise
XV	To all male citizens regardless of "race, color, or previous condition of servitude" over 21 years of age
XIX	To all female citizens over 21 years of age
XXIII	To citizens who reside in the District of Columbia
XXIV	To all citizens by abolishing the poll tax for federal elections
XXVI	To all citizens over the age of 18

- Three amendments relate to the functioning of the electoral system. Passage and ratification of the **Twelfth Amendment** were a direct result of the confusion in the electoral college in the election of 1800. The **Seventeenth Amendment** replaced election of senators by state legislatures with direct election by the people. The original method reflected the unease of the Framers with direct representation and their concern about the possibility of "tyranny of the majority." The **Twentieth Amendment** acknowledged the change in the nation's communications and transportation systems since the eighteenth century.

- The **Twenty-second** and **Twenty-fifth Amendments** relate to the presidency. George Washington's two terms had established the precedent for presidential terms until Franklin Roosevelt's four terms. The Twenty-Second Amendment ensured that Washington's example would continue. The Twenty-Fifth Amendment governs filling the presidency should the president die or become disabled in office. Roosevelt's death and Dwight Eisenhower's heart attacks made the need for an orderly succession apparent, especially with regard to filling the vice presidency.

KEY TERMS/IDEAS DEFINED

- **elastic clause:** Article I, Section 8; also known as the **"necessary and proper clause"**; grants Congress the right to make all laws "necessary and proper" in order to carry out the federal government's duties; this is an expressed power and the constitutional basis for implied powers

- **supremacy clause:** part of Article VI; the Constitution, laws passed by Congress, and treaties of the United States have superior authority over laws of state and local governments

- **concurrent powers:** powers, such as the right to tax and to establish and maintain courts, that are shared by the federal and state governments but exercised separately and simultaneously

- **denied powers:** powers denied to all government; Article I, Sections 9 and 10

- **enumerated powers:** powers stated directly in the Constitution as belonging to the federal government; Article I, Section 8; Article II, Section 2; Article III; Sixteenth Amendment

- **expressed powers:** also called **enumerated powers**

- **implied powers:** based on the "necessary and proper" or elastic clause; powers required by the federal government to carry out its duties as stated in the Constitution; not listed, but based in expressed powers, such as the power to collect taxes implies the power to establish the Internal Revenue Service

- **inherent powers:** belong to the federal government by virtue of being the federal government

- **reserved powers:** powers that belong to the states; Tenth Amendment

- **judicial activism:** theory that the Supreme Court, through its decisions, should shape national social and political policies

- **judicial restraint:** theory that the Supreme Court, through its decisions, should avoid an active role in shaping national social and political policies

- **loose constructionist:** one who argues that the Constitution needs to respond to changing times; the **Warren Court,** for example

- **strict constructionist:** one who argues that the judiciary's decisions need to be based on the Framers' intent; Justice Clarence Thomas, for example

SECTION 3. FORM OF GOVERNMENT

Three distinguishing characteristics of the government system of the United States are **federalism, separation of powers,** and **checks and balances** to ensure the separation of powers. Through an amendment process, the Framers of the Constitution provided for future changes in the Constitution to reflect changes in the nation. In addition, over time, informal ways of changing the Constitution have grown up.

FAST FACTS
Federalism

- Federalism is characterized by (1) two levels of government (national and states), (2) a constitutional division of powers between the two levels, and (3) a blurred line between national and state powers. A more detailed description of federalism includes the following points:

  - both the national and the state governments govern the people directly

  - states have certain rights outside the control of the national government **(Tenth Amendment)**

  - every state has legal equality within the system (but not necessarily political equality because of disparity in population) **(Article IV)**

  - the judiciary interprets the Constitution and hears disputes between the national government and the states and between states **(Article III)**

Review Strategy

For purposes of comparison, tables were used here. But creating a Venn diagram when you study is another way to show overlapping powers.

- By giving power to both the federal government and the states, the Framers established **dual federalism.** Certain powers were **delegated** to the national government, and certain powers were **reserved** to the states. Other powers were to be held **concurrently.**

Powers Delegated to the National Government	Concurrent Powers	Powers Reserved to the States
Based on Articles I, II, III, IV, and VI	Tenth Amendment	Tenth Amendment
Expressed Powers (enumerated powers) • Article 1, Section 8 (27 powers) **Implied Powers** • Implied in Article I, Section 8, Clause 18, **"necessary and proper clause"** **Inherent Powers** • Belong to the federal government by virtue of its existence as the federal government	Powers neither delegated to the national government exclusively nor denied to the states	Powers neither granted by the Constitution to the states exclusively nor denied to them; the national government may not exercise these powers
Examples: Coin money, regulate commerce with other nations and among the states, declare war, establish lower federal courts, establish post offices	**Examples:** Tax; borrow money, establish state and local courts, charter banks	**Examples:** Regulate commerce within the state, conduct elections, ratify amendments to the U.S. Constitution, establish school systems and local government units

- The Constitution also denies certain powers to both levels of government.

Powers Denied to the National Government	Powers Denied to Both the National Government and the States	Powers Denied to the States
Article I, Section 9 and the First through Eighth Amendments	Combination of Article I, Sections 9 and 10 and the Thirteenth, Fourteenth, Fifteenth, Nineteenth, Twenty-Fourth, and Twenty-Sixth Amendments	Article I, Section 10 and the Thirteenth, Fourteenth, Fifteenth, Nineteenth, Twenty-Fourth, and Twenty-Sixth Amendments
Powers expressly denied to the national government by the Constitution and those not expressed in the document as being within the provenance of the national government, such as establishing a national educational system		Powers expressly denied to the states by the Constitution
Examples: Tax articles in interstate commerce, violate the Bill of Rights	Examples: Grant titles of nobility; pass bills of attainder or *ex post facto* laws; deny citizens the right to vote on the basis of race, color, previous condition of servitude, or sex	Examples: Coin money, enter into treaties with other nations, infringe on the privileges of due process

- **Article I, Section 4** and **Article V** set out the states' obligations to the national government. States must conduct federal elections, and the states are the designated unit that addresses the ratification of amendments to the U.S. Constitution.

- **Article IV** deals with relations among the states. It (1) sets out the **"full faith and credit clause" (Section 1)** that establishes reciprocity between the states for laws, records, and court decisions in civil proceedings; (2) requires states to provide the same **immunity and privileges** for citizens of other states as it affords its own citizens; and (3) requires that states **extradite** suspected criminals to the requesting states. The article also outlines the obligations of the national government to the states. These are (1) to guarantee a **republican form of government** to all the states, (2) to protect them against invasion and domestic violence, and (3) to admit new states.

- **Article I, Section 10, Clause 3** deals with **interstate compacts,** including agreements with foreign nations. The approval of Congress is needed for such arrangements.

- The **"supremacy clause" (Article VI, Section 2)** establishes the Constitution as the law of the land, overriding any provision in a state constitution or any state or local law.

- Beginning in 1937, the relationship between the states and the national government began to change. Dual federalism began to give way to **cooperative federalism.** Instead of the older **layer cake** simile to describe the system, political scientists now use a **marble cake** simile. Powers and responsibilities are mixed together rather than clearly delineated, and policies are characterized by shared costs, federal mandates and guidelines, and shared management. The reliance on government programs based on grants in aid to states—**revenue sharing, categorical grants (project** and **formula),** and **block grants**—since the 1970s are one illustration of this change.

Separation of Powers

- Not only are powers divided between the national government and the states, but the powers of the national government are divided among **legislative, executive,** and **judicial branches.** Congress (legislative branch) makes the laws; the president (executive branch) carries out the laws; and the federal courts (judicial branch) interpret and apply the laws. Since the administrations of Franklin Roosevelt, the president has done much to shape the national policy agenda, so this description is somewhat simplistic. The **separation of powers** concept reflects the concern of the Framers with the possibility of factions gaining too much power.

- The separation of powers rests on (1) the source of authority of each branch, (2) the method of selection of each branch, and (3) terms of office. (1) The Constitution lays out the duties and obligations for each of the three branches, so it is the source of authority for each and all three are equal. (2) The federal judiciary is appointed by the president with the consent of the Senate, but the executive and legislative branches are elected. (3) The four-year terms of the president and vice president overlap with the six-year terms of the Senate but are longer than the two-year terms of the House, thus ensuring the potential for both change and continuity. Federal judges are appointed for life, barring some impeachable offense for which they can be removed.

Checks and Balances

- To further ensure that no one faction could take control of the national government, the Framers established a system of **checks and balances.**

System of Checks and Balances

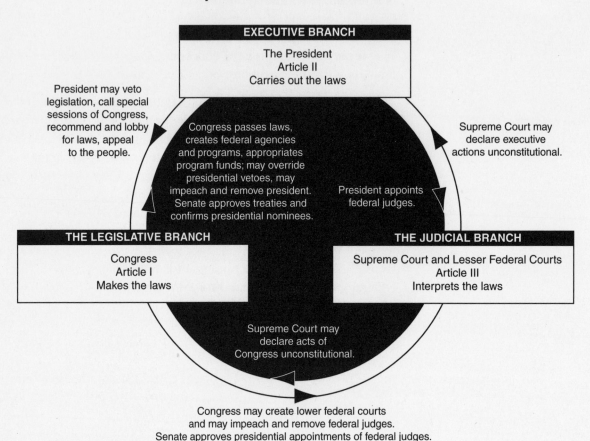

EXECUTIVE BRANCH

The President
Article II
Carries out the laws

President may veto legislation, call special sessions of Congress, recommend and lobby for laws, appeal to the people.

Congress passes laws, creates federal agencies and programs, appropriates program funds; may override presidential vetoes, may impeach and remove president. Senate approves treaties and confirms presidential nominees.

Supreme Court may declare executive actions unconstitutional.

President appoints federal judges.

THE LEGISLATIVE BRANCH

Congress
Article I
Makes the laws

THE JUDICIAL BRANCH

Supreme Court and Lesser Federal Courts
Article III
Interprets the laws

Supreme Court may declare acts of Congress unconstitutional.

Congress may create lower federal courts and may impeach and remove federal judges. Senate approves presidential appointments of federal judges.

Amending the Constitution

- In order to ensure that the Constitution would remain relevant, the Framers established a **formal amendment process.** There are four ways to amend the wording of the Constitution. An amendment may be

    - proposed by Congress by a two-thirds vote in the House and in the Senate **and** ratified by the legislatures in three quarters (38) of the states.

    - proposed by Congress by a two-thirds vote in the House and in the Senate **and** ratified by conventions in three quarters (38) of the states.

    - proposed by a national convention called by Congress at the request of two thirds (34) of the states for the purpose of proposing an amendment **and** ratified by the state legislatures in three quarters (38) of the states.

    - proposed by a national convention called by Congress at the request of two thirds (34) of the states for the purpose of proposing an amendment **and** ratified by conventions held in three quarters (38) of the states.

- Although all four methods are possible, twenty-six of the Constitution's twenty-seven amendments have been proposed by Congress and ratified by state legislatures. Only the Twenty-first Amendment, dealing with terms of office for members of Congress and the president and vice president, have followed the route of a Congressional proposal and then ratification by state conventions. The Constitution itself was proposed and ratified following the process outlined in the fourth method.

- In addition to formal methods of amendment, the Constitution can be changed **informally** through

    - legislation.

    - executive action (executive orders).

    - party practices (for example, the Constitution does not mention political party conventions to nominate presidential and vice-presidential candidates, but parties hold conventions every four years).

    - custom (heads of executive departments make up the president's Cabinet).

    - court decisions.

None of these ways change the wording of the Constitution, but they can extend, expand, or reinterpret provisions. This body of informal change is known as the **unwritten constitution.**

KEY PEOPLE

Review Strategy

See if you can relate this person to his correct context in the "Fast Facts" section.

- **Montesquieu,** *philosophe,* influence on the Constitution

Chapter 4

INSTITUTIONS OF THE FEDERAL GOVERNMENT: CONGRESS, THE PRESIDENCY, THE BUREAUCRACY, THE JUDICIARY

The AP Course Description guide for U.S. Government and Politics states that students should become familiar with "organizations and powers, both formal and informal, of the major political institutions in the United States." This chapter reviews basic information about Congress; the presidency; the federal bureaucracy, which the president oversees as chief executive; and the federal court system. The linkages between these institutions and public opinion, interest groups, political parties, the media, and subnational governments will also be explored.

It is the connections between and among institutions and how they play out in the American political system that are the most important ideas and concepts to understand. Remember: In addition to how well you know the facts, the AP exam will assess your "understanding of typical patterns of political processes and behavior and their consequences (including . . . the principles used to explain or justify various government structures and procedures and the political effects of these structures and procedures)."

	NUMBER	SELECTION/ ELECTION	TERM OF OFFICE
LEGISLATIVE BRANCH			
Member of House of Representatives	435	Direct popular vote	2 years
Member of Senate	100	Direct popular vote	6 years
EXECUTIVE BRANCH			
President/Vice President	1 each	Electoral College based on popular vote	4 years
Secretaries of Departments/ Attorney General (Cabinet)	14	Appointed by the president with the consent of the Senate	"At the pleasure of the president"
Top-level managers of Cabinet departments; boards/heads of commissions, corporations, and regulatory agencies	Approximately 4,000	Appointed by the president with the consent of the Senate	"At the pleasure of the president"
All other civilian employees of the federal government (including U.S. Postal Service)	Approximately 4.1 million (excluding employees of the legislative branch [30,000] and the judicial branch [30,000])	Civil service competitive examinations	Career employees
JUDICIAL BRANCH			
Federal judiciary	9 Supreme Court Justices Approximately 880 lower court judges	Appointed by the president with the consent of the Senate	For life; a few exceptions appointed for long terms (U.S. Claims Court, Court of Military Appeals, Tax Court, Territorial Courts)

SECTION 1. CONGRESS

Review Strategy

See Chapter 5 for information on the election of Congress.

As established by Article I of the Constitution, the legislative body of the United States is **bicameral,** consisting of the **House of Representatives** and the **Senate.** While the Constitution did not set the number of members of each house, it did establish that each state would have two senators and that the representation in the House would be proportional—that is, based on state population. With fifty states, the Senate has 100 members, and in 1929, House membership was set at 435. Although members of both houses are now elected by direct popular vote, the Constitution originally called for the election of senators by the legislature of each state.

FAST FACTS
Redistricting in the House

- As noted above, the House has 435 members. As a result of shifts in population, states may gain or lose House seats after each decennial **census.** This is known as **reapportionment** and results in the need for **redistricting.**

- If a state is to gain or lose seats after the census, the state legislature is charged with drawing up new Congressional districts to match the new number of seats. Because of the importance of holding a majority in the House, political parties in the state, with help from the national parties, vie with each other to have districts drawn in their favor. When the final bill designating new district boundaries is voted out of the legislature, it is sent to the governor, who either signs the bill or vetoes it. Opponents may appeal the law to the state and to the federal courts.

- One method of redistricting in order to gain political advantage is **gerrymandering.** This results in the creation of often unusually shaped districts that favor the party in power, either by squeezing the opposition party's members into a single district or by separating the opposition party's members into a number of districts to dilute their strength at the polls.

See the list of Supreme Court cases on p. vii to find information on other key court decisions.

Review Strategy

- A second method of redistricting creates districts of vastly unequal populations. This has been the subject of a series of cases heard by the Supreme Court that established the principle of **"one man, one vote."**

Baker v. *Carr* (1962)

Case: Tennessee federal court refused to hear a request to compel the Tennessee legislature to re-draw state legislative districts to accommodate Nashville's growth. The case was appealed to the Supreme Court.

Decision: The Supreme Court held that there was cause for a trial under the **equal protection clause** of the Fourteenth Amendment and that federal courts could hear redistricting cases for state legislatures.

Significance: Federal courts began hearing redistricting cases, which ultimately led to *Wesberry* v. *Sanders.*

Wesberry v. *Sanders* (1964)

Case: The size of Georgia's Congressional districts varied from 400,000 to 800,000. As a result, voters in the Fifth District sued their Congressman, claiming that the size of the district deprived them of equal representation.

Decision: The Supreme Court, citing Article I, Section 2, ruled that the disparity in the size of the population of the ten Congressional districts violated the Constitution.

Significance: This ruling established the principle of "one man, one vote"; led to the redistricting of federal, state, and local election districts; and ended the pattern of rural overrepresentation and urban underrepresentation in legislatures.

- In 1982, amendments were passed to the Voting Rights Act of 1965 to encourage the drawing of Congressional districts to ensure the election of more minority members to the House. After the 1990 census, some Southern state legislatures used what has become known as "benign gerrymandering" to create districts with concentrations of minority voters. Sometimes it was done to achieve the purpose that was intended, and sometimes it resulted in the loss of seats by Democrats who found incumbents running against one another. Whatever the results, this new type of gerrymandering has been ruled unconstitutional by the Supreme Court.

Shaw v. *Reno* (1993)
Case: White voters in North Carolina contested the boundaries of a new Congressional district.
Decision: The Supreme Court held that the rights of white voters under the Fourteenth Amendment had been violated by the state legislature's redistricting. The only reason that the justices could find to explain the shape and boundaries of the district was that it was meant to ensure the election of a minority member to the House. Districts must be based on the proportion of minorities to the general voting-age population.
Significance: The decision led the way for other challenges by white voters to race-based redistricting.
Similar cases:
Miller v. *Johnson* (1995), *Bush* v. *Vera* (1996), *Shaw* v. *Hunt* (1996), *Abrams* v. *Johnson* (1997), and *Easley* v. *Cromartie* (2001)
Significance: Race may be one factor in determining district boundaries, but it cannot be the major factor.

Duties and Powers of Congress

Review Strategy

See Chapter 3 for the duties of Congress relating to the passage of Constitutional amendments.

- Both senators and representatives have a number of duties. Their major duties are to (1) represent their constituents and (2) to make laws. In order to do this, members of Congress must (3) build consensus among themselves as well as their constituents. The latter includes (4) educating the public about policy issues and defending their party for its positions on policy. Congress also (5) oversees the operations of the bureaucracy and (6) may investigate the other branches through its powers of impeachment (the House) and trial (the Senate). Both houses share in these duties, but the two houses have separate duties as well. The House initiates all revenue bills, and the Senate confirms or rejects presidential appointments and treaties with other nations. In fulfilling (1) above, members of Congress also provide services to those constituents with Congressional staffs routinely fielding requests from voters for assistance in dealing with federal agencies.

- **Article I, Section 8, Clauses 1** through **18** of the Constitution list the **expressed powers** of Congress. **Clause 18, the necessary and proper clause,** is the basis for Congress's **implied powers.** For example, Article I, Section 8, Clause 11 expressly states that Congress has the power to declare war. The power to raise troops to fight that war is not directly stated but is implied through Clause 18. Another example of an implied power is Congress's use of the commerce clause, Article I, Section 8, Clause 3, to establish the minimum wage.

- The following are two important Supreme Court cases to know about Congressional powers:

McCulloch v. *Maryland* (1819)
Case: In 1816 as part of a political fight to limit the powers of the federal government, Maryland placed a tax on all notes issued by banks that did business in the state but that were not chartered by the state. The target was the Second Bank of the United States. In a test case, the bank's cashier, James McCulloch, refused to pay the tax. Maryland won in state court, but McCulloch appealed. **Decision:** In upholding the constitutionality of the Second Bank, the Court cited the **"necessary and proper clause."** The Court ruled that the Bank was necessary to fulfill the government's duties to tax, borrow, and coin money. **Significance:** The Court's opinion broadened the powers of Congress to include **implied powers** in addition to those listed in the Constitution. This ruling has had a major impact on the development of the government, allowing it to evolve as needed to meet new circumstances.

Gibbons v. *Ogden* (1824)
Case: The case revolved around the Commerce Clause, Article I, Section 8, Clause 3, of the Constitution. The state of New York had awarded Aaron Ogden an exclusive permit to carry passengers by steamboat between New York City and New Jersey. The federal government had issued a coasting license to Thomas Gibbons for the same route. Ogden sued Gibbons and won in a New York court. Gibbons appealed to the Supreme Court. **Decision:** The Supreme Court ruled in Gibbons's favor that a state cannot interfere with Congress's power to regulate interstate commerce. It took a broad view of the term *commerce*. **Significance:** Marshall, dealing a blow to the arguments of states' rights advocates, established the superiority of federal authority over states' rights under the Constitution. This ruling, which enlarged the definition of commerce, became the basis of the Civil Rights Act of 1964 prohibiting discrimination in public accommodations.

- **Nonlegislative duties** of Congress include electoral duties relating to the selection of the president and vice president, should the need arise; **legislative oversight** of the federal bureaucracy; confirmation of presidential appointments and treaties with foreign nations; and impeachment and trial of federal judges and high-level federal government officials.

Review Strategy

See the discussion of filibusters later in this section.

- There are some basic **differences** between the House and the Senate, especially regarding influence and operation. (1) Traditionally, because of its assigned duties in the Constitution, the Senate has had more influence in foreign affairs whereas the House has had more influence in budgetary matters. (2) The House has less prestige than the Senate, which is considered an elite club. (3) Because the House is a larger body, it has a stronger hierarchical leadership. (4) A major difference revolves around floor debate. The House **Rules Committee** determines the rules, including time limits for debating bills in the House, whereas debate in the Senate is not restricted.

The Organization of the House

Review Strategy

Like the vice president who presides over the Senate, the speaker of the House must vote to break a tie.

- The chief officer of the House is the **speaker of the House.** Although elected by the full House, the person is always a member of the majority party elected along party lines and, thus, becomes the spokesperson for the majority party in the House. The speaker is third in line of succession should the president die in office; be impeached, found guilty, and removed; or resign. The speaker's formal duty is to preside over the House when it is in session. Informally, the speaker can exert great influence over (1) committee assignments and (2) the choice of the majority party's leaders in the House as well as (3) which bills get to the floor for debate.

- Other elected positions in the House are the **majority leader** and the **minority leader,** who manage their party's strategies in the house. They are chosen in separate party **caucuses** (Republicans call it a **party conference**). These positions are also known as **floor leaders.**

- Next come **majority** and **minority whips** and **deputy whips** for both parties. The duties of the whips are (1) to ensure that party members are present to vote; (2) to keep track of how party members will vote on bills, thus helping the leadership decide whether to call for a vote right away or to postpone it; and (3) to attempt to persuade party members to vote the way the leadership wants.

- The **caucus/conference** has several activities in addition to (1) electing leaders. It also (2) approves committee assignments, (3) elects committee leaders, and, (4) to a degree, seeks to build consensus on the party's legislative agenda. A successful example of this was Newt Gingrich's "Contract with America" that the House speaker attempted to push through after the 1994 elections.

- Next comes the **Committee on Committees** (Republicans) and the **Policy and Steering Committee** (Democrats). The speaker chairs the majority party's committee and the minority leader chairs the minority party's committee. Their tasks are twofold: (1) to assign new members of the House to committees and (2) to reassign members who wish to change committees.

The Organization of the Senate

- The president of the Senate is the **vice president of the United States.** Unlike the speaker of the House, the vice president may not participate in floor debates or vote except to break a tie. The vice president spends little time presiding over the Senate. On a daily basis, a senator elected from the majority party sits in the vice president's place and acts as **president pro tempore,** meaning "president for the time being."

- Like the House, the majority and minority party **caucuses/conferences** in the Senate elect a **majority leader** and a **minority leader** as well as **whips** to assist them in managing their party's strategy. The **majority** and **minority leaders** have great influence over the legislation that the Senate considers. Unlike the House's **Rules Committee,** the two leaders decide which bills the Senate will debate and vote on. Each party has a **Policy Committee** that determines committee assignments.

The Committee Process

- Congress has four types of committees, each with its own purpose: (1) **standing committees/subcommittees** are organized according to specific policy areas and are charged with considering legislation and providing **legislative oversight** to the federal agencies under their policy area; (2) **joint committees** have members from both houses to oversee certain specialized areas, such as the Library of Congress; (3) **conference committees,** made up of members from the sponsoring committee/subcommittee, meet on an as-needed basis to reconcile differences between House and Senate bills; and (4) **select committees** operate for a period of time for a specified investigative purpose, such as determining the possibility of governmental wrongdoing (Senate Watergate Committee) or conditions that affect Americans (the Senate and the House Select Committees on Aging). Standing committees also hold hearings for investigative purposes.

- **Standing committees** are the workhorses of the legislative process. The policy areas, or jurisdiction, of standing committees are similar to the departments and major agencies within the executive branch; for example, there are a House Banking and Financial Services Committee and a Senate Banking, Housing and Urban Affairs Committee and their various subcommittees that deal with issues of the Treasury Department. Bills for consideration are assigned to committees and then to subcommittees based on subject.

- In both houses of Congress, members generally are assigned to the committees/subcommittees that they request and can remain on those **committees/subcommittees** until they wish to change. Members choose assignments that deal with issues of importance to their constituents so that they can show the "folks back home" that they are working for their interests. The benefits that members can reap for their voters will help **incumbents** when they run for reelection. Some committees are more likely than others to put their members in the national spotlight, also reaping publicity for reelection campaigns.

- Until a series of actions beginning in the 1970s, the **seniority rule,** an unwritten custom, dictated the way that committee chairs were chosen. The longest serving member of a committee or subcommittee from the majority party served as chair until retirement, defeat at election time, or a change in majority party in the chamber. An increase in the number of subcommittees to spread power and influence among younger members as well as an effort to strengthen party leadership undercut aging and entrenched chairs. For the first time, chairs were removed from their positions. Although seniority is still generally the method by which chairs are chosen, both the Republicans and Democrats in the House choose committee chairs by secret ballot, and Senate Democrats use secret ballots at the request of 20 percent of a committee. One advantage of the seniority rule is that it encourages longevity on committees/ subcommittees and thus the development by members of expertise in the subject matter.

- In addition to the formal structure of Congress, there are informal networks of legislators. Once formally organized as the **Legislative Service Organizations (LSO's),** these caucuses of like-minded senators and representatives were established to further the agenda of their groups by lobbying Congress from within Congress. Some caucuses are the **Congressional Black Caucus, Hispanic Caucus, Congressional Caucus for Women's Issues,** and such regional and economic groups as the **Sun Belt Caucus** and the **Travel and Tourism Caucus.**

Making Laws

Review Strategy

See Chapter 6 for information on how Congress and the president vie to control the public policy agenda through the budget process.

- There are a few basic facts to know about lawmaking:

  - Most Congressional work is done in subcommittees.

  - Most bills die in committee, not through a vote to kill but by languishing from lack of interest.

  - A bill does not go to the floor of either the House or the Senate until the leadership is fairly certain it will pass.

- In a two-year term, Congress may deal with some 30,000 bills of varying types: (1) a **public bill** deals with issues of concern to the nation in general; (2) a **private bill** applies to an individual or a place and often represents a claim against the government; (3) a **rider** is an amendment attached to a bill, which on its own probably would not be passed, but rather than defeat the original measure opponents accept the rider; (4) a **joint resolution** deals with an unusual or temporary circumstance and is the form in which constitutional amendments are passed; (5) a **resolution** affects only one chamber, such as a rule change, and is passed by that chamber alone; and (6) a **concurrent resolution** deals with matters affecting both houses and must be acted on by both, such as setting the date for the adjournment of Congress. The House has set strict limits on attaching riders to unrelated bills, whereas the Senate is less strict. Resolutions and concurrent resolutions do not have the force of law and are not sent to the president for signing.

Review Strategy

See Section 2 of this chapter for more on the presidential veto.

- The diagram, "How a Bill Becomes a Law," on the following page, shows the general route a bill takes from introduction by a member in the House or the Senate for consideration until it becomes law after signing by the president or a two-thirds override of a presidential veto.

- Once a bill is reported out by a committee for a floor vote, the **Rules Committee** in the **House** sets the rules for debate. If the Rules Committee declines to set a rule, the bill is not debated and voted on, and so it dies. If the Rules Committee agrees to allow the bill to be debated, the committee establishes a format for debate, including (1) when the bill will be debated, (2) how long debate will last, and (3) whether amendments may be offered. If a **closed rule** is invoked, the offering of floor amendments may be limited to members of the committee sponsoring the bill or no amendments may be allowed. An **open rule** permits amendments to be offered from the floor during debate.

How a Bill Becomes a Law

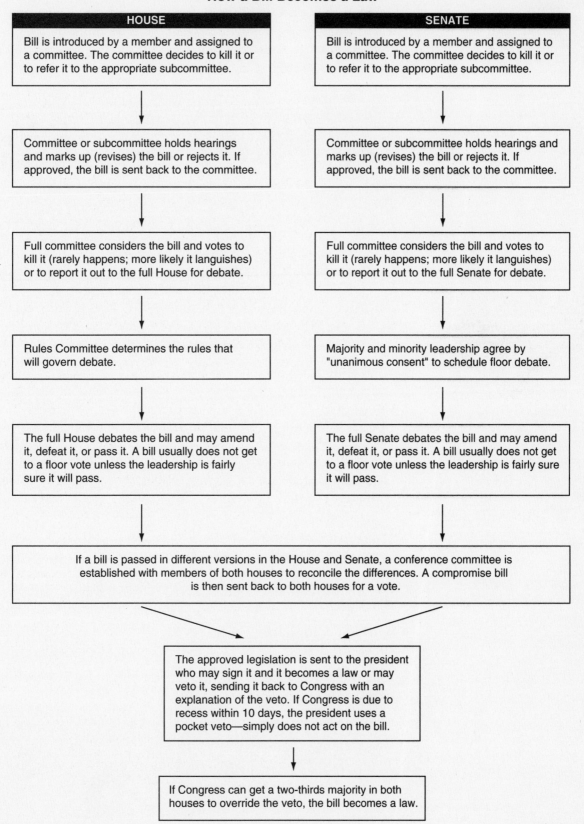

HOUSE	SENATE
Bill is introduced by a member and assigned to a committee. The committee decides to kill it or to refer it to the appropriate subcommittee.	Bill is introduced by a member and assigned to a committee. The committee decides to kill it or to refer it to the appropriate subcommittee.
Committee or subcommittee holds hearings and marks up (revises) the bill or rejects it. If approved, the bill is sent back to the committee.	Committee or subcommittee holds hearings and marks up (revises) the bill or rejects it. If approved, the bill is sent back to the committee.
Full committee considers the bill and votes to kill it (rarely happens; more likely it languishes) or to report it out to the full House for debate.	Full committee considers the bill and votes to kill it (rarely happens; more likely it languishes) or to report it out to the full Senate for debate.
Rules Committee determines the rules that will govern debate.	Majority and minority leadership agree by "unanimous consent" to schedule floor debate.
The full House debates the bill and may amend it, defeat it, or pass it. A bill usually does not get to a floor vote unless the leadership is fairly sure it will pass.	The full Senate debates the bill and may amend it, defeat it, or pass it. A bill usually does not get to a floor vote unless the leadership is fairly sure it will pass.

If a bill is passed in different versions in the House and Senate, a conference committee is established with members of both houses to reconcile the differences. A compromise bill is then sent back to both houses for a vote.

The approved legislation is sent to the president who may sign it and it becomes a law or may veto it, sending it back to Congress with an explanation of the veto. If Congress is due to recess within 10 days, the president uses a pocket veto—simply does not act on the bill.

If Congress can get a two-thirds majority in both houses to override the veto, the bill becomes a law.

- The **majority** and **minority leaders** in the **Senate** determine whether or not a bill will reach the floor for debate and a vote. There are no rules limiting debate in the Senate, but the two leaders generally agree to a time when discussion will end and a when vote will take place.

- Senators, however, can use a **filibuster,** a stalling tactic in which senators refuse to yield the floor except to sympathizers, in order to prolong debate and defeat or drastically alter a proposed bill by wearing down the opposition. Only **cloture,** a three-fifths vote of the Senate, can end a filibuster—after another 30 hours of debate. Cloture is seldom used because senators worry that should they wish to stage a filibuster in the future, those senators against whom they invoked cloture will retaliate by invoking cloture against them.

- There are many influences on how a member of the House or the Senate votes: (1) a member's constituents for issues that directly affect them, (2) the advice of other lawmakers for issues that do not affect a member's own constituents, (3) a member's own beliefs, (4) party leadership, (5) interest groups, and (6) presidential appeal and/or bargaining power.

- **Logrolling** takes number 2 (above) and turns it into a reciprocal arrangement. Lawmaker A agrees to support lawmaker B's bill if B will support A's bill when it is introduced. Another legislative practice is **pork-barrel legislation,** the name given to projects funded by Congress not because they are needed in a congressman's district but because the project will help the member in his or her reelection bid.

Key Words and Terms

Review Strategy

See if you can relate these terms and ideas to their correct context in the "Fast Facts" section.

- **Congressional staff agencies: Congressional Budget Office, Congressional Research Service, General Accounting Office**

- **different views of Congressional representation: formal, descriptive or demographic, symbolic, substantive**

- **markup: editing, rewriting, revision of a bill in committee/ subcommittee**

- **four positions a member of Congress might take in voting: trustee, delegate, partisan, politico**

- **"sunshine rule": open committee hearings**

SECTION 2. THE PRESIDENCY

The president has many **roles**: head of state, chief executive/chief administrator, chief legislator, party leader, chief diplomat, and commander in chief. The balance among these roles has changed since George Washington's day, most radically since the presidency of Franklin Roosevelt. Sections 2 and 3 of Article II of the Constitution set out a number of duties and responsibilities of the presidency, but it is Section 1 that provides latitude in how presidents interpret their office ("Executive power shall be vested in a president . . ."). One should not forget, however, that the relationship between the president and Congress as drafted by the Framers is one of **shared powers.**

FAST FACTS
Presidential Powers and Limits

Review Strategy

See Chapter 3 for the constitutional provisions dealing with the presidency: Article II and the Twelfth, Twenty-second, and Twenty-fifth Amendments.

- In addition to the Constitution, presidents derive **informal power** from (1) precedents set by past presidents (for example, Washington's use of the Cabinet for advice); (2) by actions of Congress granting presidents power (for example, the Gulf of Tonkin Resolution, which gave President Lyndon Johnson power to commit troops and thus widen the war in Vietnam); and (3) by the media as a vehicle for the "bully pulpit." The latter is a way for the president to take his case directly to the people. (Congressional leaders in recent decades have learned the power of the media as well and attempt to use it to counter presidential appeals.)

- Limits on presidential power come from (1) the constitutional **system of checks and balances,** such as overriding presidential vetoes and rejecting or holding up presidential appointments; (2) actions of Congress, such as passing laws to limit what the president may do (such as the War Powers Act to counter the Gulf of Tonkin Resolution); (3) decisions of federal courts affecting programs and policies that the president favors; (4) ineffectiveness of the bureaucracy in carrying out presidential programs; (5) the realities of global politics that make it difficult for the United States to "go it alone" and that require international cooperation; and (6) public opinion.

President as Head of State

- Another way to look at presidential powers is to categorize them as either (1) domestic or (2) foreign. In the role of **head of state,** the president represents the nation and has (1) military, (2) judicial, and (3) diplomatic responsibilities. These include the president's roles as (1) commander in chief and (2) chief diplomat. Judicial tasks involve granting **reprieves, pardons,** and **amnesties** to those who threaten national security. It was under this authority that President Gerald Ford pardoned former President Richard Nixon after Watergate.

President as Chief Executive/Chief Administrator

Review Strategy

See Section 3 of this chapter for more on the federal bureaucracy.

- Every president since Washington has assembled the heads of the government departments as a circle of advisers known as the **Cabinet.** From the original three departments, the top level of the government has grown to fourteen departments (thirteen secretaries and the attorney general). Presidential appointment of these department heads is subject to Senate confirmation. The Cabinet-level departments are:

  - State

  - Treasury

  - Defense

  - Justice

  - Interior

  - Agriculture

  - Commerce

  - Labor

  - Health and Human Services

  - Housing and Urban Development

  - Transportation

  - Energy

  - Education

  - Veterans Affairs

  At times the secretaries of state and defense may find their areas of responsibility overlapping. In reality, Cabinet meetings include the vice president and various other executive department members, such as the **White House chief of staff** and the **director of the Office of Management and Budget.**

- While the secretaries/attorney general of the departments are chosen by the president on the basis of party and personal loyalty (which is often related to their roles in the previous election), secretaries can become staunch advocates of their departments to the detriment of developing coherent administration policy. This is one reason that presidents in recent years have included nondepartment-level officials, such as the U.S. trade representative, in Cabinet meetings.

- Two separate structures serve the president. The **White House staff** includes (1) top-level aides (such as the **chief of staff, national security assistant, counsel to the president, press secretary)** and (2) several hundred anonymous people who function in support services (such as making travel arrangements). President Franklin Roosevelt organized the **Executive Office** to serve the policy-making needs of his presidency, and it, like the White House staff, has grown as the roles of the president and the government have grown. The Executive Office houses three major offices—the **National Security Council (NSC),** the **Council of Economic Advisors (CEA),** and the **Office of Management and Budget (OMB)**—and six smaller offices, such as the **Office of the U.S. Trade Representative** and the **Office of National Drug Control Policy.** Both the White House staff and the Executive Office are made up of presidential appointees and career civil service employees, with more of the latter than the former.

- The **Office of Management and Budget (OMB)** (1) develops the president's annual budget by compiling the budgets of each unit within the executive department, (2) reviews legislative and regulatory proposals from the departments, (3) oversees how departments are spending their appropriations and implementing the programs they are charged with managing, and (4) makes policy recommendations to the president.

- Membership on the **National Security Council (NSC)** includes the president, vice president, secretaries of state and defense, chairman of the joint chiefs of staff, the director of the Central Intelligence Agency, and other advisers, including the **national security advisor,** who operates the staff assigned to the council and provides information and policy recommendations.

Review Strategy

See Section 3 of this chapter for more information on the structure of the federal bureaucracy.

- In addition to the Cabinet-level departments and the Executive Office and White House staff, independent regulatory agencies (commissions), government corporations, and independent executive agencies report to the president as chief executive.

President as Chief Legislator

- The role of the president as chief legislator has grown dramatically since the administrations of Franklin Roosevelt. In the nineteenth century, presidents usually allowed Congress to shape the policy agenda. However, Franklin Roosevelt took an active role in expanding the responsibilities and programs of the federal government and the role of the president. For the first time, the federal government began to manage the economy and provide services for the poor and needy. To implement its legislation, Congress often created new agencies and placed them under the executive branch, even leaving the responsibility for filling in the details of how the agencies would enact policy to the president or to the agencies themselves.

- The success of a particular president in the legislative arena depends on the president's ability (1) to shape the public policy agenda rather than to allow the opposition to do it; (2) to consult with Congress, especially the leaders of the opposition party if they are in the majority; (3) to bargain with Congress and individual members; (4) to appeal personally to members of Congress—especially to party members—and the public; and (5) to use the "honeymoon" period to his policy advantage.

- When a bill arrives on the president's desk, the president (1) may sign it so that it becomes law or the president (2) may **veto** the bill. If Congress is in session and will remain in session for more than ten days, the president returns the bill to Congress with an explanation of why he is refusing to sign it. To **override the veto**—pass the bill over the president's veto—Congress must muster a two-thirds vote of both houses. If Congress is due to adjourn within ten days, the president simply does not act on the bill, exercising what is called a **pocket veto.**

- It is usually difficult for Congress to override a presidential veto, and if the president uses a pocket veto, the bill must be reintroduced into Congress in the next session. Often, just the president's threat to veto a bill will cause Congress to reconsider it.

- In order to rein in the budget, **line-item veto** legislation was introduced that would allow the president to veto just parts (line items) of appropriations bills that related especially to **pork-barrel legislation**. Without this law, the president had to either sign a bill and accept something that he did not agree with or veto the whole bill. Usually, the president signed the bill. In 1996, Congress passed and President Clinton signed the **Line-Item Veto Act,** but the court challenge was not long in coming.

Clinton v. *City of New York* (1998)

Case: New York City sued the government over the president's use of the line-item veto when President Clinton cut from an appropriations bill federal program funds earmarked for New York City.

Decision: The Line-Item Veto Act of 1996 was held unconstitutional on the basis of Article I. In passing the bill, Congress had delegated to the president the power to make law by striking budget items already approved by Congress.

Significance: This removed from the president a power that many state governors hold. Only a constitutional amendment can give this power to the president.

- How well Congress and the president work together, especially when the party that holds the White House is not the majority party in Congress, affects how much and what kind of legislation is passed. The shutdown of the federal government in the mid-1990s over the budget dispute between President Clinton and the Republicans, who were in the majority in Congress, is an example of the problems of **divided government.** But even when the president and the majority in control of Congress are from the same party, there is still no guarantee of a smooth working relationship. Then it can be a matter of trying to keep party members focused on the agenda and dealing with divergent views.

- Using an **executive order** is one way that presidents are able to get around a recalcitrant opposition party. Similar strategies are **executive agreements, proclamations,** and **regulations.** These have the force of law but do not require Congressional approval. President Clinton used these measures frequently in his last years in office in the face of a resistant Republican majority. President Harry Truman used an executive order to desegregate the armed forces when the Dixiecrats opposed him, and President Lyndon Johnson used an executive order to establish affirmative action as a basis for the awarding of federal contracts.

President as Party Leader

- The president is the de facto head of his party and uses the resources of the party in trying to get his agenda through Congress. But as noted above, party identification and even party feelings do not guarantee that the president and his party will agree on policy. This was especially true of a number of President Clinton's initiatives, such as welfare reform.

- (1) Bargaining, (2) appeals to party members, (3) assistance in fund-raising, (4) help in electioneering, and (5) the dispensing of perks are all methods that presidents may use to curry favor—and votes—from party members in Congress.

President as Chief Diplomat

- The president has the responsibility for maintaining national security. Presidential powers include (1) recognizing the sovereignty of other nations, (2) ending relations with other nations, (3) negotiating treaties, and (4) acting as a negotiator for other nations (President Jimmy Carter for Egypt and Israel; President Clinton for the Palestinians and Israel).

President as Commander in Chief

- The Framers entrusted control of the military to the president as a civilian, although the power to declare war resides with Congress. However, presidents have sent combat troops into battle without official declarations of war.

- One example of an **undeclared war** is Vietnam. To counter the commitment of U.S. forces to warfare, Congress passed the **War Powers Resolution** in 1973 over President Nixon's veto. The Act states (1) that the president must inform Congress of the purpose within 48 hours of committing troops to action, (2) that the troop commitment is for 60 days unless Congress agrees to a longer deployment, and (3) that Congress may end the commitment at any time through a **concurrent resolution.**

KEY WORDS AND TERMS

Review Strategy

See if you can relate these terms and ideas to their correct context in the "Fast Facts" section.

- **approval ratings: "rallying effect" during foreign crises; loss of Congressional seats by president's party in midterm elections**

- **bully pulpit**

- **chief of staff of the White House Office: runs day-to-day operations, influential aide to the president**

- **Congressional gridlock**

- **"going public": presidential appeal directly to the people for support**

- **photo opportunities, sound bites, the presidential press conference**

- **political patronage as presidential bargaining chip**

SECTION 3. THE FEDERAL BUREAUCRACY

The federal bureaucracy is made up of (1) Cabinet-level departments operated through bureaus, services, administrations, branches, and divisions; (2) independent regulatory agencies, also called administrations and commissions; (3) government corporations; and (4) independent executive agencies. Although the top-level managers may be presidential appointees, the vast majority of federal government employees—in Washington, in large metro areas, in small cities, and in national parks—are **civil service employees.**

FAST FACTS
Origins of the Bureaucracy

- The authority of the president to manage the executive branch resides in Article II, Section 3, "[the president] shall take care that the laws be faithfully executed"; but the Constitution does not define how the president is to do this. Over time, fourteen Cabinet-level departments have been organized as well as more than 200 other agencies and commissions. Once established, government units tend not to die, as presidents intent on cutting back the government have found. The federal government did decline in size in the 1990s, while state and local governments continued to grow. This was in part a function of the **devolution** of programs from the federal government to state and local governments.

Oversight and Accountability

- Even though the president is the head of the executive branch, he has little control over the operations of the departments and agencies, although the OMB provides some review of their program implementation. Congressional committees and subcommittees are charged with **legislative oversight** of the departments and agencies that are within their policy area. Standing committees and subcommittees hold appropriations hearings to review budget requests and public hearings to investigate how effectively departments and agencies are operating.

- In addition, the House has an **Oversight Committee** and the Senate has a **Rules and Administration Committee** to deal with oversight. Congress has also established the **General Accounting Office, Congressional Research Service,** and **Congressional Budget Office** to provide additional information about executive branch execution of legislation.

Cabinet Departments

Review Strategy

See Section 2 of this chapter for the list of Cabinet departments.

- Each department operates in a specific policy area with its own staff and budget. Day-to-day operations are carried out through bureaus. Most department employees are not located in Washington, D.C., but in regional and local offices where they serve the public. Most bureaucrats are career civil service employees, including those who head up the individual bureaus, agencies, and other administrative units within the Cabinet departments.

- Aside from the independent regulatory agencies discussed in the next section, the agencies and bureaus housed within Cabinet departments, (for example, the Occupational Safety and Health Administration in the Department of Labor), may also have regulatory functions if Congress has given them the power to make rules and procedures to guide the businesses within their jurisdiction. These regulations have the force of law.

Independent Regulatory Agencies

- These agencies vary in their independence from presidential control, but all are considered independent even though the president appoints the board's or commission's members with Senate confirmation and may remove members. In practice, (1) the terms of office are longer than a presidential term, (2) terms are staggered, and (3) neither party may have a majority on a board or commission.

- The function of all the federal bureaucracy is to implement the programs authorized by Congressional legislation. In doing this, the **independent regulatory agencies** may exercise **quasi-legislative** and **quasi-judicial powers.** At times, Congress leaves the details of implementation to the agency to fill in, thus allowing the bureaucracy to interpret what Congress meant. This is known as **rule-making,** and these rules have the force of law. These agencies also undertake **administrative adjudication.** They use rules and procedures to settle claims.

- Because the independent regulatory agencies have executive, legislative, and judicial powers, they are outside the regular system of checks and balances. Most regulatory agencies have been established since the 1930s, as the functions of government have expanded.

- The ten independent regulatory agencies are

  - Board of Governors for the Federal Reserve System
  - Commodity Futures Trading Commission (CRTC)
  - Consumer Product Safety Commission (CPSC)
  - Federal Communications Commission (FCC)
  - Federal Energy Regulatory Commission (FERC)
  - Federal Maritime Commission (FMC)
  - Federal Trade Commission (FTC)
  - National Labor Relations Board (NLRB)
  - Nuclear Regulatory Commission (NRC)
  - Securities and Exchange Commission (SEC)

  Note that the areas these agencies oversee all have to do with some sector of the economy, such as financial services or the shipping industry. One persistent concern about these agencies is that they have become too sympathetic to the areas they were established to oversee, with commission members being chosen from the industries and then going back to work in them after their terms in office.

- Beginning with President Carter but gaining momentum under President Ronald Reagan, a number of industries were **deregulated,** among them airlines, interstate bus companies, and financial services. The trend continued into the 1990s with the deregulation of the telecommunications and utility industries. The goals of deregulation were (1) to increase competition and (2) to cut the costs associated with the enforcement of regulation, which would, therefore, (3) decrease consumer prices.

Government Corporations

- Like the other agencies of non-Cabinet status, **government corporations** are part of the executive branch, but rather than regulate business, these fifty or so businesses provide services to the general public for a fee. Some, like the Resolution Trust Corporation and Amtrak, bailed out failing industries. Others, like the Public Broadcasting Corporation and Comsat, established and now manage new business organizations.

Independent Executive Agencies

- The duties of the **independent executive agencies** range from operating government facilities (General Services Administration) to overseeing federal elections (Federal Election Commission) to monitoring civil rights (Civil Rights Commission). Executive agencies perform services for the government and for the public.

Subgovernments

- The term **iron triangle (or rectangle)** refers to the shared web of interests that have come to connect Congressional committees and subcommittees with agencies in the executive branch and interest groups served by the agencies.

Iron Triangles (Subgovernments)

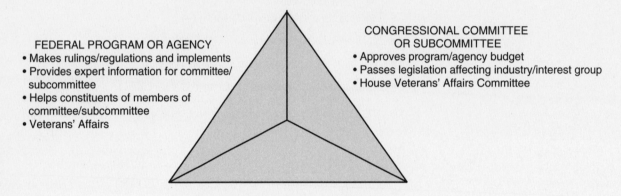

FEDERAL PROGRAM OR AGENCY
- Makes rulings/regulations and implements
- Provides expert information for committee/subcommittee
- Helps constituents of members of committee/subcommittee
- Veterans' Affairs

CONGRESSIONAL COMMITTEE OR SUBCOMMITTEE
- Approves program/agency budget
- Passes legislation affecting industry/interest group
- House Veterans' Affairs Committee

INDUSTRY/INTEREST GROUPS
- Supports appropriations for program/agency
- Provides expert information to program/agency
- Provides expert information to committee/subcommittee
- Makes campaign contributions to members of committee/subcommittee
- Veterans of Foreign Wars

KEY WORDS AND TERMS

Review Strategy

See if you can relate these terms and ideas to their correct context in the "Fast Facts" section.

- **clientele agencies:** executive departments that promote the interests of specific groups such as farmers

- **Hatch Act:** limits the political activities of civil service (classified) employees

- **issues networks:** less formalized than iron triangles; environmental and welfare activists

- **National Performance Review (NPR):** reinventing government to make it smaller and more efficient; initiative of the Clinton administration

- **Pendleton Act:** established civil service

- **"revolving door" in regulatory agencies**

SECTION 4. THE FEDERAL JUDICIARY

Although Article III established the Supreme Court, the Framers charged Congress with determining the type of lower court system that should be set up. The **Judiciary Act of 1789** established federal district courts, and, over time, Congress added to these by establishing courts of appeal and the Court of International Trade. These courts and the Supreme Court are called **constitutional courts** because they were established under Article III. Over time, Congress also created **special courts,** or **legislative courts,** such as the U.S. Tax Court, that deal with issues relating to the powers of Congress as designated in Article I.

FAST FACTS

Jurisdictions of Federal Courts

Review Strategy

See the heading on the Supreme Court in this section for information on how it chooses to hear cases.

- The United States has a dual system of justice—state and federal. The Constitution and the Judiciary Act of 1789 deal only with the federal system. However, cases tried in state courts that go up through the state appeals system may end on appeal to the U.S. Supreme Court. On the diagram showing the federal court system, you could draw a box labeled "Highest State Courts" to the right of the federal court system and link it with an arrow to the Supreme Court. Most law cases in the United States are tried in state courts, and most criminal cases end in **plea bargains,** not trials.

- Courts in the federal system may have **original jurisdiction** or **appellate jurisdiction.** District courts have original jurisdiction, and courts of appeal have only appellate jurisdiction. The Supreme Court has both.

- The types of cases that federal courts hear are based on provisions of Article III. They hear cases that arise from or involve any of the following:

    - application of the Constitution, federal law, or a federal treaty

    - interpretation of the Constitution, federal law, or a federal treaty

    - admiralty and maritime laws

    - the United States, a federal government official, or a federal agency

    - a representative of a foreign government, such as an ambassador or consul

    - a state suing another state, a citizen of another state, or a foreign government or one of its subjects (but states cannot be sued in federal court by an individual or a foreign nation)

    - a suit in which a citizen of one state sues a citizen of another state (but the floor for such suits is $50,000)

    - land claimed under grants by two or more states

Federal Court System

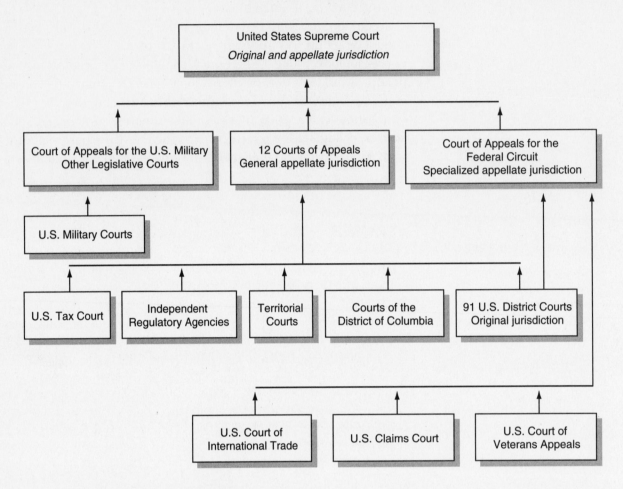

Appointment of Federal Judges

- All federal judges, like Supreme Court justices, are appointed by the president with the "advice and consent of the Senate." While the norm is **life tenure,** a few federal judges—those in the special courts—are appointed for specified terms that range from fifteen years for the Court of Military Appeals to four years for Superior Court judges in the District of Columbia. The Framers' purpose in having federal judges appointed for life was to remove them from the political arena of elections and from undue influence from those who might reappoint them.

- Presidential appointments can be blocked by a tradition known as **senatorial courtesy (blue slip).** If the senator of the president's party objects to the appointment of a federal judge who will preside in the senator's state, the Senate does not confirm the nominee. This unwritten rule is also applied to other court officers, such as U.S. attorneys and federal marshals.

- The nomination and confirmation of **Supreme Court justices** has become highly politicized as liberals and conservatives vie over the public policy agenda. The ideological leanings of potential justices are important in a president's decision to nominate a person and in the Senate's questioning of that person in a confirmation hearing.

Judicial Activism versus Judicial Restraint

- In questioning a prospective justice, the Senate delves into the person's philosophy regarding the role of the Court in interpreting the Constitution. Some nominees will adhere to a philosophy of **judicial activism,** believing that the Constitution must be viewed in the light of current circumstances and its decisions should help to mold national policy. Other nominees will hew to the line of **judicial restraint** and believe that justices should avoid an active role in shaping national policies in their decisions. These views, of course, permeate the whole of the judicial system, not just the Supreme Court, but since that court is the last word on the interpretation of the Constitution, it has a great deal of influence.

- Judicial activism versus judicial restraint should not be confused with arguments about **liberal** versus **conservative.** The arguments are more complex and nuanced. Participants may be on either side depending on whether the issue is school prayer or abortion. As some political scientists have said, the argument today is about what is the "proper balance between government authority and individual rights."

Role of the Supreme Court

Review Strategy

See Chapter 3 for a discussion of Alexander Hamilton's defense of judicial review in The Federalist, *No. 78.*

- Through the long-established principle of **judicial review,** the Supreme Court is the **final arbiter** of the Constitution and of federal laws and treaties. It has the final word on the constitutionality of any federal action and any action by a state, but it can exercise this right only on appeal. The Supreme Court also has **original jurisdiction** in a few instances: (1) cases in which one of the parties is a state, (2) in which two or more states are parties, and (3) in which an official representative of a foreign nation, such as ambassador or consul, is a party.

Marbury v. *Madison* (1803)

Case: As the Federalists were leaving office in 1800, President John Adams appointed a number of Federalists as justices to lesser federal courts for terms of five years each. The appointments were confirmed, and Adams signed the commissions in the last hours of his term. Several of the commissions were not delivered, and the new president, Thomas Jefferson, had his Secretary of State James Madison withhold them. William Marbury asked the Supreme Court to issue a **writ of mandamus** to force Madison to give him his commission. Marbury's case was based on that section of the Judiciary Act of 1789 that created the federal court system.

Decision: The Supreme Court ruled that the section of the Judiciary Act that Marbury cited was in conflict with the Constitution and was, therefore, unconstitutional. Chief Justice John Marshall based the Court's opinion on the premise that the Constitution is the supreme law of the land (**supremacy clause**) and all other laws are subordinate to it. Judges take an oath to uphold the Constitution and, therefore, cannot enforce any act ruled to be in conflict with the Constitution.

Significance: In this decision, John Marshall led the Court in establishing its power to review laws and declare them unconstitutional, if necessary.

- Almost all of the cases that the Supreme Court hears come under its **appellate jurisdiction.** At least four justices—the **rule of four**—must agree to hear a case in order for the Court to issue a **writ of certiorari** ordering a lower court to send up the case records for review. Most cases come from the highest state courts, after they have wound their way through the lower state courts, or from federal courts of appeal rather than from the special federal courts. Either side in a case may petition the Court for a "cert."

- The justices choose to hear only those cases that have broader significance for the general good. If the Court denies the petition for a writ of certiorari, the Court has not ruled on the merits of the case, so the lower court's ruling stands. The Supreme Court has merely decided not to hear the case. There are several reasons why the Court may decline to hear a case. (1) The constitutional issue involved may not be important enough or broad enough for it to consider (the justices only hear about 100 cases each term), (2) the case may not be the best crafted upon which to decide the issue involved, or (3) the Court may not choose to take up the subject at that time. The justices' law clerks have a hand in the decisions about which cases the justices will review because the law clerks read the cases and select for the justices' review those cases they think have merit.

- Another important actor in the decision about which cases to take up is the **U.S. solicitor general,** who represents the United States in any case involving the federal government that is heard before the Supreme Court.

Checks and Balances

Review Strategy

See Chapter 3 for the diagram on the checks and balances among the three branches of the federal government.

- The major influence of the president on the federal court system is the appointment of federal judges and lesser officers, subject to the confirmation of the Senate. Senators may use their power to try to shape the federal benches to their own ideological interests. Both the president and Congress have tried to influence the courts by changing the number of justices on the Supreme Court and by changing the number of lower court judges.

- In addition, Congress may pass bills that curtail the Court's ability to hear certain kinds of cases or its ability to order certain kinds of remedies for actions. Congress may revise a bill and reintroduce it after the Supreme Court has struck down the original law as unconstitutional.

- The judiciary has no power to implement and enforce its rulings. Here it must rely on the other two branches, which may defy it as President Andrew Jackson did in ignoring the Supreme Court rulings in favor of the Native American nations in Georgia.

Judicial Revolution

Review Strategy

See Chapter 7 for more on civil liberties and civil rights.

- In the second half of the twentieth century, the federal court system began to shape national policy in the area of civil rights and civil liberties. It also introduced **structural remedies** to ensure that its rulings were carried out. That is, federal courts began to oversee a case until the directed remedy had been accomplished; this oversight might continue for ten or more years after the original decision was handed down. School desegregation and the rights of people with disabilities are two areas where structural remedies have been used.

KEY PEOPLE

Review Strategy

See if you can relate these people to their correct context in the "Fast Facts" section.

- **John Marshall: Marshall Court, established principle of judicial review**

- **Warren E. Burger: Burger Court, considered a more conservative court but decided in favor of abortion in *Roe* v. *Wade***

- **Earl Warren: Warren Court, considered liberal and activist**

KEY WORDS AND TERMS

Review Strategy

See if you can relate these terms and ideas to their correct context in the "Fast Facts" section.

- **class-action suits:** a tool in shaping public policy

- **"court packing":** Franklin Roosevelt's scheme to gain a friendly Supreme Court

- **"midnight judges":** Federalist scheme to increase the number of Federalist judges at the end of John Adams's last term

- **per curiam opinion:** Supreme Court does not request arguments but bases its ruling on available written records

- **stare decisis:** application of precedents (prior decisions) to a current ruling

- **types of cases heard in federal courts:** civil law (including equity law), criminal law, constitutional law

- **statutory construction:** Congress's passage of a law to clarify a court decision about a previously passed law

- **Supreme Court opinions:** majority, concurring, dissenting

Chapter 5
POLITICAL BEHAVIOR AND POLITICAL GROUPS

The subtitle for this chapter could be "Political Participation." The chapter describes political behavior, including voter behavior; the formation and reporting of public opinion; the influence of the mass media in shaping the political agenda; the influence of interest groups on the election process; the election system itself; and the functions of political parties.

SECTION 1. POLITICAL BEHAVIOR, PUBLIC OPINION, AND THE MASS MEDIA

Political culture includes the basic beliefs, values, and norms about a nation and its government that are widely shared within that society. Most Americans, if asked, would agree that among the basic values of this nation are (1) liberty, (2) freedom of opportunity, (3) equality, and (4) belief in the value of the individual. Yet, how people think that these values should be safeguarded and supported vary greatly.

FAST FACTS

Acquiring One's Political Beliefs

- The process by which people develop their political ideas, attitudes, and values is called **political socialization.** The factors that influence this development are (1) family, (2) school, (3) peers (friends, coworkers, organizations), (4) the mass media, and (5) opinion leaders. Socioeconomic factors also are important: (1) educational level, (2) age, (3) race, (4) income, (5) occupation, and (6) religion. These factors also affect party choice and one's tendency to vote. The major influence is **family.** As people grow older, their income level wields greater influence on political decisions.

Differences Among Political Beliefs

- Political ideological differences can be classed as (1) **conservative** or (2) **liberal.** Political differences play out in party politics as Democrat, Republican, or independent, although a person may qualify his or her ideology as a moderate Republican or a conservative Democrat—or a socialist, a member of the Reform Party, or a libertarian, and so on. The **moderate** label does not signify an ideology but a way of looking at government problems and solutions. In general, U.S. conservatives advocate a limited role for government, especially the federal government, whereas liberals in this country view the government's role as that of an active advocate for economic and social change.

- Certain blocs of voters are powerful influences on the outcome of elections. **Older Americans**, who tend to vote more than younger Americans and tend to be more conservative, became a force in politics in the last two decades of the twentieth century. Traditional supporters of the Democratic Party are the less powerful and less well-off economically—organized labor, farmers, African Americans, and other minority groups. Republicans tend to gain support from wealthier people and the business community. The **gender gap** appeared for the first time in the 1980 election and helped elect Bill Clinton to his second term in office in 1996.

- There are other generalizations about voting behavior. (1) Men tend to be influenced in their voting by economic and military issues and women by social issues, such as education. (2) The better educated a person is, the greater the likelihood the person will vote. (3) The higher a person's income, the greater the likelihood the person will vote. (4) People in the suburbs are more likely to vote than urban dwellers, and rural people are the least likely to vote.

Political Participation

- People may participate in the political process in a variety ways, such as (1) voting, (2) running for elected office, (3) volunteering to work in an election campaign, (4) getting signatures on a petition, (5) writing to an elected official to effect some change, or (6) marching in a demonstration or a protest. But the primary way in which people participate is by voting.

Nonvoters

- The basic requirements to vote are that one must be a citizen of the United States, must be a resident of the voting district for a minimum of 30 days, and must be 18 years of age. States also have registration requirements, but the **Motor Voter Act of 1993** has made this process much easier by making it possible to register to vote when getting or renewing a driver's license.

- Still, many citizens do not register to vote. The major reason why people who are eligible to vote choose not to is because they lack a sense of **political efficacy.** As far as they are concerned, their vote has no influence. Big business, big money, and special interests control politics and the government. Those with the least amount of political power—the political know-how to organize and the money to underwrite lobbying efforts and campaign donations—are the least likely to vote and to participate in general in the political process. They are also the least likely to be heard in national policy debates.

Public Opinion

- **Public opinion** is the aggregate of many different publics on a range of issues. Parties measure it by (1) direct contact—letters, telephone calls, e-mail messages—between constituents and elected officials; (2) media coverage of issues and the public's reaction; and (3) elections, the ultimate referendum on what people think. In the last few decades, **public opinion polling** has become singularly important.

- In evaluating the validity of an **opinion poll,** one should consider (1) sampling method, (2) the wording of the questions that might suggest bias or leading questions, (3) the margin of error, and (4) any bias in interpretation of the results. Public opinion survey results are useful in developing public policy if they demonstrate (1) direction—positive or negative—of the public's opinion on an issue; (2) intensity, or depth, of opinion; and (3) stability. Public opinion polls may also show (1) latency, which may develop into intensity about an issue, and (2) salience, or relevance.

The Mass Media

Review Strategy

See Chapter 7 for information on freedom of expression, including the press.

- The **mass media** includes television, cable, radio, newspapers, news magazines, movies, books, and the Internet. To a large degree, the media (1) **shape the political agenda** by choosing the stories, issues, candidates, and campaign events to cover and (2) **frame** how the information is presented. Politicians, in turn, use the media to frame issues.

- The mass media—especially the broadcast media—is one of the factors that political scientists cite for the decline of political parties. It is now easier for candidates to appeal directly to voters; they are less in need of the party apparatus to get their messages out. The importance of the Internet as a tool to reach voters directly became apparent in the 2000 election.

KEY WORDS AND TERMS

Review Strategy

See if you can relate these terms and ideas to their correct context in the "Fast Facts" section.

- **bandwagon effect:** poll results that influence people to support the person who appears to be the running candidate

- **exit polling:** polling of voters as they leave the polling place; concern that it influences those who have not yet voted

- **focus groups:** candidates and political parties question small groups of voters about candidates and issues

- **image making:** use of the media to establish an image, or persona, for a candidate

- **presidential use of the media:** appeal to the people, Saturday morning radio addresses, televised press conferences, photo ops

- **push polling:** polling to leave a negative opinion of the opponent

- **regional, or sectional, differences in political attitudes:** once "solid South" for Democrats, but voted Republican beginning with Reagan; Sun Belt, Rust Belt, Snow Belt

- **sound bites:** few catchy sentences from a candidate or politician for TV or cable news

SECTION 2. INTEREST GROUPS, POLITICAL PARTIES, AND ELECTIONS

Political parties, interest groups, and elections as well as the mass media are **linkage institutions** in the United States. They are the means through which issues and public opinion reach government.

FAST FACTS

Interest Groups

Review Strategy

See Chapter 4 for more information on special interest groups as elements of iron triangles.

- An **interest group** is a group of people organized around a shared cause for the purpose of influencing government policy. Interest groups have certain characteristics in common: (1) membership, (2) financial resources to support the organization, (3) an organizational structure, and (4) leadership. How successful any interest group is depends on the number of competing groups in its area of concern and how large and powerful—in membership and/or financial support—its base is.

Types and Functions of Interest Groups

- Interest groups can be divided into several categories: (1) business and industry, (2) trade associations, (3) organized labor, (4) agriculture, (5) professional associations, (6) public interest (especially environmental and consumer protection groups), (7) government, and (8) a variety of cultural, ethnic, and religious groups, such as the National Council of Catholic Bishops and the National Organization for Women (NOW). The first five categories are known as **economic interest groups.** Some groups, such as the National Rifle Association, are **single-issue groups.**

Review Strategy

As you read about interest groups, connect them to James Madison's concern with factions.

- Interest groups and their **lobbyists** influence policy by (1) providing information to legislators and to agency employees through public hearings and through informal meetings, office appointments, and the distribution of reports and position papers; (2) by helping to draft legislation, rules, and regulations; (3) by instituting lawsuits or other litigation to achieve their goals; (4) by educating and mobilizing the public for support; and (5) by acting as watchdogs on the government.

- Interest groups also influence political parties and candidates by (1) making campaign contributions to candidates and political parties and by (2) **electioneering** on behalf of candidates.

Political Action Committees (PACs)

- **Political action committees (PACs)** are the political arm of interest groups, business, and labor unions and may be major contributors to election campaigns. Because of campaign finance reform instituted in 1974, corporations and labor unions may not make contributions directly to election campaigns, but their PACs may.

- The Federal Election Commission (FEC) administers federal election laws. The laws (1) regulate the **disclosure** of campaign financing, (2) restrict the amount of campaign contributions, (3) limit the amount that can be spent on campaigns, and (4) provide federal matching funds for preconvention primaries and caucuses and for the general election to candidates who qualify and who are willing to accept in return certain requirements, such as a spending limit.

Campaign Finance Reform

- The major legislation dealing with campaign finance reform for federal elections for some thirty years was the **Federal Election Campaign Act of 1971** and its amendments passed in 1974, 1976, and 1979. Among other things, these laws:

  - prohibit foreign campaign contributions.

  - require that all campaign advertisements include the name of the group sponsoring it.

  - require that all contributions by PACs be reported to the FEC.

- The laws also set limits on the amount of **hard money** individuals ($1,000) and groups ($5,000) could make to a candidate in federal elections, both primaries and general elections. Contributors early on found a way around the contribution limits. The political parties began to accept contributions for **"party building"** efforts such as registering voters and getting out the vote on election day. The parties then used this so-called **soft money** to support candidates as long as they did not coordinate their efforts with candidates' campaign committees—that is, the party could run TV ads that touted candidate A's abilities, but the party could not pay for ads that candidate A's campaign committee ran. For years, efforts to reform the soft money loopholes were stymied by members of Congress who are the beneficiaries of these contributions and by special interest groups that use campaign money to increase their influence over Congress. Finally, in 2002 after seven years of fighting, Congress, prodded by the collapse of Enron, the giant energy corporation that had supported several politicians' election campaigns, passed the Campaign Finance Reform Act of 2002. Popularly known as the McCain-Feingold bill, it:

- bans soft money contributions to national parties.

- limits soft money contributions to state and local parties to $10,000, which must be used for get-out-the-vote and voter registration drives only.

- raises to $2,000 the hard money contributions individuals may contribute to federal campaigns.

- indexes raises for future hard money contributions to inflation.

- the limit on hard money contributions is tripled for candidates running against wealthy and often largely self-financed candidates. Although he signed the bill into law, President George W. Bush claimed it was flawed. Opponents immediately said they would contest it in the courts.

Political Parties

- Since its beginning, the United States has had a **two-party system.** This dates from the division between Federalists and Anti-Federalists over ratification of the Constitution and continued into Washington's Cabinet.

- That is not to say that the United States has never had **third parties.** Third parties have served as innovators and stimulators of ideas and reforms. Once their ideas have proved popular, one or other of the major parties has co-opted the innovation and the third party has collapsed. U.S. third parties have been of four types: (1) ideological parties (Socialist Party), (2) single-issue parties (Free-Soilers), (3) economic-protest parties (Greenback Party), and (4) splinter parties (Bull Moose Party).

- One or other of the two major parties dominated the national political scene from 1800 to 1968. Each change is referred to as a **party realignment.** Since 1968, national politics has been known as the **era of divided government.** Either the Republicans held the White House and the Democrats one or both houses of Congress or vice versa.

  - Democrats from 1800 to 1860
  - Republicans from 1860 to 1932
  - Democrats from 1932 to 1968
  - Divided government from 1968 to the present

Divided government tends to create **legislative gridlock.**

Functions of Political Parties

- Political parties at all levels (1) recruit people to run for office; (2) nominate candidates through **caucuses, conventions,** or **primaries;** (3) inform the public about candidates and issues; (4) vouch for candidates through **party identification;** (5) manage the government at local, state, and federal levels; and (6) turn public opinion into policy.

Weakening of Political Parties

- A number of factors are seen as indications of the weakening, or **dealigning,** of the political parties: (1) the increasing number of **independents,** (2) **split-ticket** rather than **straight-ticket** voting, (3) the independence of candidates from the party organization as a result of different campaign strategies (such as courting television coverage and the use of candidate Web sites), and (4) the cost of campaigns that make candidates beholden to some degree to special interests.

Elections

Review Strategy

See Section 1 of this chapter for information on voter behavior.

- Most elections today begin with a **nominating process,** by which candidates are chosen in **direct primaries** to run in the general election. The convention system is still used by some states for some offices, and, as a prelude to the general election, presidential nominees from the same party contend in state primaries and caucuses to win **delegates** to compete in a **national party convention.**

- Primaries may be (1) **closed** or (2) **open.** The former restricts voting to registered party members; the latter allows a person to choose to vote for candidates in either party. A by-product of the latter is **crossover voting.**

Incumbents

Review Strategy

Consider how redistricting and midterm elections may affect this generalization.

- Most often an **incumbent** will win against a challenger. Incumbents have certain advantages in a race: (1) name recognition, (2) the goodwill and good public relations that come with the assistance that their staffs give to constituents **(credit claiming),** (3) larger amounts of campaign financing, and (4) their positions on issues.

How Voters Choose

- Voters choose for whom to vote based on (1) party identification, (2) issues, and (3) the candidate's personality and appearance. **Party identification** is a more important factor in races on the state and local level than on the federal level. A candidate's record comes into play as an indication of where a candidate stands on the current issues.

Election Reform

- Since the 1968 presidential election, the two parties (and especially the Democratic Party) have written new rules governing the selection of delegates to the national party's nominating convention. The aim of the Democratic Party reforms was to include more women and minorities as delegates. The changes have resulted in new laws being written at the state level, since state laws actually govern the primaries.

- The Democratic Party has eliminated **winner-take-all primaries** and replaced them with a **proportional representation** formula that enables a candidate with at least 15 percent of the vote to receive a percentage of the delegates. The Republicans still use the winner-take-all primary in many states. Both parties also use a **preference primary,** in which voters vote their preference for president, and the delegates to the national conventions are chosen in state conventions in proportion to the outcome of the presidential preference primary.

- An unintended result of the reforms has been the **frontloading** of the primary schedule because states that previously voted late in the primary season found that the candidates had already been chosen.

Key Words and Terms

Review Strategy

See if you can relate these terms and ideas to their correct context in the "Fast Facts" section.

- **blanket primary:** California legislation to have one ballot with all candidates; lawsuit to block it making its way through the courts as *Democratic Party et al* v. *Jones* (1999)

- **class-action lawsuits, file *amicus curiae* briefs:** attempts to influence policy by interest groups

- **cross lobbying:** joining with other groups to try to influence legislators

- **electoral college:** actual selection of the president and vice president; flaws; proposed reforms; effect of viable third-party candidates

- **honeymoon period after an election:** muted criticism by the opposition

- **influence peddling, corridoring**

- **Lobbying Disclosure Act of 1995:** expands the definition of lobbyist; requires registration and information disclosure

- **McCain-Feingold bill to reform campaign finance:** defeated

- **midterm elections:** loss of seats by the president's party; Clinton's second term is an exception

- **patronage:** somewhat restricted by civil service

- **stealth/secret donors:** phony nonprofit groups that hide contributions from people who do not wish to be disclosed; vote to require full disclosure, one aspect of campaign reform to make it through the Senate in 2000

- **superdelegates:** delegates to the Democratic National Convention who represent the old line of state and city elected officials and party leaders in contrast with the new, younger, female, and ethnically and racially mixed popularly chosen delegates

Chapter 6

THE PUBLIC POLICY AGENDA

Public policy is all the actions that a government takes. It may be a law, a rule, a regulation, a court order, or an executive order and is backed by some government sanction—either a reward or a punishment. Most public policy today is rooted in decisions and actions taken by government decades ago. For example, Social Security dates to the Great Depression. Once programs are established, it is very difficult for government to end them or even to substantially amend them. An example is the welfare program, which underwent major changes during the Clinton administration despite criticism from liberals. Some important terms that you should know relating to public policy are **deregulation** and **devolution.**

SECTION 1. ECONOMIC POLICY

The federal government sets **fiscal** and **monetary policies** for the nation. But before looking at these aspects of the policy agenda, it is necessary to look at the budget-making process, because without revenue, the federal government—or any government—cannot carry out its policy agenda. Related to economic policy is **regulatory policy,** which establishes sanctions to ensure compliance. This section examines the environment as an example.

Fast Facts
The Budget Process

Review Strategy

See Chapter 3 for more information on the Constitution.

- The basis of the national government's power to tax and spend rests in the Constitution.

    - Article I, Section 8, Clause 1: Congress is given the power "to lay and collect taxes, duties, imposts (taxes on imports) and excises, to pay the debts, and provide for the common defense and general welfare of the United States . . ."

    - Article I, Section 7, Clause 1: "All bills for raising revenue shall originate in the House of Representatives . . ."

    - The Sixteenth Amendment: This established the income tax, the only **direct tax.**

    Note that Article I, Section 9, Clause 5 prohibits the levying of export taxes.

Review Strategy

As you read, make note of how linkage institutions affect policy making, in the cases of the budget, interest groups, and political parties.

- The stakeholders in the budget process include (1) the president, (2) the Office of Management and Budget, (3) federal agencies, (4) the House and Senate Budget Committees, (5) the Congressional Budget Office, (6) the Appropriations Committee in each house, (7) committees and subcommittees in Congress, (8) interest groups, (9) each house sitting as a whole to approve appropriations bills, and (10) the **General Accounting Office**, which monitors how federal agencies use their budgets.

- The budget process begins with the president. The **Office of Management and Budget (OMB)** in the Executive Office of the President pulls together budget requests from each agency and department within the executive branch and, after a review and revision of these separate budgets, submits a final document to Congress. (This document also includes the federal judiciary's budget but without an OMB review.) The **Budget Committee** in each house, with the assistance of the **Congressional Budget Office**, studies the budget while the **Appropriations Committee** in each house holds hearings and takes testimony from government agencies and from **interest groups** about the requested budgetary needs. At the end of the process, Congress passes thirteen major appropriations bills each year. The government's fiscal year begins on October 1, and if all the appropriations bills are not passed, Congress may pass a **continuing resolution** that allows a department to operate on the basis of the previous year's budget.

Review Strategy

See Section 2 of this chapter for information on entitlements.

- For a number of years it had been difficult to balance the budget, so Congress passed the **Gramm-Rudman-Hollings Act of 1985** to try to force fiscal responsibility. The purpose of the bill was to control the size of the national debt. In 1990, after part of the bill was declared unconstitutional, Congress changed its tactics and began to try controlling spending. If spending in one area of the national budget increased, then spending in another part of the budget had to be cut to offset the increase. The fight over priorities between the Republican Congress and the Democratic president (Bill Clinton) led to the shutdown of the government.

Fiscal Policy

- **Fiscal policy** relates to the impact of the government's taxing, spending, and borrowing policies on the nation's economy. Presidents and political parties espoused two major economic theories in the twentieth century. According to **John Maynard Keynes's theory,** the government should pour money into the economy to stimulate demand; this policy has been followed by Democrats since Franklin Roosevelt. Ronald Reagan championed Arthur Laffer's **supply-side economics**, which held that the government should stimulate the supply of goods by cutting taxes and encouraging investment.

Monetary Policy

Review Strategy

See Chapter 4 for more information on regulatory agencies.

- The government's management of the economy by manipulating the supply of money and credit in private hands is known as **monetary policy.** Credit is manipulated by increasing, decreasing, or holding steady **interest rates.** The main agency in determining the nation's monetary policy is the **Federal Reserve System,** an **independent regulatory agency.** The **Fed** manages monetary policy by (1) setting the **discount rate** for money borrowed from Federal Reserve banks, (2) setting the **reserve requirements** that determine the amount of money banks must keep on hand, and (3) buying and selling government securities.

Issues in Economic Policy Making

- Economic policy is affected by and concerned with (1) **inflation,** (2) the rate of **unemployment,** (3) the **trade deficit,** and (4) the **national debt.**

- Various constituencies look to the federal government to enact laws that (1) increase the **minimum wage,** (2) **deregulate** industries, (3) protect the environment and consumers, (4) stimulate industrial and agricultural growth, and (5) promote trade with other nations by eliminating trade barriers.

The Environment

- A major area of concern to many is the environment. The **Environmental Protection Agency** is the regulatory agency charged with protecting the environment. Important legislation related to the environment is (1) the **Clean Air Act of 1970**, (2) the **Water Pollution Act of 1972**, (3) the **Endangered Species Act of 1973**, and (4) the **Comprehensive Environmental Response, Compensation, and Liability Act of 1980** (the law that established the **Superfund**). The removal of **toxic wastes** continues to be of major concern, as is **global warming.**

- Various groups have vested interests in any environmental policies that are created. Among these groups are (1) environmentalists; (2) property owners, including lumber, mining, and oil companies and ranchers; (3) workers employed in industries affected by proposed legislation; and (4) foreign nations.

Key Words and Terms

Review Strategy

See if you can relate these terms and ideas to their correct context in the "Fast Facts" section.

- **balanced budget amendment, entitlement cap**

- **Budget Impoundment and Control Act of 1974: a way to force presidents to spend the money Congress appropriates for programs; refusing to spend the money was a president's way of getting around programs he did not support**

- **environmental impact statements**

- **influences on the budget-making process: iron triangles, issues networks, interest groups**

- **income tax: largest source of government revenue, progressive tax**

- **indirect taxes: customs duties, excise (luxury, hidden), estate, gift**

- **laissez-faire economics**

- **line-item veto: declared unconstitutional**

- **Love Canal**

- **national debt: huge increase in debt since the Reagan administration; surplus in the 1990s; major policy issue is how to use the surplus—pay down the debt, protect Social Security and Medicare, provide a tax cut**

- **Old Age, Survivors, and Disability Insurance (OASDI), Medicare, unemployment compensation: regressive taxation**

- **proportional taxes**

SECTION 2. SOCIAL AND DOMESTIC POLICY

Social and domestic policy includes all matters regulating and supporting public housing, health care, education, and housing. In Article I, Section 8, Clause 1 the Constitution admonishes Congress "to provide for . . . the general welfare of the United States." Today, much of the government's activity is meant to provide for equality of opportunity—whether it be in education, housing, or employment.

FAST FACTS
Social Insurance

- (1) **Social security** (Old Age, Survivors, and Disability Insurance, OASDI), (2) unemployment compensation, and (3) **Medicare** are **social insurance programs** intended to help the elderly, the unemployed, and the sick. The first two programs began during the **New Deal.** Unemployment compensation programs are administered jointly by the states and the federal government, whereas Social Security is a federal program. Employers and employees pay into the **trust fund** through the **Federal Insurance Contribution Act (FICA).** Medicare was established in 1965 as part of Lyndon Johnson's **Great Society** programs.

Public Assistance

- What has become known as **welfare** also began in the New Deal as part of the social security authorizing act. The **Aid to Families with Dependent Children (AFDC)** was replaced in 1996 by the **Temporary Assistance to Need Families (TANF),** a **block grant** program for the states. **Means testing** is used to establish **eligibility.** Recipients have a five-year time limit for benefits and must enter a work program after two years to remain eligible. This is known as **welfare to work.**

- Some 13 percent of the population live under the official **poverty line.** They are most likely to be (1) single women, (2) children under the age of 18, (3) Hispanic or African American, (4) urban dwellers, and (5) living in the South.

Entitlements

- **Entitlements** are programs that provide a specified level of benefits to all persons who meet certain qualifications as defined by law. Among entitlement programs are social security, Medicare, Medicaid, food stamps, and TANF. Entitlements along with the interest on the national debt make up about 80 percent of the nation's annual budget and are known as **uncontrollable expenditures.** Some entitlements like Social Security have annual built-in **cost of living adjustments (COLAS).**

Education

- The system of public education in the United States has a mixed record in educating its children. While the children of European immigrants used the public school system as a way to acculturate, African-American and Hispanic children have found the system less welcoming and less successful as a way to enter mainstream society. By the beginning of the twenty-first century, the public policy debate about education involves (1) the proper role for the federal government, (2) higher academic standards, (3) better preparation for teachers, (4) the best use of technology in education, (5) **school vouchers,** and (6) **charter schools.**

Health Care

- A major issue in the national debate over public policy is the nation's health-care system and the proper role for the government. Problems with the current way health care is delivered are (1) the high cost of health care; (2) the more than 40 million Americans who have no health insurance, many of whom are children; (3) the uneven quality of care allowed by **health maintenance organizations;** (4) the amount of paperwork required to obtain permission for procedures and then to file claims; and (5) the malpractice and litigation costs.

Stakeholders

Review Strategy

For more information on voting behavior and interest groups, see Chapter 5.

- In determining social policy, the government must consider competing interest groups. For example, older people are a well-organized lobby who vote. The poor tend not to be organized and tend not to vote. Professional organizations like the American Medical Association and the National Education Association are also powerful lobbies who influence legislation.

KEY WORDS AND TERMS

Review Strategy

See if you can relate these terms and ideas to their correct context in the "Fast Facts" section.

- **contributory programs:** "forced savings," social insurance programs
- **food stamps**
- **income redistribution**
- **job training as part of welfare reform**
- **Medicaid**
- **noncontributory programs:** public assistance
- **Omnibus Budget Reconciliation Act (OBRA) of 1981:** Ronald Reagan's plan to cut welfare funding and welfare rolls
- **public housing policies**
- **Supplementary Security Income (SSI):** additional assistance for the elderly poor, the blind, and those with disabilities; COLA

SECTION 3. FOREIGN AND DEFENSE POLICY

The United States moved from a policy of isolationism in the early twentieth century to one of internationalism by the end of the century. Changing political alliances and a globalization of the economy were two factors that moved the nation in this direction.

FAST FACTS
The Basis of U.S. Foreign and Defense Policy

- **Foreign policy** is the sum total of a nation's actions in world affairs. This policy has diplomatic, military, and economic aspects to it. The chief responsibility for U.S. foreign and defense policy rests with the **president,** according to the Constitution and to tradition. The president is (1) chief diplomat and (2) commander in chief.

- However, Congress, especially the Senate, has important roles in the conduct of foreign affairs. Congress (1) has the power to declare war; (2) must approve troop commitments **(War Powers Resolution Act)**; and (3) appropriates all funding for foreign policy projects, including troop commitments and foreign aid. In addition, the Senate must (1) approve all treaties and (2) confirm all appointments of top-level officials, such as ambassadors and envoys, for foreign posts. The president can get around the treaty provision by making an executive agreement with another nation, which does not require Senate approval.

Setting Policy

Review Strategy

For more information on the Executive Office of the President, see Chapter 4.

- In setting foreign policy, the president uses the **National Security Council (NSC)** for advice and as a sounding board. The (1) president chairs the council and its other members are (2) the vice president, (3) the secretary of state, and (4) the secretary of defense. Additional attendees at the meeting may be (1) the **Joint Chiefs of Staffs,** who are the commanding officers of the four branches of the armed forces, and (2) the director of the **Central Intelligence Agency (CIA),** which is responsible for gathering intelligence information.

- U.S. foreign policy today may involve interaction with (1) other nations; (2) international organizations, such as the United Nations; (3) regional economic and/or military (security) organizations, such as the Association of South East Asian Nations (ASEAN); (4) multinational corporations (MNCs), such as Microsoft and Toyota; and (5) nongovernmental organizations (NGOs), such as Amnesty International.

Review Strategy

Read newspapers and news magazines to find foreign policy issues that you might use to support your opinions in the essays.

- In determining foreign policy, the president and his advisers must also consider domestic politics: (1) public opinion, especially the views of any interest groups or ethnic groups with ties to the foreign nation and (2) Congress's views on involvement in the particular issue or area of the world.

- There are three major ways to carry out foreign policy decisions: (1) military action, (2) economic policies, and (3) diplomacy. Military action means the use of force—whether **conventional warfare** or **covert operations**—whereas diplomacy involves negotiation but may also mean **political coercion.** Economic policies may include (1) foreign aid, (2) **economic sanctions,** (3) tariff regulations, and (4) monetary policies.

Defense Policy from 1950 to the Present

Review Strategy

This section deals with defense issues. See the list of "Key Words and Terms" to identify other foreign policy issues that the United States is wrestling with in the twenty-first century.

- World War II brought an end to the nation's long-standing policy of **isolationism,** first advocated by George Washington in his Farewell Address. The **Cold War** initiated the **nuclear arms race** and the **containment doctrine.** Richard Nixon launched **détente** with the Soviet Union, but Ronald Reagan, calling the Soviet Union the "evil empire," favored rearmament.

- Current foreign policy includes the principle of **collective security** and the policy of **deterrence,** both of which actually began after World War II.

- **President George W. Bush** is attempting to change U.S. foreign policy by scraping the 1972 **Anti Ballistic Missile Treaty (ABM)** and resurrecting **Star Wars (Missile Defense Shield),** first proposed by President Ronald Reagan. Bush's view and those of his advisers is that the 1972 treaty is no longer valid in today's post-Cold War world. U.S. allies, especially Russia, reacted negatively. Time will tell if Bush is successful in getting the necessary money from Congress and easing the fears of allies.

KEY WORDS AND TERMS

- arms limitation treaties: START I, II

- brinksmanship, domino theory: Secretary of State John Foster Dulles

- civilian control of the military

- Foreign Service

- dilemma of "guns versus butter": ended Lyndon Johnson's "Great Society" programs

- economic interdependence: globalization of the market, International Monetary Fund (IMF), the Internet and e-commerce, telecommunications; trade barriers, General Agreement on Tariffs and Trade (GATT), World Trade Organization (WTO), North American Free Trade Agreement (NAFTA)

- environmental interdependence: global warming, ozone layer

- military-industrial complex

- most-favored-nation trade status, balance of trade

- nuclear proliferation

- peacekeeping

- Selective Service: the draft, women in combat

- Strategic Defense Initiative (SDI): Star Wars, later scrapped when its funding was withdrawn

- terrorism as a global security issue

Chapter 7

CIVIL LIBERTIES AND CIVIL RIGHTS

Civil liberties is a collective term for those protections, or safeguards, that citizens enjoy against the abusive power of the government. **Civil rights** are the obligations that government has to protect citizens from discrimination and to guarantee equal citizenship—in other words, to put the promises of the Constitution into practice. The first section of this chapter deals with civil liberties, and the second section deals with civil rights. As you study the chapter, consider how the legislation and court decisions discussed reflect the public policy agenda at any given time.

SECTION 1. CIVIL LIBERTIES

Because the United States is built on the concept of federalism, the **Bill of Rights** applies only to the federal government. It took various decisions by the Supreme Court to extend and apply the guarantees of the first ten amendments to the actions of the states.

FAST FACTS
The Nationalization of the Bill of Rights

Review Strategy

See Chapter 3 for more information on the Constitution.

This process began with the passage and ratification of the **Fourteenth Amendment** and the Supreme Court's interpretation of its **due process clause** to apply to the states. This is known as the **nationalization,** or **incorporation, of the Bill of Rights.** It is a **selective incorporation,** however, because a few provisions of the Bill of Rights have not been included as yet, such as the limit on excessive fines and bail in the Eighth Amendment.

Gitlow v. *New York* (1925)

Case: Under the Criminal Activity Law of New York State, Benjamin Gitlow was arrested and convicted for distributing pamphlets calling for the overthrow of the government. He appealed, claiming that his conviction and sentence deprived him of due process under the Fourteenth Amendment.

Decision: While the Supreme Court upheld the conviction and sentencing, it also made constitutional law. The Court applied the First and Fourteenth Amendments to state law for the first time and concluded that the First Amendment was **"incorporated"** into the Fourteenth Amendment. The Court held that freedom of speech is a basic right that no state may deny.

Significance: This decision began the process of **nationalizing** the Bill of Rights, which was speeded up by the **Warren Court.**

Freedom of Religion

Review Strategy

See Chapter 3 for more information on the amendments to the Constitution.

- The **First Amendment** guarantees the freedom of religion by setting up "a wall of separation between church and state." Through the **establishment clause,** it forbids Congress from establishing a religion, and through its **free exercise clause,** the amendment guarantees the right of people to practice—or not practice—a religion of their own choosing. While this may seem simple, it has led to a number of court cases.

- The appeals that have gotten to the Supreme Court involve: (1) school prayer (denied), (2) school funding and support for student religious groups (upheld), (3) released time (mixed), (4) seasonal displays with religious themes (denied), (5) government aid to parochial schools computers for student use in parochial schools (upheld), and (6) use of school vouchers to pay for a parochial school education (upheld). In school aid cases, the Court applies what is known as the *Lemon* test (*Lemon* v. *Kurtzman, 1971):* (1) the aid must be used for secular purposes; (2) the aid must be neutral—that is, it may not advance or inhibit religions; and (3) the aid must not "entangle" the government in religion. On the basis of this test, the Court has allowed the use of Title I funds for remedial help for parochial school students and the purchase of textbooks and computers for student use in parochial schools. The key is that the funding must directly impact the student. In 2002, the Court in *Zelman* v. *Simmons-Harris* ruled in favor of a Cleveland program that allowed children to use publicly funded vouchers to pay tuition to attend parochial schools, saying that the program offered "true private choice." The majority opinion held that the program "was neutral in all respects toward religion" because children could and did use vouchers to attend private nonsectarian schools and public magnet schools as well as private schools.

Freedom of Expression

- While the First Amendment guarantees **freedom of speech** and **freedom of press,** there are limitations. **Unprotected speech** includes (1) obscenity, (2) defamatory speech (libel and slander), (3) pornography, (4) fighting words, and (5) seditious speech. It is worth noting that the definition of *press* has been increased to include many things the Framers never dreamed of, such as movies, cable, faxes, and e-mails. One significant case involving the **Internet** is *Reno* v. *ACLU.* In 1997, the Supreme Court struck down provisions of the Communications Decency Act and extended the First Amendment to the Internet.

- Various standards are used to determine whether a law or action is in violation of freedom of speech and of the press: (1) bad tendency, (2) clear and present danger, (3) preferred position, (4) prior restraint, (5) vagueness, (6) least drastic means, (7) neutral content and viewpoint, and (8) commercial speech.

Freedom of Assembly and Petition

- The **freedom of assembly** includes (1) the right to assemble and (2) the **right to associate.** Gathering like-minded people together in a group to underwrite the costs of a lobbying effort to influence Congress as well as assembling a group of marchers on the Capitol grounds to picket Congress in protest of the same bill are examples of the freedoms of assembly and of **petition** and are covered by the First Amendment.

- Freedom of petition covers literal petitions as well as letters, ads, lobbying, marches, and similar demonstrations—as long as they are **lawful** and **nonviolent.** The same strictures apply to the right of assembly. Protesters who march after being denied a parade permit are breaking the law.

- In order to ensure the peace and protect government and private property, governments may set certain limits on these two freedoms. Regulations to maintain public order on **public property** cover (1) time, (2) place, and (3) manner, and they must be (1) precise, (2) fairly administered, and (3) content neutral. Freedom of petition or assembly does not give anyone the right to trespass on **private property.**

The Rights of the Accused

- The principle of **due process** is guaranteed on the federal level by the **Fifth Amendment** and on the state level by the **Fourteenth Amendment.** Due process has evolved into **procedural due** and **substantive due process.** The first deals with how laws are administered and the second with what the laws contain—whether or not they are fair.

- On both the federal and state levels, due process entitles the accused to:

  - freedom from **unreasonable search and seizure** of suspected evidence (Fourth Amendment; **probable cause** is required for the issuance of a **search warrant;** evidence taken without a valid search warrant may not be used in court under the **exclusionary rule).**

  - the right to counsel in a criminal trial (Sixth Amendment).

- the right to counsel and to remain silent (Sixth Amendment).

- freedom from self-incrimination and forced confessions (Fifth Amendment).

- freedom from excessive bail (and fines) (Eighth Amendment; applies only to the federal government).

- right to a speedy and public trial (Sixth Amendment).

- right to a trial by jury in a criminal case (Article III, Section 2; a jury trial in a civil case has not been incorporated on the state level, Seventh Amendment).

- freedom from double jeopardy (Fifth Amendment).

- freedom from **cruel and unusual punishment** (Eighth Amendment).

Mapp v. *Ohio* (1961)

Case: Looking for a fugitive, the police broke into the home of Dollree Mapp. In the process, the police found and seized obscene materials without a search warrant and arrested Mapp. Mapp appealed her conviction on the grounds that the Fourth and Fifteenth Amendments protected her from unlawful police actions.

Decision: The Supreme Court reversed the conviction on the basis that the evidence was seized illegally.

Significance: This decision incorporated the **exclusionary rule** into the Fourteenth Amendment and extended it to the states.

Gideon v. *Wainwright* (1963)

Case: Earl Gideon was charged with robbing a Florida pool hall—a felony. Indigent, Gideon asked for and was denied a court-appointed attorney. Convicted and sentenced to five years in jail, Gideon crafted his own appeal and sent it to the Supreme Court.

Decision: The Court overturned the conviction, stating that the **due process clause** of the Fourteenth Amendment protects individuals against state encroachments on their rights. Represented by counsel, Gideon was tried and acquitted.

Significance: As a result of *Gideon,* everyone accused of a crime must be represented by an attorney. If a person is too poor to afford one, then the court must appoint one. This is one of several cases dealing with the rights of the accused that the Warren Court agreed to hear. Many of the decisions earned the Court the reputation among conservatives for being soft on criminals.

Miranda v. *Arizona* (1966)

Case: Ernesto Miranda was arrested on charges of kidnapping and rape and was identified by the victim. He was not informed of his right to have an attorney present during questioning. After 2 hours of interrogation, he confessed and voluntarily signed a confession, which was later used in court. Miranda was convicted and appealed. His lawyer argued that Miranda's right under the Fifth Amendment to avoid self-incrimination was violated when he was not informed of his right to have a lawyer present.

Decision: The Warren Court reversed the conviction. It ruled that a suspect must be **"read his rights" (Miranda Rule)**: the right to remain silent, that anything a suspect says may be used against him/her in a court of law, the right to have a lawyer present during questioning, the right to have a court-appointed attorney if the person cannot afford one, and the right to end questioning at any time.

Significance: The Warren Court stated that the Court would not uphold any conviction on appeal if the accused had not been informed of his or her constitutional rights before questioning. A challenge to *Miranda* in the 1999–2000 term of the Court was defeated on the grounds of **stare decisis** (precedent).

KEY WORDS AND TERMS

Review Strategy

See if you can relate these terms and ideas to their correct context in the "Fast Facts" section.

- *Barron* v. *Baltimore:* 1833 case, Bill of Rights applied only to federal government

- bills of attainder, *ex post facto* laws: forbidden by the Constitution

- civil disobedience: unprotected

- Federal Communications Commission (FCC): regulation of the public airwaves; fairness doctrine for political candidates; refusal to renew licenses, fines

- freedom of the press: issue of fair trial, public's right to know; shield laws, protection of sources

- *Near* v. *Minnesota:* 1931, incorporation of freedom of the press into the Fourteenth Amendment; prohibited prior restraint

- Ninth Amendment: not all rights belonging to the people are stated in the Constitution; basis of right to privacy

- plea bargain

- right of eminent domain: right of state and federal government to take private property in return for compensation

- symbolic speech: burning the U.S. flag, First Amendment, would require a Constitutional amendment

- writ of *habeas corpus:* recently limited by Antiterrorism and Effective Death Penalty Act of 1996—curtails ability of death row inmates to appeal their convictions and sentences

SECTION 2.   CIVIL RIGHTS

The idea of civil rights was introduced into the Constitution with the passage and ratification of the **Fourteenth Amendment,** which defined the terms of citizenship and guaranteed to all citizens **"equal protection under the law."** However, discrimination on the basis of race, gender, age, disability, and sexual orientation has continued into the twenty-first century. Some of it has been based on the law—**de jure segregation**—but much of it has been **de facto segregation,** having evolved through differences in income, housing patterns, educational opportunities, and similar socioeconomic factors.

FAST FACTS
Separate but Equal

- Two of the more famous civil rights court cases rested on de jure segregation, however, and show the differences in public attitudes and judicial policy over time.

Plessy v. *Ferguson* (1896)

Case: In a test of the Jim Crow laws, Homer Plessy, an African American, was arrested in Louisiana for riding in a whites-only railroad car. Plessy was found guilty in state court and appealed to the U.S. Supreme Court on the basis of the Fourteenth Amendment's **equal protection under the law** guarantee.

Decision: Establishing the principle of **separate but equal,** the Court ruled that as long as the facilities were equal, it was not unconstitutional to segregate whites and blacks.

Significance: The Court's ruling led to new and more comprehensive segregation laws across the South.

Brown v. *Board of Education* (1954)

Case: African Americans had won several Supreme Court cases involving segregation in colleges and universities but needed a case involving public elementary and secondary schools. In 1954, the future Supreme Court Justice Thurgood Marshall and the National Association for the Advancement of Colored People (NAACP) found their case in *Brown* v. *Board of Education of Topeka, Kansas,* filed on behalf of Linda Brown by her father. According to the law, Linda could not attend her neighborhood school, which was all-white, but had to go across town to an all-black school. Marshall based his argument on expert testimony demonstrating that segregated schools damaged the self-esteem of African-American children. As such, segregated schools violated the **equal protection clause** of the Fourteenth Amendment.

Decision: The Warren Court agreed with Marshall's argument, overturning the decision in *Plessy* v. *Ferguson.*

Significance: The Court ordered schools to desegregate "with all deliberate speed." It would take court orders, more laws, and the civil rights movement to desegregate public education in both the South and the North.

Judicial Test for Civil Rights Cases

- The Supreme Court has extended the **equal protection clause** of the **Fourteenth Amendment** to cover the actions of states. The Court has also held that the **due process clause** of the **Fifth Amendment** extends to the federal government the same protections for citizens.

- In order to write and apply laws, governments set up categories or **classifications** of people; for example, the rate of income tax to be paid is based on different levels of income, and companies that do not flush pollutants into water sources are not regulated by the Clean Water Act. In this way, governments discriminate against certain groups, or classes, in certain contexts and not against other groups in the same context. As a result, classification has become the basis for determining **equal protection** cases under the **Fourteenth Amendment.** Does a state or federal law discriminate unjustly against a group or classification?

- The Supreme Court has established different tests, or standards, for different types of classifications. The underlying question is whether the law or action of government meets a standard of **reasonableness.**

    - **Rational basis test:** This is the traditional test. Governments must show that a reasonable relationship exists between the purpose of the law or action and the classification that is being made.

    - **Heightened/medium scrutiny:** This test is applied to **quasi-suspect classifications** (based on gender). Governments must prove that "important government objectives" exist for the gender-based law and how the classification is closely related to those purposes.

    - **Strict scrutiny test:** This is the highest standard and is applied to laws or actions that deal with **suspect classifications** (based on race and national origin) or **fundamental rights** (rights guaranteed under the Constitution). To have these laws upheld, the government must prove a "compelling" need and no other way to achieve it except through the classification.

Affirmative Action

- In 1964, President Lyndon Johnson issued an executive order stating that all contractors working on federal projects "take **affirmative action**" to ensure that they did not discriminate in hiring or promoting members of minority groups. This order was meant to enforce the provisions of **Title VII** of the **Civil Rights Act of 1964** for federal projects. The concept became institutionalized when President Richard Nixon set specific **quotas** for federally financed construction projects.

- The concept of affirmative action had actually begun in higher education, and a major test case involved a student who claimed that he was denied admission to medical school because he was white.

Regents of the University of California v. *Bakke* (1978)

Case: Alan Bakke, a white student seeking admission to the medical school at the University of California, was denied a place. The medical school reserved a certain number of openings—a quota—for minority students, and some minority students with lower test scores were admitted ahead of Bakke. Bakke claimed that, as a white applicant, he was the victim of **reverse discrimination.**

Decision: The Supreme Court upheld the notion of affirmative action, but it said that race could be only one factor in determining admissions. Strict quota systems based on race were unconstitutional and in violation of the Civil Rights Act of 1964. Bakke was admitted.

Significance: Race could no longer be the predominant factor, but it could be a factor in attempting to redress the wrongs of the past. While the Court has reviewed a number of affirmative action cases since 1978, its rulings have been mixed—upholding some affirmative action plans and striking down others as unconstitutional.

Women's Rights

- The road to **gender equity** has been long and hard. The first laws dealing with equal pay, equal housing, and equal work and educational opportunities for women were not passed until the civil rights movement of the 1960s. While some laws have been passed specifically for women, such as the **Equal Credit Opportunity Act of 1974,** most civil rights laws have included women within their provisions. The first Supreme Court case to be decided on the basis of gender discrimination did not occur until 1971.

Reed v. *Reed* (1971)

Case: A mother in Idaho filed to become the administrator of the estate of her dead child. When the father also filed, he was made the administrator based on an Idaho state law that gave preference to fathers over mothers when both parents had equal claims.

Decision: The Supreme Court struck down the law, holding that the preferential treatment given to fathers without regard to qualifications violated the **equal protection clause** of the **Fourteenth Amendment.**

Significance: This is the first case in which the Supreme Court struck down a law on the basis of gender discrimination and marked the beginning of more scrutiny of gender-based laws.

- A major issue in establishing women's rights has dealt with a woman's reproductive rights. There are two landmark cases in this area.

Griswold v. *Connecticut* (1965)

Case: A Connecticut law forbade the use of any drug or method of preventing conception by married people and any distribution of birth control information. When the director of a Planned Parenthood clinic was convicted under the law, he appealed.

Decision: The Supreme Court overturned the law, stating that the guarantees in the Constitution created "zones of privacy," including the right to marital privacy.

Significance: The decision in this case led the way to a consideration of the concept of **unenumerated rights** in the Ninth Amendment and to the decision in *Roe* v. *Wade.*

Roe v. *Wade* (1973)

Case: This was a test case. A Texas law banned all abortions except those to save the life of the mother. An unwed pregnant woman sought an abortion and was denied.

Decision: The Supreme Court ruled that the state may not ban abortions in the first six months of pregnancy. A fetus is not a person and, therefore, is not protected by the **Fourteenth Amendment.** However, the amendment does protect a **woman's right to privacy.** Therefore, the state may not interfere in a woman's decision to have an abortion. At the same time, the right to an abortion is not absolute. After the first trimester, the state may regulate abortion procedures to protect women who elect to have the procedure. During the final three months, the state may regulate and even ban abortions in the interest of the unborn, except in cases to save the life of the mother.

Significance: The decision expanded the right to privacy, decriminalized abortions nationwide, created a political division along pro-life and pro-choice lines, and sparked a movement to add an anti-abortion amendment to the Constitution.

- Another issue that affects mostly—but not solely—women is **sexual harassment.** The Supreme Court has ruled that sexual harassment is gender and employment discrimination and and that it violates the **Civil Rights Act of 1964.** The harassment, however, must be so "pervasive" that it creates a hostile or abusive work environment. The Court has since clarified and qualified its ruling in several cases. If a business has a sexual harassment policy in place and the employee does not use it to make known the harassment, the company is not legally liable. If the business had no policy in place, the company may be held liable for any sexual harassment of employees.

Constitutional Amendments Enlarging Civil Rights

Review Strategy

See Section 1 of this chapter for a discussion of the Fourteenth Amendment and the nationalization, or incorporation, of the Bill of Rights.

- The **Thirteenth, Fourteenth,** and **Fifteenth Amendments**—the **Civil War Amendments**—were passed to ensure the rights of newly freed slaves. While figuring prominently in Reconstruction history, these amendments have also proved to be important tools in the continuing struggle for civil rights—and civil liberties. (1) The **Thirteenth Amendment** provides a national definition for U.S. citizenship. (2) The **due process** and **equal protection** clauses of the **Fourteenth Amendment** have been used to expand the guarantees of the Constitution to the dealings of the states with their citizens. (3) The **Fifteenth Amendment** guarantees the right to vote to all male citizens of voting age regardless of race, color, or previous condition of servitude.

- In addition to the Civil War Amendments, four other amendments have expanded the civil rights of citizens. (1) The **Nineteenth Amendment** extended the suffrage to women, and (2) the **Twenty-sixth Amendment** expanded it to eighteen-year-old citizens. (3) The **Twenty-third Amendment** entitles citizens of the District of Columbia to vote for electors to the electoral college and, therefore, for the president. (4) The **Twenty-fourth Amendment** prohibits the use of poll taxes or any tax in federal elections, which had been a tool for keeping African Americans from voting.

Some Civil Rights Laws

Test-Taking Strategy

As you read the table, consider the public policy issues that each law addresses.

• The table below illustrates the range of rights and of laws to protect those rights that Congress passed and various presidents signed in the latter half of the twentieth century as more Americans demanded equal access and equal treatment under the law.

SOME IMPORTANT CIVIL RIGHTS LEGISLATION

Legislation	Major Benefiticiaries	Major Provisions
Civil Rights Act of 1957	African Americans	Bans discrimination in voting in federal elections
Equal Pay Act of 1963	All employees (women)	Equal pay for male and female workers doing the same job
Civil Rights Act of 1964	African Americans, other minorities, women	• Prohibits discrimination in public accommodations (Title II) • Authorizes U.S. Attorney General to intervene on behalf of victims of discrimination • Forbids employers and unions to discriminate against minorities and women (Title VII) • Enables the federal government to withhold funding from projects in which discrimination exists (Title VII) • Forbids the use of different standards for whites and African Americans applying to registering to vote
Voting Rights Act of 1965	African Americans	Allows the federal government to register voters in localities where literacy tests and similar restrictions were in effect as of November 1, 1964, and where less than half the eligible voters had been registered and voted in the 1964 federal election (most of the South)

SOME IMPORTANT CIVIL RIGHTS LEGISLATION—*continued*

Legislation	Major Benefiticiaries	Major Provisions
Age Discrimination in Employment Act of 1967, 1978	Older Americans	• Prohibits job discrimination against workers 40 to 65 • Changed compulsory retirement age to 70 (compulsory retirement age since eliminated)
Civil Rights Act of 1968 Title VIII (Open Housing Act)	African Americans, minorities, women	• Prohibits discrimination in the sale or rental of housing
Higher Education Act of 1972, Title IX	Women	Prohibits discrimination on the basis of gender in any educational program using federal funding
Education of All Handicapped Children Act of 1975	Children with physical and mental disabilities	Entitles all children, regardless of disability, to an education at public expense
Voting Rights Act of 1982	Minorities	Requires states to redistrict in such a way that majority-minority representation will be ensured (See Chapter 4 for court decisions dealing with **racial gerrymandering.**)
Civil Rights Act of 1988	African Americans, Hispanics, Asians, women	• Amended 1968 law against discrimination in the sale or rental of housing • Removes from the victims the responsibility for bringing charges against those who discriminated against minorities in renting or selling housing and placed it with the Justice Department

SOME IMPORTANT CIVIL RIGHTS LEGISLATION—*continued*

Legislation	Major Benefiticiaries	Major Provisions
Americans with Disabilities Act of 1990	People with disabilities	• Prohibits discrimination in employment because of a disability • Requires businesses and public agencies to make facilities accessible to those with disabilities • Requires employers to make reasonable accommodations to employees' and potential employees' disabilities
Civil Rights and Women's Equity in Employment Act of 1991	Women	Requires proof from employers that any differences in hiring and promotion are because of the requirements of the job
Family and Medical Leave Act of 1993	Families	Requires employers of 50 or more workers to grant up to twelve weeks of unpaid leave for the birth or adoption of a child or the illness of a close family member; a man or woman may request the leave

KEY WORDS AND TERMS

- **age:** protected class rather than suspect class

- **class-action suits to end discrimination**

- **comparable worth:** factor in compensation discrimination suits

- **Equal Employment Opportunity Commission (EEOC):** established under Title VII of the Civil Rights Act of 1964 to enforce the Act

- **Equal Rights Amendment:** arguments pro and con; defeated

- *Harris* v. *Forklift:* 1993, sexual harassment case

- **Illegal Immigration Restrictions Act of 1996:** deportation of undocumented aliens easier, prohibited undocumented aliens from receiving various government benefits

- **Immigrant Control and Reform Act of 1986:** amnesty program, illegal to hire an undocumented alien

- *Korematsu* v. *United States:* evacuation of Japanese from the West Coast constitutional under war powers granted to Congress and president by the Constitution

- **Proposition 209:** California state law, bans state affirmative action, constitutionality to be decided

- **restrictive covenants:** method of segregating housing

GLOSSARY OF TERMS

The following glossary is a good summary of important terms and concepts associated with government on the federal, state, and local levels in the United States. You won't find any definition questions on the test, but knowing the terminology of government will help you remember the concepts they represent. Read through the glossary and review any terms that you don't know or can't explain.

A

affirmative action—a policy that requires public and private organizations to take positive steps to overcome the effects of past discrimination against women and minorities, especially in employment and education

Albany Plan of Union—a plan introduced by Benjamin Franklin in 1754 that aimed at uniting the thirteen British colonies for trade, military, and other purposes; never enacted

alien—a person who is not a citizen of the country in which he or she lives

ambassador—a government official appointed by the head of a nation to represent that nation in diplomatic matters

amendment—a change in, or addition to, a constitution or law

amnesty—a general pardon offered to a group of individuals for an offense against the government, such as draft evasion during the Vietnam War

Anti-Federalists—those persons who opposed the adoption of the federal Constitution in 1787-1788

appellate jurisdiction—the authority of a court to review decisions of inferior (lower) courts

apportionment—the process of determining the number of seats that each electoral district receives in a legislative body

appropriations bill—a proposed law to authorize spending money

Articles of Confederation—document by which the first U.S. government was established after the American Revolution; it delegated few important powers to the central government

at-large—the election of an officeholder by the voters of an entire governmental unit, such as a state or county, rather than by the voters of a subdivision, such as a district, of that unit

B   **balanced budget**—a financial plan in which spending does not exceed its income

bench trial—a trial in which the judge decides questions of fact and of law; there is no jury

bicameral—a two-house legislative body

bill—a proposed law

bill of attainder—a law that establishes guilt and punishes people without a trial

Bill of Rights—the first ten amendments to the U.S. Constitution

blanket primary—a nominating election in which candidates for the same office are grouped without regard to party affiliation

block grant—a large grant of federal funds to a state or local government to be used for a particular area of public policy, such as education

C   **cabinet**—an advisory body that helps the president make decisions and set government policy; members head the departments of the executive branch

categorical-formula grant—the means by which federal funds are distributed to states on the basis of a state's wealth

caucus—a meeting of party leaders or like-minded individuals to select the candidates they will support in an election

censure—a vote of formal disapproval of a member's actions by other members of a legislative body

certiorari, writ of—an order issued by a higher court directing a lower court to send up the record of a case for its review

checks and balances—the system of overlapping the powers of the three branches of government—executive, legislative, judicial—thereby permitting each branch to check the actions of the others

civil law—that body of law relating to disputes between two or more individuals or between individuals and government that is not covered by criminal law

civil liberties—the guarantees of the safety of persons, opinions, and property from arbitrary acts of government

civil rights—the nonpolitical rights of citizens, such as the right to not to be discriminated against

civil service system—the principle and practice of government employment on the basis of open, competitive examinations and merit

closed primary—a form of the direct primary in which only declared party members of a political party may vote

cloture—a procedure that may be used to limit or end floor debate in a legislative body by limiting the time a member is allowed to speak about one bill

coattail effect—the effect that a popular candidate for a top office can have on the voters' support for other candidates in his or her party on the same ballot

collective security—a system in which participating nations agree to take joint action against a nation that attacks or threatens another member

commerce power—the exclusive power of Congress to regulate interstate and foreign trade

commission form—a form of municipal government in which elected commissioners serve together as a city council and separately as administrative heads

committee chairman—a member who heads a standing committee in a legislative body

Committee of the Whole—a committee that contains the entire legislative body; used in the House of Representatives

common law—that body of law made up of generally accepted standards of right and wrong developed over centuries by judicial decisions

concurrent jurisdiction—the authority shared by federal and state courts to hear certain cases

concurrent powers—the powers held by both federal and state governments

concurrent resolution—a measure passed by both the House and the Senate that does not have the force of law nor requires the president's approval; often used for internal rules or housekeeping

confederation—a form of government in which an alliance of independent states creates a central government of limited powers; the states maintain authority over all matters except those specifically designated to the central government; first government of the United States

conference committee—a temporary joint committee created when the House and the Senate have passed different versions of the same bill

Connecticut Compromise—the agreement made during the Constitutional Convention that the Congress should be composed of a Senate, in which the states would be represented equally, and a House, in which representation would be based upon a state's population

conservative—a person who believes that the role of government in society should be very limited and that individuals should be responsible for their own well being

constructive engagement—the policy of a country to try to bring about a change in the policy of another government by offering economic incentives; an element of the Clinton administration's foreign policy

containment—the policy of keeping Soviet communism from expanding its power beyond Eastern Europe as a way to force its own eventual collapse; an element of the Eisenhower administration

continuing resolution—a measure that, when signed by the president, allows an agency to function on the basis of appropriations made the prior year

council-manager form—a form of municipal government in which an elected council serves as the policy-making body and an appointed administrator responsible to the council oversees the running of the government

custom duty—a tax or tariff imposed on goods imported into the United States

D

de facto **segregation**—segregation that exists "in fact," not as a result of law or governmental actions

de jure **segregation**—segregation that exists as a result of law or governmental action

delegated powers—the powers granted the national government by the Constitution

deportation—the legal process by which aliens are legally required to leave the country

deterrence—a basic feature of U.S. foreign policy; to maintain massive military strength in order to prevent any attacks on this country or its allies; in the past, related to nuclear weaponry

direct primary—an election in which party members select their party's candidate to run in the general election

direct tax—a tax that must be paid by the person on whom it is levied; income tax, for example

discharge petition—a petition to put a bill back into consideration after it has been tabled by a legislative body

dissenting opinion—the written explanation of one or more justices opposing the majority opinion in a judicial ruling

division of powers—the basic principle of federalism; the constitutional provisions by which governmental powers are distributed geographically (in the United States, between the federal and state governments)

double jeopardy—the retrial of a person found not guilty in a previous trial for the same crime (prohibited by the Fifth and Fourteenth Amendments)

due process/Due Process Clause—the constitutional guarantee, set out in the Fourteenth and Fifteenth Amendments of the U.S. Constitution and in every state's constitution, that government will not deprive any person of life, liberty, or property by any unfair, arbitrary, or unreasonable action and that government must act in accord with established principles

E

elastic clause—Article 1, Section 8, of the Constitution, which gives Congress the right to make all laws deemed "necessary and proper" to carry out the powers granted to the federal government

electoral college—the group of persons chosen in every state and the District of Columbia every four years who make a formal selection of the president and vice president

enabling act—the first step toward admission as a state into the Union, the congressional act that allows a U.S. territory to prepare a constitution

entitlement—a required government expenditure, such as Social Security payments, that must be made to those persons who meet the eligibility requirements set for those payments

enumerated powers—those government powers listed in the Constitution; also called expressed powers; most relate to Article 1, Section 8

establishment clause—the First Amendment guarantee that Congress shall make no law respecting establishment of religion

estate tax—a tax levied on the estate of a deceased person

excise tax—a tax levied on the production, transportation, sale, or consumption of goods or services

exclusionary rule—the rule, based upon Supreme Court interpretation of the Fourth and Fourteenth Amendments, that evidence obtained by illegal or unreasonable means cannot be used at the trial of the person from whom it was seized

exclusive jurisdiction—the power of the federal courts alone to hear certain cases

exclusive powers—those held by the federal government alone in the federal system; most of the delegated powers

executive agreement—a pact made by the president with the head of a foreign nation; a binding international agreement with the power of law but does not require Senate consent

executive order—regulations issued by a chief executive or his or her subordinates, based upon either constitutional or statutory authority and having the force of law

executive privilege—the president's right to refuse to testify before, or provide information to, Congress or a court

ex post facto law—a criminal law applied retroactively to the disadvantage of the accused; prohibited by the Constitution

expressed powers—those powers that are directly stated in the Constitution; also called enumerated powers

extradition—the legal process by which a fugitive from justice in one state is returned (extradited) to the state in which the crime was committed

F

federal budget—a detailed estimate of federal income and spending for the upcoming fiscal year and a plan for the execution of public policy

federalism—a system under which power is divided between a national government and state governments

Federalists—those persons who supported the adoption of the federal Constitution in 1787–1788

filibuster—various methods (usually lengthy speeches) aimed at defeating a bill in the U.S. Senate by preventing a final vote on it

foreign policy—the strategies and principles that guide a nation's relations with other countries; everything a government says and does in world affairs

formal amendment a modification of the Constitution by one of the four methods set forth in the Constitution

free exercise clause—the First Amendment guarantee that Congress will not prohibit the free exercise of religion

Full Faith and Credit—the Constitution's requirement (Article IV, Section 1) that each state accept the public acts, records, and judicial proceedings of every other state

G

general election—a regularly scheduled election at which the voters choose public officeholders

gerrymandering—the drawing of an electoral district's boundaries to the advantage of a party or group

gift tax—a tax levied on the making of a gift to a living person

grand jury—the group of persons who hears charges made against a person and decides whether there is enough evidence to bring that person to trial

grant-in-aid—a sum of money given by the federal government to the states for a specific purpose

grass roots—of or from the common people or the average voter; used to describe pressure and opinion on public policy

H

habeas corpus, writ of—a court order to bring a prisoner before the court to determine whether he or she has been legally detained

I

impeachment—the formal accusation of misconduct in office against a public official

implied powers—those powers of the federal government inferred from the expressed powers; the powers deemed "necessary and proper" to carry out the expressed powers

independent—a voter who does not support any one party

independent agency—an agency created by Congress outside of the authority of executive departments; National Aeronautics and Space Administration (NASA) and the Securities and Exchange Commission (SEC), for example

indictment—an accusation by a grand jury that declares there is sufficient evidence to bring a named person to criminal trial

indirect tax—a tax levied on one person but passed on to another for payment; tax on cigarette makers that they then pass on to cigarette purchasers

informal amendment—a change made in the Constitution, not by actual written amendment, but by legislation passed by Congress, actions taken by the president, decisions of the Supreme Court, the activities of political parties, or custom

inherent powers—those powers that the federal government may exercise because it is government

inheritance tax—a tax levied on a beneficiary's share of a deceased person's estate

initiative—the petition process by which voters may propose a law or state constitutional amendment

injunction—a court order that requires or forbids some specific action

interest group—a private organization of people who share common goals or interests and organize to influence government policy

iron triangle—the relationship between and among a Congressional committee or subcommittee, an agency of the executive branch, and an interest group that results in mutual cooperation and support

isolationism—the policy of avoiding involvement in world affairs; basis of U.S. foreign policy between World Wars I and II

item veto—the power to reject a particular section or item in a piece of legislation without vetoing the entire law; a power held by most state governors but not by the U.S. president

J

Jim Crow law—a law requiring racial segregation in places such as schools and restaurants

joint committee—a legislative committee composed of members from both the House and the Senate

joint resolution—a legislative measure that must be passed by both houses and approved by the president to become effective; similar to a bill, with the force of law, that usually deals with unusual or temporary measures

judicial review—the power of the Supreme Court to review the actions of local, state, or federal governments and declare them invalid if they violate the Constitution

jus sanguinis—the principle, or "law of the blood," that grants U.S. citizenship at birth because of the citizenship of one or both parents

jus soli—the principle, or "law of the soil," that grants U.S. citizenship to a person born in the United States

L

libel—written or published statements intended to damage a person's reputation

liberal—person who believes that the federal government should be very active in helping individuals and communities promote health, education, justice, and equal opportunity

liberal or loose constructionist—person who believes that the provisions of the Constitution, especially those granting powers to government, should be construed in broad terms

limited government—the basic principle of the U.S. system of government; that government is limited in its powers and cannot deny individuals certain rights

linkage institutions—the access points by which the public's issues are transmitted to government, that is, political parties, elections, interest groups, and the media

lobbying—making direct contact with lawmakers or other government leaders to influence government policy on the behalf of organizations or businesses

logrolling—the agreement by two or more lawmakers to support each other's bills

Magna Carta—the Great Charter; established the principle that the power of the monarchy was not absolute in England; forced upon the king by his barons in 1215; established such rights as trial by jury

majority opinion—a written statement by the majority of the justices of a court in support of a decision by that court

mandamus, writ of—a court order requiring a specific action

market economy—the economic system in which the government's role is a limited one and key decisions are made by private individuals and companies through the supply and demand of the marketplace

mass media—those means of communication that reach large audiences, such as television, newspapers, radio, magazines, and the Internet

mayor-council government—a form of municipal government in which executive power belongs to an elected mayor and legislative power belongs to an elected council

monopoly—a firm that is the only source of a good or service

N

nationalization—the process by which the government acquires private industry for public use

naturalization—the legal process by which a person born a citizen of one country becomes a citizen of another

necessary and proper clause—Article I, Section 8, Clause 18 of the Constitution, which gives Congress the power to make all laws "necessary and proper" for executing its powers

New Jersey Plan—an alternative to the Virginia Plan offered at the Constitutional Convention of 1787, differing chiefly in the matter of how states should be represented in Congress

nonresident alien—a person from another country who expects to stay in the United States for a short, specified period of time

O

open primary—an election in which any qualified voter may participate without regard to party affiliation

original jurisdiction—the authority of a trial court to be the first to hear a case

oversight function—the review by legislative committees of the policies and programs of the executive branch

P

pardon—a release from legal punishment

party caucus—a meeting of party leaders and/or members to discuss party business

patent—a license awarded to an inventor granting him or her the exclusive right to manufacture, use, and sell an invention for a specified period of time

patronage—the practice of giving government jobs to friends and supporters

payroll tax—a tax levied on employers, employees, and self-employed persons

petit jury—a trial jury of 12 persons who hear the evidence presented in court and render a decision

Petition of Right—challenged the idea of the divine right of kings, declaring in 1628 in England that even a monarch must obey the law of the land

platform—the written statement of a party's principles, beliefs, and positions on issues

plurality—the largest number of votes in an election

pocket veto—the type of veto a president may use to kill a bill passed within the last 10 days that Congress is in session by simply refusing to act on it

political action committee (PAC)—a political arm of a special interest group specifically designed to collect money and provide financial support for political candidates

political socialization—the process by which individuals learn their political beliefs and attitudes through life experiences

polling place—the location in a precinct where people vote

poll tax—money paid in order to vote; declared illegal as a way to discriminate against African-American voters

popular sovereignty—a basic principle of the American system of government; that the people are the only source of any and all governmental power

pork-barrel legislation—the money that Congress appropriates for local federal projects that may or may not be worthwhile and/or necessary projects

precedent—previous court decisions on which to base later decisions or actions

precinct—a voting district

president of the Senate—the presiding officer of a senate; in the U.S. Senate, the Vice President of the United States; in a state legislature, either the lieutenant governor or a senator

president pro tempore—the member of the U.S. Senate, or of the upper house of a state's legislature, chosen to preside in the absence of the president of the Senate

probable cause—reasonable ground, or a good basis, for believing that a person or premise is linked to a crime

progressive tax—a tax that varies with a person's ability to pay; federal personal income tax, for example

propaganda—a technique of persuasion aimed at influencing public opinion to create a particular popular belief

property tax—a tax levied on real property (land and buildings) or personal property (tangible and intangible wealth, such as stocks)

public-interest group—an organization that tries to influence public policies for the good of the public

public opinion—the ideas and attitudes that a significant number of Americans hold about such things as government and political issues

public policy—a law, rule, statute, or order that expresses the goals of the government

Q　**quorum**—the minimum number of members who must be present for a legislative body to conduct business

quota sample—in scientific polling, a group chosen to be interviewed in which members of each of several groups are chosen in proportion to their percentage in the actual population; for example, groups representing men and women aged 24 to 30 and 31 to 40; blue-collar and white-collar workers; high school graduates, college graduates, and people with some postgraduate work

R　**random sample**—in scientific polling, a sample to be interviewed in which each member of the population has an equal chance of being included

ratification—the formal approval of a constitution, constitutional amendment, or treaty

reapportionment—the redistribution of political representation on the basis of population changes

recall—the procedure by which voters may remove elected officials before their terms expire

recognition—the exclusive power of the president to recognize, or establish formal diplomatic relations with, foreign states

redress—the satisfaction of a claim brought to court

referendum—the procedure by which voters approve or disapprove of a measure passed by a state legislature

regressive tax—a tax that affects people with low incomes more than those with large incomes; for example, a state sales tax

representative democracy—a system of government in which people elect delegates to make laws and conduct government

republic—a government in which voters hold sovereign power; elected representatives who are responsible to the people exercise that power

reserved powers—those powers that belong to the states under the Constitution

resident alien—a person from another nation who has established permanent residence in the United States

resolution—a statement that relates to the internal business of one house of Congress that is passed by that house alone

reverse discrimination—a description of affirmative action by opponents of that policy; holds that giving preference to females and/or nonwhites discriminates against the majority group

rider—a provision, unlikely to pass on its own merit, that is added to a bill that is certain to pass so that it will "ride" through legislative approval

runoff primary—a second primary election between the two candidates who received the most votes (but not a majority of votes) in the first primary

S

sales tax—a tax levied on the sale of commodities, paid by the purchaser; the single most important source of income among the states

sedition—spoken, written, or other action promoting resistance to authority; especially advocating overthrowing the government

segregation—the separation or isolation of a racial or other minority group from the rest of the population in education and other areas of public or private activity

select committee—a temporary legislative committee created to study a specific issue and report its findings to the Senate or the House

seniority rule—the unwritten rule in both houses of Congress that the top posts in each chamber (with few exceptions) will be held by "ranking members," or members with the longest records of service

separate-but-equal doctrine—the policy that allowed separate facilities for different races as long as those facilities were equal; established in *Plessy* v. *Ferguson;* declared unconstitutional in *Brown* v. *Board of Education*

separation of powers—the division of power among the legislative, executive, and judicial branches of government

shield law—a law in some states that gives reporters some protection against disclosing confidential information or sources

single-interest group—a political action committee that focuses on a single public policy issue

slander—false speech intended to damage a person's reputation

social insurance taxes—the money the federal government collects to pay for major social programs, such as Social Security, Medicare, and unemployment insurance

sound bite—a short, sharply focused comment from a public official or candidate for public office that is meant to be picked up and carried on television news

Speaker of the House—the presiding officer of the House of Representatives, chosen by and from the majority party in the House

special district—a unit of local government that deals with a specific function, such as a school or library district

split-ticket voting—voting for candidates of more than one party in the same election

soft money—money given directly to political parties for party-building activities rather than to elect particular candidates; unregulated money

spoils system—the practice of rewarding friends and supporters with government jobs, contracts, and other favors

standing committee—a permanent committee in a legislative body that oversees bills in a specific area

straight-ticket voting—voting for the candidates of one party only in an election

strict constructionist—someone who advocates a narrow interpretation of the Constitution's provisions, especially those areas granting power to government

strong-mayor government—a type of mayor-council government in which the mayor has broad executive powers

supply and demand, laws of—a basic feature of a capitalist economy; when supplies of goods and services become plentiful, prices tend to drop; when supplies become scarce, prices tend to rise

sunshine law—a law that prohibits public officials from holding meetings not open to the public

T

Three-fifths Compromise—an agreement at the Constitutional Convention of 1787 that slaves should be counted as three fifths of a person for purposes of determining the population of a state and representation in the House of Representatives

township—a term used for a subdivision of a county in many states

treason—crime of disloyalty to a nation that involves waging war against the nation or giving aid and comfort to its enemies, that is, turning over national secrets

trust—a form of business consolidation in which several corporations combine their stock and allow a board of trustees to run the corporation as one enterprise

U

unemployment insurance—programs in which federal and state governments cooperate to provide help for people who are out of work

unicameral—a single-house legislative body

V

veto power—a constitutional power that enables the president (or a governor) to return legislation to the Congress (or state legislature) unsigned and with reasons for his or her objections

Virginia Plan—a plan offered at the Constitutional Convention of 1787; called for a bicameral legislature in which representation in both houses would be based on population

W

ward—a large district comprised of several adjoining precincts

weak-mayor government—a type of mayor-council government in which the mayor has little real power

whip—an assistant to party floor leaders in a legislature, responsible for monitoring and marshalling the party's votes according to the wishes of the party's leaders

Z

zoning—the practice of dividing a city or other unit of government into districts and regulating the uses of land in each district

Practice Test 1
AP GOVERNMENT AND POLITICS

On the front page of the test booklet, you will find some information about the test. Because you have studied this book, none of it should be new to you, and much of it is similar to other standardized tests that you have taken.

The page will tell you that the following exam will take 2 hours and 25 minutes—45 minutes for the multiple-choice portion, Section I, and 100 minutes for the essay part, Section II. There are two booklets for the exam, one for the multiple-choice section and one for the essays.

The page in your test booklet will also say that SECTION I

- is 45 minutes.

- has 60 questions.

- counts for 50 percent of your total score.

Then you will find a sentence in capital letters telling you not to open your exam booklet until the monitor tells you to open it.

Other instructions will tell you to be careful when you fill in the ovals on the answer sheet. Fill in each oval completely. If you erase an answer, erase it completely. If you skip a question, be sure to skip the answer oval for it. You will not receive any credit for work done in the test booklet, but you may use it for making notes.

You will also find a paragraph about the guessing penalty—a deduction of one-quarter point for every wrong answer—but also words of advice about guessing if you know something about the questions and can eliminate several of the answers.

The final paragraph will remind you to work effectively and to pace yourself. You are told that not everyone will be able to answer all the questions and it is preferable to skip questions that are difficult and come back to them if you have time.

GOVERNMENT AND POLITICS

SECTION I	TIME—45 MINUTES	60 QUESTIONS

Directions: Each question or incomplete sentence is followed by five suggested responses. Select the best answer and fill in the corresponding oval on the answer sheet.

1. *Wesberry* v. *Sanders* established the principle of

    (A) the exclusionary rule.
    (B) "one man, one vote."
    (C) race as a factor for admitting students to institutions of higher education.
    (D) judicial review.
    (E) the right to counsel.

2. Of the following voters, which is the least likely to vote?

    (A) A Northerner
    (B) A college graduate
    (C) A regular attendee at religious services
    (D) A person with a high sense of civic duty
    (E) A person who lives in a rural area

3. The original jurisdiction of the Supreme Court does not include which of the following?

    (A) A case between two or more states
    (B) A case involving an appeal based on denial of due process
    (C) A case between one state and citizens of another state
    (D) A case involving a foreign diplomat
    (E) A case between a state and a foreign nation

4. The indirect purpose of the Pendleton Act was to

    (A) establish a civil service system for the federal government.
    (B) make the assassination of the president a federal crime.
    (C) make the federal government more efficient and less susceptible to corruption.
    (D) prohibit political parties in power from soliciting campaign contributions from federal officeholders.
    (E) limit the level of federal officeholders who were appointed rather than elected.

5. All of the following are true statements about the presidential nominating process since reforms began in 1972 EXCEPT

    (A) primaries are the major way delegates are selected for the nominating conventions.
    (B) favorite son candidates are rare.
    (C) the primary calendar is front-loaded.
    (D) candidates typically announce their intention to run at least a year before the convention.
    (E) New Hampshire primaries and Iowa caucuses are no longer important.

6. The significance of the Immigration Act of 1965 is that the act

(A) abolished the national quota system for immigration.

(B) reinstated the elements of the Gentlemen's Agreement of 1906.

(C) continued the system of preferences for skilled workers and relatives of U.S. citizens.

(D) provided an amnesty under which undocumented aliens could become legal citizens.

(E) made it easier for the INS to deport illegal aliens.

7. The informal organization of interests in Congress is dominated by

(A) subcommittees.
(B) select committees.
(C) networks.
(D) caucuses.
(E) congressional staffs.

8. Which of the following was instituted to limit the power of the presidency?

(A) Line-item veto
(B) War Powers Resolution of 1973
(C) National Performance Review
(D) Law authorizing the appointment of an independent counsel
(E) National Security Advisor

9. In voting on legislation, a member of Congress is more likely to vote

(A) based on party loyalty.

(B) based on the interests of his or her constituents.

(C) based on what the president wants, regardless of which party the president belongs to.

(D) based on what the president wants if the Congress member and the president belong to the same party.

(E) based on the urging of the party's whip.

10. To say that the American people tend to be "ideologically conservative but operationally liberal" means that

(A) Americans favor conservative moral values but also favor the latest in management techniques to supervise government bureaucracy.

(B) Americans are both conservative and liberal.

(C) Americans are likely to support limited government in theory but support social programs in practice.

(D) Americans are likely to talk about the need for social welfare programs but to vote for legislators who will restrain government spending.

(E) ideology has little impact on American politics.

11. Public opinion is

I. the sum total of the opinion of everyone in the nation.

II. made up of many different publics.

III. related to a specific issue.

(A) I
(B) II
(C) III
(D) I and II
(E) II and III

GO ON TO THE NEXT PAGE

12. Which of the following statements best describes government under the Articles of Confederation?

    (A) The Confederation government established guidelines for settling new territories and admitting new states.

    (B) Because of the colonists' experiences with Great Britain, the Articles of Confederation had been written so that real power remained with the states.

    (C) States could not make treaties without Congress's approval, nor could the states pass laws that conflicted with treaties made by the central government.

    (D) The Confederation government was hampered in its ability to levy taxes.

    (E) Because of sectional interests, the central government could not agree on whether or not to set customs duties or how high the tariff should be.

13. All of the following are clientele agencies EXCEPT the

    (A) Department of Agriculture.

    (B) Department of Labor.

    (C) Department of Housing and Urban Development.

    (D) Department of Defense.

    (E) Department of Education.

14. The major difference between interest groups and political parties is that

    (A) interest groups want to influence specific policies whereas political parties want to control government.

    (B) interest groups lobby government officials whereas members of political parties are elected or appointed officials.

    (C) interest groups raise money to donate to political parties.

    (D) interest groups have no allegiance to the general public whereas political parties have allegiance at least to their constituents.

    (E) interest groups work behind the scenes whereas political parties are open to anyone.

15. The statement "It is emphatically the province and duty of the judicial department to say what the law is" relates to which of the following cases?

    (A) *Brown* v. *Board of Education*

    (B) *Plessy* v. *Ferguson*

    (C) *Miranda* v. *Arizona*

    (D) *Marbury* v. *Madison*

    (E) *McCulloch* v. *Maryland*

16. Senatorial courtesy refers to the practice

    (A) of appointing senators to the committees they wish to sit on.

    (B) whereby a nominee to a federal court is rejected if opposed by the senator from the state where the nominee will serve if the senator is from the president's party.

    (C) of relinquishing the floor to a senator who wishes to speak.

    (D) of senators' supporting pork-barrel legislation for one another.

    (E) of inviting the president to deliver the State of Union address in the Senate chamber.

17. All of the following are examples of conventional political participation EXCEPT

    (A) making a campaign contribution to a candidate for public office.

    (B) testifying at a public hearing.

    (C) voting.

    (D) participating in a march to protest pending legislation.

    (E) volunteering as a campaign worker to stuff envelopes for a mailing.

Questions 18 and 19 refer to the following figure.

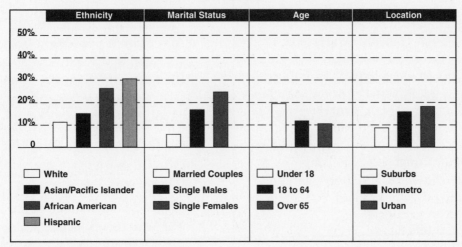

Source: *U.S. Census Bureau*

18. Based on the graph above, which of the following statements is the most inclusive description of poverty in the United States?

    (A) The face of poverty in the United States is young, female, and African American.

    (B) Most Americans of African-American and Hispanic descent live at or below the poverty level.

    (C) Children under the age of 18 and unmarried African-American and Hispanic women who live in cities are more likely to be at or below the poverty line.

    (D) African-American and Hispanic women and children who live in cities in the South are more likely to live at or below the poverty line.

    (E) The major characteristics of persons living at or below the poverty level are being African American or Hispanic, female, under the age of 18, and a Southerner.

19. Faced with the inequality of income that the poverty level illustrates, most Americans favor

    (A) income redistribution to reduce income inequality.

    (B) a flat federal income tax.

    (C) creating equal educational, employment, and housing opportunities rather than income redistribution.

    (D) federalization of welfare benefits.

    (E) an increase in federal and state governments to better manage the social welfare program.

GO ON TO THE NEXT PAGE

20. All of the following help to explain the decline in voter turnout EXCEPT

(A) the difficult process involved in registering to vote.

(B) a decline in Americans' sense of political efficacy.

(C) a decline in political parties.

(D) lack of interest.

(E) a decline in the belief that government is responsive to citizens' concerns.

21. All of the following are linkage institutions in the United States EXCEPT

(A) political parties.

(B) elections.

(C) the media.

(D) interest groups.

(E) Congress.

22. All of the following benefit congressional subcommittees in an iron triangle EXCEPT

(A) contributions by client groups to the election campaigns of subcommittee members.

(B) expert information from government agency witnesses at subcommittee hearings.

(C) assistance from the government agency with complaints from constituents.

(D) the seniority of the committee chair.

(E) expert testimony at subcommittee hearings from the client groups' representatives.

23. Which of the following demographic changes is the most likely to affect public policy in the future?

I. Graying of America

II. Shift of population from the North and Midwest to the South and West

III. Growth of a minority-majority population

(A) I only

(B) II only

(C) III only

(D) II and III

(E) I and III

24. The elite theory of politics posits which of the following?

(A) The need for coalition building

(B) Compromise

(C) Republicanism

(D) A strata of wealthy people

(E) Civil disobedience

Question 25 refers to the following cartoon.

"My grandson, needless to say, is also pro-Reagan."

25. The above cartoon makes reference to

   (A) the Republican Party symbol.
   (B) the political socialization process.
   (C) age as the major determinant in acquiring party affiliation.
   (D) tradition as an important factor in party identification.
   (E) the importance of family income in choosing one's political party.

26. The relationship between the print media and the federal government is defined by the

   (A) role of the Federal Communications Commission.
   (B) doctrine against prior restraint.
   (C) fairness doctrine.
   (D) commerce clause.
   (E) equal time rule.

27. All of the following are true of the federal bureaucracy EXCEPT

   (A) the bureaucracy is responsible for implementing federal legislation.
   (B) the bureaucracy is responsible for interpreting how legislation should be implemented.
   (C) the bureaucracy has rule-making and administrative adjudication authority.
   (D) the executive branch provides oversight to the federal bureaucracy.
   (E) the power of bureaucratic agencies can be checked by the appropriations authority of Congress.

28. According to the Constitution, the number of justices on the Supreme Court

   (A) cannot be changed.
   (B) can be changed by amending the Judiciary Act of 1789.
   (C) can be changed by Congress.
   (D) can only be changed through a Constitutional amendment.
   (E) can be changed by a voter referendum.

29. All of the following are powers and duties of the president as set forth in the Constitution EXCEPT the power to

   (A) appoint justices to the Supreme Court subject to the advice and consent of the Senate.
   (B) receive foreign ministers with the advice and consent of the Senate.
   (C) serve as commander in chief of the armed forces.
   (D) act as chief legislator.
   (E) fill open positions in the executive branch when Congress is in recess.

GO ON TO THE NEXT PAGE

30. Federal block grants are an example of

(A) the deregulation of some industries.
(B) the increasing federal oversight of state activities.
(C) revenue sharing.
(D) the devolution of federal power.
(E) pork-barrel legislation.

31. All of the following are true about standing committees in Congress EXCEPT

(A) members can keep their committee assignments as long as they wish.
(B) membership on committees does not mirror the party makeup of either the House or Senate.
(C) with a few exceptions standing committees mirror the departments of the executive branch.
(D) the position of committee chair is no longer determined by length of service on the committee.
(E) most bills die in committee.

32. Electioneering is an important tool of interest groups because

(A) electioneering is more effective than lobbying in gaining support from legislators.
(B) PACs don't always achieve their goals.
(C) electioneering projects a good public relations image for interest groups.
(D) working to elect sympathetic candidates can help ensure support for a group's views in future legislation.
(E) incumbents usually win reelection.

33. Although the president has the primary role in foreign affairs, Congress has all of the following responsibilities in this area EXCEPT

(A) negotiating treaties.
(B) appropriating funds for national defense.
(C) approving U.S. ambassadorial appointments.
(D) authorizing foreign aid.
(E) establishing tariffs rates.

34. All of the following are steps in the lawmaking process EXCEPT

(A) the full committee usually refers a proposed piece of legislation to a subcommittee for study, hearings, revision, and approval.
(B) the House Rules Committee determines the amount of time for debate that a bill will receive.
(C) a Conference Committee reconciles differences between the House version and the Senate version of a bill.
(D) the House initiates revenue bills.
(E) the subcommittee reports the bill to the full House or Senate for debate.

35. The establishment clause relates to the

(A) First Amendment.
(B) Fifth Amendment.
(C) Eighth Amendment.
(D) Ninth Amendment.
(E) Tenth Amendment.

36. Which of the following is a power that is not shared by the federal government and state governments?

(A) Power to tax personal income
(B) Power to establish courts
(C) Power to charter banks
(D) Power to tax property
(E) Power to borrow money

37. The bandwagon effect refers to

(A) how public opinion polls are conducted.

(B) the way polls may affect people's views of candidates.

(C) the way polls may influence people to support a particular candidate because they see others supporting the candidate.

(D) the sampling error in a public opinion poll.

(E) a propaganda technique.

38. An interest group would most likely be able to influence policy

(A) where the issues require expert knowledge.

(B) when it is one of a large number of groups involved in the lobbying.

(C) when the interest group uses a "going public" strategy.

(D) when the issues involved revolve around broad national or foreign policy.

(E) when the subcommittee chair is sympathetic to the interest group's cause.

39. All of the following statements about the relationship between the president and Congress in regard to proposed legislation are true EXCEPT

(A) the president may use a pocket veto to reject a piece of legislation if Congress is due to adjourn within ten days of the president's receipt of the bill.

(B) the Senate allows for more amendments to bills than the House.

(C) a two-thirds vote of each chamber overrides a presidential veto of a bill.

(D) the president may call Congress into special session after it recesses in order to consider legislation.

(E) presidents use the power and influence of the office to cajole recalcitrant members of Congress to vote for or against legislation.

40. Conservatives would most likely support which of the following Supreme Court decisions?

(A) Upholding of the Miranda rule

(B) Ban on prayer led by students at high school football games

(C) Striking down of a law banning partial-birth abortions

(D) Decision to hear an appeal from a death row inmate

(E) Upholding of a law that allowed federal money to be used to purchase computers for parochial school students

GO ON TO THE NEXT PAGE

Questions 41 and 42 refer to the following table.

Recent Presidential Vetoes

Administration	Total Vetoes	Pocket Vetoes	Pocket Vetoes as % of Total Vetoes	Regular Vetoes	Vetoes Overridden	% of Vetoes Overridden
Kennedy, 1961–1963	21	9	43	12	0	0
Johnson, 1963–1969	30	14	47	16	0	0
Nixon, 1969–1974	43	17	40	26	7	27
Ford, 1974–1977	66	18	27	48	12	25
Carter, 1977–1981	31	18	58	13	2	15
Reagan, 1981–1989	78	39	50	39	9	23
Bush, 1989–1993	46	15	33	31	1	3
Clinton, 1993 through 1998	25	0	0	25	2	4

41. Which of the following presidents used the pocket veto more often than the regular veto?

    (A) Nixon
    (B) Ford
    (C) Carter
    (D) Reagan
    (E) Bush

42. As a percentage of vetoes, which of the following presidents had the most vetoes overridden?

    (A) Nixon
    (B) Ford
    (C) Carter
    (D) Reagan
    (E) Clinton

43. The views of male and female voters tend to differ on

  I.   abortion.
  II. spending for social services.
  III. spending on national defense.

  (A) I
  (B) II
  (C) III
  (D) I and II
  (E) II and III

44. Which of the following is a Congressional staff agency?

  (A) Office of Management and Budget
  (B) Independent Prosecutor's Office
  (C) Library of Congress
  (D) General Accounting Office
  (E) Federal Emergency Management Agency

45. All of the following are provisions of campaign law EXCEPT

  (A) unregulated use of soft money by state and local parties.
  (B) a $2,000 limit on individual contributions to a candidate for a primary or a general election.
  (C) federal matching funds for candidates in federal elections who meet certain requirements.
  (D) full disclosure of all money raised by presidential candidates.
  (E) spending limits by state for all candidates who accept government funding.

46. The determining factor in the public's approval rating of the president is

  (A) the economy.
  (B) identification with the incumbent president's political party.
  (C) the honeymoon effect.
  (D) foreign relations.
  (E) the leadership effect.

47. The most powerful influence on public opinion in the nation is

  (A) the president.
  (B) Congress.
  (C) political parties.
  (D) the news media.
  (E) public interest groups.

48. All of the following are checks on the judicial branch EXCEPT

  (A) the president appoints federal judges.
  (B) Congress can decrease or withhold appropriations for the judicial branch.
  (C) the Senate can withhold approval of presidential appointments to the judiciary.
  (D) Congress can create additional courts.
  (E) congressional committees exercise oversight on the judiciary.

49. Which of the following is less a predictor of one's political ideology than it once was?

  (A) Gender
  (B) Religion
  (C) Social class
  (D) Ethnicity
  (E) Age

50. Gridlock in government can result from

  I.   one party controlling the House and the other party controlling the Senate.
  II. one party controlling both the House and the Senate while the president is from the minority party.
  III. having the president and both houses of Congress from the same party.

  (A) I only
  (B) II only
  (C) III only
  (D) I and II
  (E) I, II, and III

GO ON TO THE NEXT PAGE

51. Which of the following cases extended the Fourth Amendment's protection against unreasonable searches and seizures to the states?

(A) *Gideon* v. *Wainwright*
(B) *Schenck* v. *United States*
(C) *Miranda* v. *Arizona*
(D) *Mapp* v. *Ohio*
(E) *Heart of Atlanta Motel* v. *United States*

52. Which of the following has a Constitutional responsibility to participate in the budget-making process?

(A) The president
(B) The House
(C) The Senate
(D) Both the House and the Senate
(E) Congress and the president

53. To return to the notion of limited government as viewed by the Framers of the Constitution would negate laws and regulations dealing with all of the following EXCEPT

(A) the Individuals with Disabilities Act.
(B) desegregation of schools.
(C) affirmative action in awarding government contracts.
(D) the Fourteenth Amendment.
(E) a ban on school prayer.

54. The amendment process built into the Constitution by the Framers accounts for the government's

I. stability.
II. federalism.
III. flexibility.
IV. informal changes.

(A) I only
(B) II only
(C) III only
(D) I and II
(E) I, III, and IV

55. All of the following are examples of concern for the general welfare EXCEPT

(A) the Food and Drug Administration.
(B) PACs.
(C) regulation of public utilities.
(D) the Department of Housing and Urban Development.
(E) right of eminent domain.

56. Televised debates between presidential and vice-presidential candidates during the general election have relatively little effect on voters' decisions because the debates

(A) reach a narrow audience of voters.
(B) occur late in the election process when most voters have decided for whom to vote.
(C) are stage-managed by the television networks.
(D) fail to provide adequate time for the candidates to discuss their positions on issues.
(E) unfairly highlight candidates' physical qualities rather than their policies.

57. Which of the following is not a regulatory technique for ensuring the implementation of public policy?

(A) Patronage
(B) Imprisonment
(C) Taking public property for public use
(D) Tax on cigarettes
(E) Affirmative action as a prerequisite to awarding federal contracts to construction companies

58. Which of the following statements best describes the purpose of the Fourteenth Amendment?

(A) The Fourteenth Amendment overrode the provision of Article I, which counted African Americans as three fifths of a person for apportioning representatives in the House.

(B) The federal government used the Civil War amendments to prosecute civil rights cases in the twentieth century.

(C) The Fourteenth Amendment limits the power of the federal government in cases involving a person's civil rights within a state.

(D) The Fourteenth Amendment protects people from acts of the state.

(E) Together, the Fourteenth and Seventeenth Amendments have extended the franchise to all Americans of voting age.

59. Reducing the budget deficit through across-the-board budget cuts was the goal of the

(A) creation of the Office of Management and Budget.

(B) Gramm-Rudman-Hollings Act.

(C) Congressional Budget and Impoundment Act.

(D) balanced budget amendment.

(E) government shutdown in 1995.

60. The decisions of the Federal Reserve Board directly affect

(A) the money supply and interest rates.

(B) inflation and recession.

(C) the money supply and recession.

(D) interest rates.

(E) political campaigns.

STOP If you finish before time is called, you may check your work on this section only. Do not turn to any other section in the test.

SECTION II	TIME—100 MINUTES

Directions: You have 100 minutes to answer all four of the following questions. It is suggested that you take a few minutes to outline each answer. Spend approximately one fourth of your time (25 minutes) on each question. Support the ideas in your essay with substantive examples where appropriate. Make sure to number each of your responses with the number that corresponds to the question.

1. Walter Lippmann, in *A Preface to Politics,* is quoted as saying, "It is perfectly true that the government is best which governs least. It is equally true that the government is best which provides most." To what extent do you agree or disagree with this statement? Give examples of current government programs to support your position.

2. In 1996, California voters passed Proposition 198, which created a blanket primary. In the 1999–2000 court term, the United States Supreme Court ruled 7–2 that Proposition 198 was unconstitutional, stating that the proposition violated the First Amendment associational rights of political parties. Critically evaluate the decision by presenting arguments that both support and oppose the Court's position on open primaries.

3. Since the 1950s, Congress has passed landmark legislation that has advanced the civil rights of its citizens. Select three pieces of legislation from the list below and discuss the impact of each on the rights of U.S. citizens.

   Equal Pay Act of 1963
   The Twenty-fourth Amendment
   Civil Rights Act of 1964
   Age Discrimination Act of 1967
   Title IX, Higher Education Act (1972)
   Voting Rights Act of 1982
   Civil Rights Restoration Act of 1988
   Americans with Disabilities Act of 1990
   Civil Rights Act of 1991

4. The media has become an integral part of U.S. culture and society. Analyze the effects of the media on modern political campaigns. Consider how the media may shape the agenda of elections and influence their outcomes.

STOP If you finish before time is called, you may check your work on this section only. Do not turn to any other section in the test.

ANSWERS AND EXPLANATIONS

Quick-Score Answers

1. B	11. E	21. E	31. D	41. C	51. D
2. E	12. B	22. D	32. D	42. A	52. E
3. B	13. D	23. C	33. A	43. E	53. E
4. C	14. A	24. D	34. E	44. D	54. C
5. E	15. D	25. B	35. A	45. A	55. B
6. A	16. B	26. B	36. D	46. B	56. B
7. D	17. D	27. D	37. C	47. D	57. A
8. B	18. C	28. C	38. A	48. E	58. B
9. B	19. C	29. B	39. B	49. C	59. B
10. C	20. A	30. D	40. E	50. E	60. A

PRACTICE TEST 1

1. **The correct answer is (B).** *Wesberry v. Sanders* was one in a series of court cases filed against redistricting procedures. Choice (A), the exclusionary rule, was established in *Mapp* v. *Ohio*. Choice (C) restates the decision in *Regents of the University of California* v. *Bakke*. *Marbury* v. *Madison* established the principle of judicial review, choice (D). *Gideon* v. *Wainwright* extended the Sixth Amendment to include the right to an attorney, choice (E), in any trial in state as well as in federal courts. It was part of the nationalization of the Bill of Rights into the Fourteenth Amendment.

2. **The correct answer is (E).** Common sense will tell that you someone who attends religious services regularly, choice (C), and someone with a high sense of civic duty, choice (D), would most likely translate those values into voting, so these choices would be incorrect. Choice (A), a Northerner, is more likely to vote than a Southerner. The higher the level the education, the more likely that a person will vote, so choice (B) is incorrect. This process of elimination leaves choice (E) as the correct answer. A person who lives in rural America is less likely to vote than an urban dweller.

3. The correct answer is (B). The original jurisdiction of the Supreme Court includes choices (A), (C), (D), and (E). The word *appeal* should have been your clue. The Supreme Court has original jurisdiction and appellate jurisdiction. An appeal case comes under the appellate jurisdiction. Cases may be appealed from both state courts and federal courts, but for the former there must be a matter of Constitutional law involved for the Supreme Court to hear the case.

Test-Taking Strategy

The key words are indirect results.

4. The correct answer is (C). Choices (A), (C), and (D) are all true statements, but (A) and (D) are specified in the act. Choice (C) was the underlying reason for passing the act. Choice (B) is incorrect, as is choice (E). The Pendleton Act set up competitive examinations for hiring employees; it did not deal with elected officeholders.

5. The correct answer is (E). Although at some time in the future the Iowa caucuses and the New Hampshire primary may be less important, they have remained important through the end of the twentieth century and into the twenty-first. Thus, choice (E) is the only incorrect response and, therefore, the correct answer to the question. Choices (A), (B), (C), and (D) have come about since the parties rewrote their party rules.

Test-Taking Strategy

The key word here is significance.

6. The correct answer is (A). The quota system had been established by the immigration laws of 1921, 1924, and 1929. Choice (C) is incorrect because the 1965 act established the preference system for relatives. The Immigration Reform and Control Act of 1986 provided for an amnesty program, so choice (D) is incorrect. The Illegal Immigration Restriction Act of 1996 made it easier for the Immigration and Naturalization Service (INS) to deport illegal aliens, so choice (E) is incorrect. Choice (B) is incorrect.

7. The correct answer is (D). Caucuses have come to dominate the informal organization of Congress. Caucuses are formed around shared interests and may include members of both parties and both houses of Congress. Caucuses lobby to hold hearings on issues of interest to them, push for legislation, and gather votes to pass that legislation. Choice (C) is a word that could be used to characterize caucuses, but networks is not the correct term. Choices (A) and (B) are formal organizations of Congress, not informal. Choice (E) is illogical.

8. **The correct answer is (B).** The War Powers Resolution, choice (B), was passed over President Nixon's veto in response to the commitment of troops to the Vietnam War by Presidents Johnson and Nixon without congressional approval. Choice (A) increased the president's power by allowing him to veto certain items in appropriations bills after Congress had passed them; the Supreme Court struck down the law as a violation of the separation of powers. Choice (C), also known as the Reinventing Government program, was instituted by President Bill Clinton in an effort to reduce the federal bureaucracy; it has nothing to do with limiting power but rather with improving efficiency and cutting costs. Choice (D), the independent counsel, or special prosecutor, law, officially the Ethics in Government Act of 1978, was authorized to investigate suspected wrongdoing by any official of the executive branch; it was not aimed solely at the president, making choice (D) also incorrect. The National Security Advisor, choice (E), is a member of the president's staff and advises him on national security and defense issues.

9. **The correct answer is (B).** Although choice (A), party loyalty, and choice (D), the wishes of the president of the same party have some effect on how a member of Congress votes, legislators most often will vote with their constituents because the legislators have to face their constituents in the next election. Choice (C) is illogical. Choice (E) is similar to choice (A) and is also incorrect.

10. **The correct answer is (C).** Choice (A) is a distracter. Choice (B) is a true statement but does not relate to the question; it does not describe the equation of theory versus practice, ideology versus operations. Choice (D) is the opposite of what the phrase means. Common sense will tell you that choice (E) is an incorrect statement. Ideology greatly impacts American politics, which is different from American government, the topic of the phrase in the question.

11. **The correct answer is (E).** Public opinion is the opinion of the majority who hold similar views on a particular issue. Public opinion is not a general viewpoint but must be related to a specific issue. With this in mind, you can eliminate point I. Points II and III correspond to the definition of public opinion, and the only answer choice that contains both points is choice (E).

12. **The correct answer is (B).** While choices (A), (B), and (C) are all true about government under the Articles of Confederation, choice (B) is the most inclusive answer. Choices (A) and (C) state specific instances of government policy. Choice (D) is incorrect because the central government could not levy taxes at all. Choice (E) is incorrect because the central government had no power to establish customs duties or tariff rates; only the states had these powers.

13. **The correct answer is (D).** A clientele agency is one that is directed by law "to foster, promote, and develop" the interests of those individuals and groups for whom the agency was established to serve. Choices (A), (B), (C), and (E) all have distinct clients—farmers and those involved in agriculture, workers, homeowners and urbanites, and teachers and students—whereas choice (D), the Defense Department, serves the interests of the nation as a whole rather than the members of its armed forces.

14. **The correct answer is (A).** Choices (A) and (B) are both correct statements about the difference between interest groups and political parties, but choice (A) is the broader, or more inclusive, answer. Choice (B) is a detail that supports choice (A). Choice (C) is also a true statement, but it does not follow through on the comparison that the question sets up. Interest groups raise money, but what do political parties do? Choice (D) is incorrect because public interest groups work for what they perceive to be the public good. The elements in choice (E) are not comparable. The answer choice states that interest groups work behind the scenes, but stating that political parties are open to anyone is not comparable. The statement would need to say either that membership in interest groups is limited to those who share the same viewpoint as the group or that political parties work in the open as well as behind the scenes.

15. **The correct answer is (D).** This is the central point of John Marshall's opinion in *Marbury* v. *Madison,* which established the principle of judicial review. Chief Justice William Rehnquist used this same argument in handing down the decision upholding *Miranda* in *Dickerson* v. *United States* in 2000. The statement does not relate to the opinion in *Miranda,* however, making choice (C) incorrect. Choices (A), (B), and (E) are illogical.

16. **The correct answer is (B).** The answer is somewhat convoluted, but this is the definition of senatorial courtesy. Senators typically receive the assignments that they wish, choice (A), but this is not the definition of senatorial courtesy. Choice (C) is a distracter; it seems to make sense and could confuse you. The practice described in choice (D) is known as logrolling. Choice (E) might give you pause too, but the president delivers the State of the Union address in the House; the Senate chamber is too small.

Test-Taking Strategy

The key word is conventional.

17. **The correct answer is (D).** The question asks about conventional political participation. Choices (A), (B), (C), and (E) are all conventional activities that voters perform. Participating in a political protest, choice (D), is an example of an unconventional activity, as are civil disobedience and violence.

18. **The correct answer is (C).** A person is more likely to be one of the 13.3 percent of Americans living at or below the poverty level of $16,276 (1997 level) if one is African American or Hispanic, an unmarried woman, or a child under the age of 18, and a city dweller. Choice (A) omits Hispanic, the word *unmarried* to describe female, and city dweller. Choice (B) is incorrect because 73.5 percent of African Americans and 69.7 percent of Hispanics live above the poverty line. Choices (D) and (E) are incorrect because the graph does not include regions of the country; Southerner is another characteristic that could be added to round out the description, however. Both choices (D) and (E) also omit the word *unmarried* as a qualifier.

19. **The correct answer is (C).** Americans tend to believe that providing equal opportunities rather than equalizing income through transfer payments or other social engineering is the better course, thus making choice (A) incorrect and choice (C) correct. Choices (B), (D), and (E) are illogical.

20. **The correct answer is (A).** Registering to vote has been made easier in many states, for example, by allowing people to register in supermarkets or on election day. The 1993 Motor Voter Act requires that states allow people to register to vote when they apply for a driver's license. Choices (B), (C), (D), and (E) are true statements about why voter turnout has declined, but none of them answer the question, which asks for the answer choice that is not correct. Choice (D) is the major reason why people don't vote.

21. **The correct answer is (E).** Linkage institutions are those that provide access to government for people's views on policy. Political parties, choice (A); elections, choice (B); the media, choice (C); and interest groups, choice (D), are the linkage institutions in a democracy. Choice (E), Congress, is the government, so it is an illogical answer and in this *not/except* question, the correct answer.

22. **The correct answer is (D).** The seniority of the committee chair does not benefit the subcommittee as much as it benefits the interest groups that do business with the subcommittee and the agency. Influence in government depends upon having access, and a member of a committee or subcommittee with a number of years' experience on the committee or subcommittee who supports a particular group provides that access for the group. Choices (A), (B), (C), and (E) are all ways that committees or subcommittees benefit from their participation in an iron triangle.

Test-Taking Strategy

The key words are most likely.

23. **The correct answer is (C).** The question asks about the future. The graying of America (I) and the population shift from the "frost belt" or "rust belt" states to the "sunbelt" (II) are already affecting public policy and will undoubtedly continue to affect it. The potential minority-majority population (III), in which the majority of citizens will no longer be white and European in background, will greatly affect public policy decisions in the future, even though some effects of point III, such as the debates over bilingual education and affirmative action, are already challenging public policy. Choice (C) contains only point III and is, therefore, the correct answer.

24. **The correct answer is (D).** The elite theory of politics holds that a single group holds power over the policy agenda. Choices (A) and (B) are characteristics of the pluralist theory of politics. According to this theory, groups holding minority viewpoints compete for power; in order to achieve their goals, groups must compromise. Choice (C), republicanism, is a third form of government in which people indirectly assert power by electing representatives to govern for them. Choice (E), civil disobedience, is a form of direct action politics and can be a tool of any group.

25. **The correct answer is (B).** The cartoon is drawing attention to the political socialization process, choice (B). Choice (C) is incorrect, because age is not a significant factor in choosing one's political party—at least initially; family party identification is the predominant factor. The cartoonist may seem to be making a case for tradition, choice (D), but that is not a direct factor in the political socialization process. Choice (E) is a distracter because many people think of Republicans as being wealthy, but choice (E) is incorrect. The elephant as the symbol of the Republican Party is not shown, so choice (A) is incorrect.

26. **The correct answer is (B).** Based on the First Amendment, the doctrine against prior restraint governs the relationship between the federal government and the print media, that is, the government cannot keep a newspaper or magazine from publishing anything. This principle was upheld in *New York Times* v. *United States;* this was the so-called Pentagon Papers case of the Vietnam War era. Choice (A), the role of the FCC, which is to regulate the media, does not make sense. Giving airtime to opposing viewpoints on controversial issues, choice (C), was a provision of FCC regulations until its repeal in 1987 because of the proliferation of cable channels. Choice (D), the commerce clause, might give you pause since the commerce clause allows Congress to regulate many interstate transactions, but in this case, it is a distracter. Choice (E), providing equal time to opposing candidates for public office, was repealed by the FCC in 2000.

Test-Taking Strategy

For not/except *questions, ask yourself if the answer is correct in the context of the question. If it is, cross it off and go on to the next answer.*

27. **The correct answer is (D).** Choice (D) is illogical. The federal bureaucracy is part of the executive branch, so it would not make sense that the bureaucracy would oversee itself. Congressional committees provide oversight to the federal bureaucracy, a reason why iron triangles can cause barriers to effective oversight. Choice (A) is the purpose of the bureaucracy. Choice (B) operates because Congress often leaves up to the agency authorized to handle particular legislation how to implement it. This is when choice (C), rule-making and administrative adjudication, come into play. Choice (E) is also correct.

28. **The correct answer is (C).** Choice (A) is illogical because the Constitution can be changed by amendment. Choices (B), (D), and (E) are simply incorrect because the Constitution established the Supreme Court and gave to Congress the power to set the number of justices (Article III, Section 1).

29. **The correct answer is (B).** The president does not need the advice and consent of the Senate to receive foreign ministers and heads of state, making choice (B) the correct answer in this reverse question. The Senate does provide advice and consent on the appointment of U.S. ambassadors to other nations. Choices (A), (C), (D), and (E) are all stated or implied in the Constitution. The president's role as an influence on legislation, choice (B), has expanded greatly since the era of Franklin Roosevelt but is built on the phrase "[the president shall] recommend to [Congress's] consideration such measures as he shall judge necessary and expedient."

30. **The correct answer is (D).** Beginning with Richard Nixon, presidents have attempted to return power to the states in a number of ways; this is known as devolution. Choice (A) is illogical. Choice (B) is incorrect; a part of devolution has been an attempt to decrease oversight. Revenue sharing, choice (C), was President Nixon's term for the policy of returning money to the states with fewer strings attached. Choice (E), pork-barrel legislation, refers to specific federally financed programs in states or local districts, whereas block grants are given to the states to administer, making pork irrelevant in this context.

31. **The correct answer is (D).** Despite reforms, the committee chairs are still determined by seniority on committees. Choices (A), (B), (C), and (E) are all true statements that do not answer this reverse question. Members may keep their committee assignments, choice (A), but they may also ask to change them; the decision rests with each chamber's Committee on Committees. One of the exceptions noted in choice (C) is the House Rules Committee and the House and Senate committees on appropriations.

32. **The correct answer is (D).** Interest groups use lobbying, choice (A); litigation, choice (B); and electioneering, choice (C) as tools in their efforts to influence government. Providing campaign contributions through PACs, choice (E), is one of the electioneering methods that interest groups use to elect candidates sympathetic to their cause. Choice (D) is the opposite of "going public," methods such as public relations campaigns that interest groups use to present their cause in the best possible way to the public.

33. **The correct answer is (A).** According to the Constitution, the power to negotiate foreign treaties resides with the president. However, the Senate has the power of "advice and consent," that is, the Senate has the sole power to ratify treaties. Presidents have gotten around the ratification process for unpopular treaties by entering into executive agreements with heads of other nations; executive agreements do not require Congressional approval. Choice (C) is similar to the power to ratify treaties. The Senate approves or rejects ambassadors, choice (C), that the president nominates. Choices (B), (C), and (D) relate to Congress's responsibilities in the areas of taxing and spending.

34. **The correct answer is (E).** Once a subcommittee has drafted, held hearings on, revised, and approved a proposed bill, the subcommittee reports it to the full committee. The committee then must decide whether to approve it and send it to the full House or Senate or allow it to die in committee. Rarely is a subcommittee report rejected. Choices (A), (B), (C), and (D) are all steps in how a bill becomes a law. If you were going to put the steps in order, the order would begin with choices (D) and (A). If the committee reports out the bill to the full House, then choice (B) would be next. When the two houses pass a similar but different bill on a topic, then the Conference Committee, choice (C), takes over to reconcile differences and return a new compromise bill to both houses.

35. **The correct answer is (A).** The First Amendment states that "Congress shall make no law respecting an establishment of religion." This is known as the establishment clause. The First Amendment goes on to state that Congress cannot make any law that will "prohibit the free exercise" of religion either, which is referred to as the free exercise clause. Choice (B), the Fifth Amendment, guarantees immunity from self-incrimination and from double jeopardy. Choice (C), the Eighth Amendment, prohibits excessive bail and fines as well as cruel and unusual punishment. The Ninth Amendment, choice (D), refers to the powers reserved to the people, the nonenumerated powers, whereas the Tenth Amendment, choice (E), refers to the powers reserved to the states or to the people.

36. **The correct answer is (D).** Property taxes are local tax levies. Choices (A), (B), (C), and (E) are all powers that the federal government and state governments share and exercise within their own jurisdictions.

37. **The correct answer is (C).** Upon first reading the answers, both choices (B) and (C) may appear to be correct, but choice (C) is the more specific response and, therefore, the more correct response. The bandwagon effect doesn't just affect one's view of a candidate, but it influences people to support a candidate. Choice (E) is a true statement, but it does not define the technique as choice (C) does. Always select the most complete answer. Choices (A) and (D) are distracters and untrue.

Test-Taking Strategy

The key words are most likely.

38. **The correct answer is (A).** One of the benefits to legislators that lobbyists offer is their specialized knowledge on a subject. This specific, technical knowledge can be useful to Congressional committees and subcommittees as they gather information to assess policy and write legislation. This makes choice (A) the best answer. The smaller the number of interest groups involved, the more likely a particular group will be heard, so choice (B) is illogical. Choice (C) is also illogical because the influential work of lobbyists is done at the committee and subcommittee level, not necessarily in the general arena of public relations. The broader the issue—whether domestic or foreign—the less likely the specialized knowledge of an interest group could be very influential, making choice (D) incorrect. Although a committee chair has influence over the committee and can provide access to the committee for the interest group, the members also have a voice in decisions, making choice (E) illogical.

Test-Taking Strategy

Highlight key words and phrases in the questions so that you know what you are looking for in the answer choices.

39. **The correct answer is (B).** The question asks you about the relationship between the president and Congress in terms of legislation. Choice (B) is a true statement about the Senate, but it does not relate to the question, making it incorrect. Choices (A), (C), (D), and (E) are all true statements and all relate to the duties, powers, and influence of the president and Congress as legislation is proposed, debated, and passed or vetoed.

40. **The correct answer is (E).** All the decisions in the list of answer choices occurred in the Supreme Court's 1999–2000 session. Conservatives typically supported the challenge to Miranda, choice (A), and support laws approving prayer in school, choice (B); a ban on abortion, especially what they term partial-birth abortion, choice (C); and the death penalty, choice (D). Conservatives would support, at least in theory, the use of public funding for materials for parochial school students, choice (E), because they do not support the "wall between church and state" as interpreted in the First Amendment.

41. **The correct answer is (C).** The amount of data on the table may confuse you, but this is a straightforward question and answer. You only need to read the columns labelled "Regular Vetoes" and "Pocket Vetoes" to find the correct answer.

42. **The correct answer is (A).** Again, it is a matter of finding the correct column and comparing the percentages to determine that Richard Nixon had the largest percentage of vetoes overridden, or conversely had the smallest percentage of vetoes sustained.

Test-Taking Strategy

For tiered or multistep questions, determine which point(s) answer the question correctly and then decide which answer choice contains that point(s).

43. **The correct answer is (E).** Men and women hold similar views on abortion (I), but their priorities differ on spending on social services (II) and for military defense (III), so points II and III are correct. The only answer choice that contains both points is choice (E).

44. **The correct answer is (D).** The General Accounting Office, choice (D), was established by Congress as one of three staff agencies to assist Congress in its oversight of the executive departments and in evaluating presidential programs and proposals. The other two staff agencies are the Congressional Research Service and the Congressional Budget Office. The sole function of the Office of Management and Budget, choice (A), is to prepare the budget that the president submits to Congress each year. Choice (B), the Independent Counsel's Office, is illogical; logic tells you that a prosecutor's office would most probably be housed in the Justice Department rather than with Congress. (The law that authorized the independent counsel was allowed to lapse in 1999.) Choice (C), the Library of Congress, is a good distracter because it does come under the jurisdiction of Congress, but it is not a staff agency. It is the nation's library established in 1800 by Congress, and it also administers the nation's copyright system. Choice (E), FEMA, is an independent agency in the executive branch.

45. **The correct answer is (A).** The Campaign Finance Reform Act of 2002 allows state and local parties to accept soft money contributions but regulates the size of such donations (up to $10,000 per individual or group) and how the money may be used (for get-out-vote drives and voter registration).

46. **The correct answer is (B).** People who hold the same party identification as the incumbent president tend to approve of that president's actions. Choices (A), the economy, and (D), the president's conduct of foreign affairs, can influence people's approval rating of the president for a period of time, but the primary determining factor is still party affiliation. At the beginning of a president's first four-year term, people may give the president the benefit of the doubt, the so-called honeymoon effect, choice (C), but a sudden change in the economy, a politically unpopular policy advanced by the president, or a similar event can end this effect. Choice (E) is a distracter.

47. **The correct answer is (D).** Common sense and the process of elimination would help you answer this question if you did not know the answer immediately. The amount of influence that the president has, choice (A), depends on the popularity of the president. Congress's support, choice (B), is split by partisanship. Logic and common sense will tell you that Congress's influence (and to a lesser degree, the president's) will break along ideological lines, so neither choice (A) nor (B) can be correct. The same reasoning makes choices (C) and (E) incorrect.

48. **The correct answer is (E).** Choices (A), (B), (C), and (D) are all examples of how the system of checks and balances works in terms of the judiciary. Choice (E) is incorrect because legislative oversight relates to Congress's monitoring of the executive branch's administration of laws. Legislative oversight is an example of the system of checks and balances operating between the legislative and executive branches.

Test-Taking Strategy

The key word is less.

49. **The correct answer is (C).** Social class is no longer as predictive of political ideology, whether someone is a liberal or a conservative, as it once was. First seen in the 1980 presidential election, the gender gap, choice (A), is a relatively new indicator of ideological leaning. Choice (B), religion, is not as important as it once was, but it is still more important as an indicator of an ideological position than social class. Today, however, it is less the religious denomination that is the contributing factor than the importance that religion plays in a person's life. Ethnicity, choice (D), is a good predictor of ideology because the less power a group has the more liberal the group—and its members—tends to be. Choice (E), age, is also a good indicator of ideology; the younger the person, the more likely it is that he or she is liberal but does not vote.

For a tiered or multistep question, determine which point(s) is correct, and then find the answer choice that contains that point(s).

50. **The correct answer is (E).** All three scenarios can result in gridlock. Points I and II are obvious because the House and the Senate must often compromise on legislation and the president must work with Congress on getting his agenda passed. Point III can also result in gridlock because it can be difficult for a president to hold the competing interests of his party together. This happened in the first term of President Clinton's administration and resulted, for example, in the inability to pass health-care reform.

51. **The correct answer is (D).** *Mapp* v. *Ohio* is part of a series of cases that the Supreme Court used to nationalize the Bill of Rights, that is, extend its protections to the states. If you did not know the answer immediately, you could have eliminated choices (B) and (E) because the prosecution in both cases was the federal government, not a state. That probably removes choice (A) also. Choice (C), *Miranda,* established the procedure for reading one's rights to suspects before questioning. Choice (A) established the right to counsel for those who cannot afford their own. Choice (B) established the principle of clear and present danger, while choice (E) is a case from the civil rights movement era dealing with interstate commerce.

52. **The correct answer is (E).** Article I, Sections 7, 8, and 9 set out Congress's budget responsibilities and Article II, Section 3, the president's. Both branches must work together, so choices (A), (B), (C), and (D) are incorrect. Don't be confused by choice (B). The House must initiate all revenue bills, but the president initiates the federal budget. The Senate debates and approves the budget as it must all other legislation.

53. **The correct answer is (E).** The ban on school prayer is in keeping with the establishment clause of the First Amendment as written by the Framers. Expanding the interpretation of the Constitution to include people with disabilities, choice (A); integrating schools, choice (B); affirmative action, choice (C); and the Fourteenth Amendment itself, choice (D), expands the view of government held by the Framers; however, they knew that change was inevitable and allowed for change through the amendment process.

54. **The correct answer is (C).** The amendment process reflects the Framers' desire to make the new government stable (I) yet flexible (III) enough to meet whatever situations that arose in the future. However, the government's stability is a result of the system of checks and balances, not the amendment process, so any answer choice with point I is incorrect. Federalism is the basic concept of the Constitution, so point III is incorrect. While informal changes also illustrate the flexibility of the Constitution, the amendment process is the formal process of change, so point IV is incorrect. Only choice (C) has point III and is the correct answer.

55. **The correct answer is (B).** That the government should preserve the general welfare of its citizens is one of the basic beliefs of Americans. Choices (A), (C), (D), and (E) are examples of the government's support of this belief. While some PACs are operated by public interest groups, they are not government organizations, making choice (B) incorrect.

56. **The correct answer is (B).** Choice (A) is illogical because of the number of people who have television sets. Choice (C) is incorrect. While choices (D) and (E) may be true at times with some debates, the correct answer is choice (B). Debates are more likely to influence voters during primaries than in the general election because most voters have not yet made up their minds.

57. **The correct answer is (A).** Patronage is an example of a promotional technique for implementing public policy. Choices (B), (C), (D), and (E) are all examples of regulatory techniques of public control. Choice (B) is an example of a criminal penalty. Choice (C) is known as expropriation; it exercises the government's right of eminent domain. Choice (D) is known as regulatory taxation, and choice (E) uses the government's right to offer subsidies, contracts, and licenses as a way to ensure compliance with laws, rules, and regulations. A point to remember: the first use of affirmative action outside higher education was in the construction industry.

58. **The correct answer is (B).** Choices (A), (B), and (D) are all correct statements, but choice (B) best answers the question. Choice (D) describes how the amendment is used, not what its purpose, or provisions, are. Choice (A) describes one specific provision, but choice (B) states a more significant and long-lasting effect of the law. Choice (C) is incorrect, as is choice (E). Together, the Fourteenth, Nineteenth (women's suffrage), and the Twenty-sixth (the vote to 18-year-old citizens) Amendments have extended the franchise.

59. **The correct answer is (B).** Although the across-the-board aspect of the Gramm-Rudman-Hollings Act was declared unconstitutional, its supporters claim that it focused the nation's attention on the budget deficit issue. Choice (A), the OMB, was created to assist the president in preparing the annual federal budget. Choice (C), the Congressional Budget and Impoundment Act of 1974, was passed to reform the congressional budgetary process; its success has been mixed. Choice (D) is incorrect, and choice (E) was a result of the inability of Congress and the president to agree on a budget.

60. **The correct answer is (A).** Choice (A) is a more complete answer than choice (D) and, therefore, the better choice. While the decisions of the Fed may affect political campaigns, the question asks about the *direct* consequences of the Fed's actions, so choice (E) is incorrect. Part of choice (B) is correct, inflation, but a partially correct answer is a partially incorrect answer, so choice (B) is incorrect. The same reasoning invalidates choice (C) as the answer.

SUGGESTIONS FOR FREE-RESPONSE ESSAY 1

Study Strategy

Revise your essay using points from this list that will strengthen it.

You might have chosen the following points for your essay arguing for or against more government-sponsored programs. Consider these points as you complete the evaluation of your essay.

Supporting Position

- "All men are created equal."

- Government has responsibilities to the poor, to the aged, to those with disabilities, to the underrepresented, and to those who are discriminated against.

- Long-term societal abuses are the source of social problems.

- Poverty is linked to drug abuse, crime, and lack of educational and employment opportunities.

- Only government has the resources and the will to break the cycle of poverty.

Opposing Position

- Equality means equal opportunity, not equal income.

- Entitlement programs discourage personal responsibility and personal initiative.

- Entitlement programs continue the cycle of poverty.

- Local, privately sponsored programs can best meet the challenges of overcoming poverty.

Current Government Programs that You Might Have Used as Examples

- Temporary Assistance to Needy Families

- Old Age, Survivors, and Disability Insurance

- Supplementary Security Income

- Medicare

- Medicaid

- Food stamp program

- Housing subsidies

- Student loans, educational income tax credits

- Vocational and training block grants

SUGGESTIONS FOR FREE-RESPONSE ESSAY 2

Test-Taking Strategy

Use relevant information from your own experience and reading to answer questions. For example, your reading could provide information such as, "Alaska, Louisiana, and Washington also have blanket primary systems. The Supreme Court decision affects those states as well."

You might have chosen the following points about primaries for your essay evaluating the Supreme Court's ruling that California Proposition 198 is unconstitutional. Consider these points as you complete the evaluation of your essay.

Definition: A blanket primary is one in which all voters receive one ballot on which they may vote for each office regardless of party affiliation.

Supporting the Finding of Unconstitutionality:

- Members of one party cannot "raid" the other party's primary.

- Closed primaries make the candidates more responsive to their parties and party members.

- Voters are more thoughtful in closed primaries.

- A blanket primary undercuts party loyalty.

- A blanket primary interferes with party governance.

- A blanket primary is a threat to the continuing political discussion.

- A blanket primary allows nonparty voters to influence primary elections.

Opposing the Finding of Unconstitutionality:

- Blanket primaries will help to change the tone of the political scene by diffusing some of the negativity of campaigns.

- Candidates will be able to focus on the middle ground of voters rather than on the extreme partisans who now typically support candidates in primaries.

- Closed primaries tend to exclude independent voters, whereas blanket primaries will remove the barrier to their voting.

- Blanket primaries have the potential to increase the number of citizens who vote.

- States should have the right to determine their own primary system.

- Crossover voter numbers are overemphasized.

Test-Taking Strategy

Suppose you were not familiar with the Supreme Court decision in Democratic Party et al. *v.* Jones. *You could still create a creditable essay by focusing on the issues surrounding the primary system.*

SUGGESTIONS FOR FREE-RESPONSE ESSAY 3

You might have chosen the following points about federal legislation for your essay discussing the growth of civil rights since the 1950s. Consider them as you complete the evaluation of your essay.

Equal Pay Act of 1963

- Illegal to base an employee's pay on race, gender, religion, or national origin

- Important to women's movement

- Important to minorities' battle for civil rights

The Twenty-fourth Amendment

- Outlawed poll taxes in federal elections

- Poll taxes used to prevent African Americans and poor whites from voting

Civil Rights Act of 1964

- Bans discrimination in public accommodations, interstate transportation, restaurants, theaters, etc.

- Bans job discrimination based on sex

- Prohibits discrimination in any program receiving federal funds

- Power to initiate lawsuits in school segregation cases given to the federal government

- Increased rights of African Americans and other minorities

- Federal government given greater means to enforce antidiscrimination laws

Age Discrimination Act of 1967

- Prohibits employers from discriminating on the basis of age

- Jobs in which age essential to job performance exempted

- Banned some mandatory retirement ages

- Increased some retirement ages to 70

Title IX, Higher Education Act (1972)

- Prohibits gender discrimination in any institution of higher education that receives federal funds

- Forced increased funding of women's programs, especially athletics

Voting Rights Act of 1982

- Required states to create Congressional districts with minority majorities

- Increased minority representation in House of Representatives as a by-product

- The resulting gerrymandered districts declared unconstitutional

- Unclear how to achieve more minority representation and preserve regional integrity of districts

Civil Rights Restoration Act of 1988

- Increases power of Title IX

- Cuts off funding to institutions violating the law, not just to a specific program or office

Americans with Disabilities Act of 1990

- Requires businesses with more than twenty-four employees to make offices accessible to those with disabilities

- Requires wheelchair accessibility for public transportation

- Requires wheelchair accessibility for new offices, hotels, restaurants, and other public places

Civil Rights Act of 1991

- Eased limitations on ability of job applicants to bring suit against employers for discriminatory hiring practices

- Relaxed limits on employees' lawsuits charging discriminatory behavior on part of employer

SUGGESTIONS FOR FREE-RESPONSE ESSAY 4

You might have chosen the following points about the media for your essay analyzing its effect on political campaigns and elections. Consider these points as you complete the evaluation of your essay.

Definition: In this sense, the media is television, newspapers, radio, magazines, and the Internet.

- People get most of their political information from the media rather than directly from the candidates.

- The more the information superhighway grows, the less direct influence policymakers have on average citizen.

- Public's perception of media: What media covers is important

- Media as shaper of what people think

- Distortion of candidates and their positions through focus

- Issues of biased and unbiased reporting

- Internet: more access to information—accurate or inaccurate

- Rise of news magazines and Web sites that go for the jugular, sensational material

- Equal-time provision of the Federal Communications Act

- Visual impact: candidates required to be photogenic

- Sound bites rather than real discussion of issues

- Media blamed for decline of party identity and party politics

SELF-EVALUATION RUBRIC FOR THE ADVANCED PLACEMENT ESSAYS

	8–9	5–7	2–4	0–1
Overall Impression	Demonstrates excellent understanding of U.S. government and legal system; outstanding writing; thorough and effective; incisive	Demonstrates good understanding of U.S. government and legal system; good writing competence	Reveals simplistic thinking and/or immature understanding of U.S. government and legal system; fails to respond adequately to the question; little or no analysis	Very little or no understanding of U.S. government and legal system; unacceptably brief; fails to respond to the question; little clarity
Understanding of the U.S. Government	Scholarly; excellent understanding of the question; effective and incisive; in-depth critical analysis; includes apt, specific references; acknowledges other views	Mostly accurate use of information about U.S. government and legal system; good understanding of the question; often perceptive and clear; includes specific references and critical analysis	Some inaccuracies in information regarding U.S. government; superficial understanding and treatment of the question; lack of adequate knowledge about U.S. government; overgeneralized	Serious errors in presenting information about U.S. government and legal system; extensive misreading of the question and little supporting evidence; completely off the topic
Development	Original, unique, and/or intriguing thesis; excellent use of fundamentals and principles of U.S. government; thoroughly developed; conclusion shows applicability of thesis to other situations	Adequate thesis; satisfactory use of knowledge of U.S. government; competent development; acceptable conclusion	Inadequate, irrelevant, or illogical thesis; little use of knowledge of government; some development; unsatisfactory, inapplicable, or nonexistent conclusion	Lacking both thesis and conclusion; little or no evidence of knowledge of U.S. government
Conventions of English	Meticulously and thoroughly organized; coherent and unified; virtually error free	Reasonably organized; mostly coherent and unified; few or some errors	Somewhat organized; some incoherence and lack of unity; some major errors	Little or no organization; incoherent and void of unity; extremely flawed

Rate yourself in each of the categories below. Enter the numbers on the lines below. Be as honest as possible so you will know what areas need work. Then calculate the average of the four numbers to determine your final score. It is difficult to score yourself objectively, so you may wish to ask a respected friend or teacher to assess your essays for a more accurate reflection of their strengths and weaknesses. On the AP test itself, a reader will rate your essays on a scale of 0 to 9, with 9 being the highest.

Each category is rated 9 (high) to 0 (incompetent).

ESSAY 1
SELF-EVALUATION
Overall Impression _____
Understanding of U.S. Government _____
Development _____
Conventions of English _____

TOTAL _____
Divide by 4 for final score. _____

ESSAY 1
OBJECTIVE EVALUATION
Overall Impression _____
Understanding of U.S. Government _____
Development _____
Conventions of English _____

TOTAL _____
Divide by 4 for final score. _____

ESSAY 2
SELF-EVALUATION
Overall Impression _____
Understanding of U.S. Government _____
Development _____
Conventions of English _____

TOTAL _____
Divide by 4 for final score. _____

ESSAY 2
OBJECTIVE EVALUATION
Overall Impression _____
Understanding of U.S. Government _____
Development _____
Conventions of English _____

TOTAL _____
Divide by 4 for final score. _____

ESSAY 3
SELF-EVALUATION
Overall Impression _____
Understanding of U.S. Government _____
Development _____
Conventions of English _____

TOTAL _____
Divide by 4 for final score. _____

ESSAY 3
OBJECTIVE EVALUATION
Overall Impression _____
Understanding of U.S. Government _____
Development _____
Conventions of English _____

TOTAL _____
Divide by 4 for final score. _____

ESSAY 4
SELF-EVALUATION
Overall Impression _____
Understanding of U.S. Government _____
Development _____
Conventions of English _____

TOTAL _____
Divide by 4 for final score. _____

ESSAY 4
OBJECTIVE EVALUATION
Overall Impression _____
Understanding of U.S. Government _____
Development _____
Conventions of English _____

TOTAL _____
Divide by 4 for final score. _____

Practice Test 2

AP GOVERNMENT AND AND POLITICS

On the front page of the test booklet, you will find some information about the test. Because you have studied this book, none of it should be new to you, and much of it is similar to other standardized tests that you have taken.

The page will tell you that the following exam will take 2 hours and 25 minutes—45 minutes for the multiple-choice portion, Section I, and 100 minutes for the essay part, Section II. There are two booklets for the exam, one for the multiple-choice section and one for the essays.

The page in your test booklet will also say that SECTION I

- is 45 minutes.

- has 60 questions.

- counts for 50 percent of your total score.

Then you will find a sentence in capital letters telling you not to open your exam booklet until the monitor tells you to open it.

Other instructions will tell you to be careful when you fill in the ovals on the answer sheet. Fill in each oval completely. If you erase an answer, erase it completely. If you skip a question, be sure to skip the answer oval for it. You will not receive any credit for work done in the test booklet, but you may use it for making notes.

You will also find a paragraph about the guessing penalty—a deduction of one-quarter point for every wrong answer—but also words of advice about guessing if you know something about the questions and can eliminate several of the answers.

The final paragraph will remind you to work effectively and to pace yourself. You are told that not everyone will be able to answer all the questions and it is preferable to skip questions that are difficult and come back to them if you have time.

GOVERNMENT AND POLITICS

SECTION 1	TIME—45 MINUTES	60 QUESTIONS

Directions: Each question or incomplete sentence is followed by five suggested responses. Select the best answer and fill in the corresponding oval on the answer sheet.

1. The principle of separate but equal was established by

   (A) *Brown* v. *Board of Education of Topeka.*
   (B) *Wesberry* v. *Sanders.*
   (C) *Plessy* v. *Ferguson.*
   (D) *University of California Board of Regents* v. *Bakke.*
   (E) *Heart of Atlanta Motel* v. *United States.*

2. An older population of voters would most likely not support which of the following proposals?

   (A) An increase in Medicare benefits
   (B) Government subsidies to public education
   (C) Health-care reform
   (D) COLA for Social Security
   (E) Campaign finance reform

3. Prior restraint refers to

   (A) the force used in search and seizure situations.
   (B) government actions that prevent the publication of material in print media.
   (C) injunctions issued against strikers.
   (D) slander.
   (E) reading of one's rights to a suspect before questioning.

4. All of the following are ways that executive agencies benefit from being part of an iron triangle EXCEPT

   (A) support from client groups for the agency's budget.
   (B) approval of the agency's budget by the relevant Congressional committee or subcommittee.
   (C) technical advice from the interest groups.
   (D) assistance from the Congressional committee with complaints from constituents.
   (E) support when threatened with abolishment or reorganization by Congress.

5. The ruling in *Miranda* v. *Arizona* established

(A) the right to privacy.

(B) the right to be represented by counsel.

(C) the principle of a clear and present danger.

(D) the rights of a suspect under questioning.

(E) that the defendant had been rightfully convicted for failure to relocate.

6. A political fact of life that political parties need to recognize in order to be successful at the polls is

(A) that campaign finance reform is a major issue with voters.

(B) that older voters are conservative and the population is aging.

(C) that the gender gap elected Bill Clinton in 1996.

(D) that most voters hold middle-of-the-road views on most issues.

(E) that touting their accomplishments is the best way to win.

7. Which of the following programs is outside the regular budget-making process of Congress?

(A) Entitlements

(B) Medicare

(C) The federal judiciary

(D) Social Security

(E) Secret defense arsenals

8. A writ of certiorari

(A) is issued by the Supreme Court to stay an execution.

(B) is an order to a lower court by the Supreme Court to send up a case for review.

(C) must be agreed to by five justices of the Supreme Court in order for the Court to consider a case.

(D) is a court order requiring that a specific action be taken.

(E) is handed down in cases involving civil liberties.

9. Critics of the Federal Election Campaign Act of 1974 claim that the law

I. caused backloading of the presidential primary calendar.

II. increased the power of special-interest groups.

III. increased the role of the news media.

(A) I only

(B) II only

(C) III only

(D) I and III

(E) II and III

10. Which of the following helps the president sort out the competing agendas of the various executive departments?

(A) Office of Management and Budget

(B) Council of Economic Advisors

(C) National Security Council

(D) Chief of staff

(E) Research Office of the White House Staff

GO ON TO THE NEXT PAGE

11. All of the following are true of voter behavior EXCEPT

    (A) the higher the level of education the more likely one is to vote.

    (B) women tend to be more liberal than men.

    (C) the less political power a group has the more likely it is to be liberal.

    (D) parental affiliation is the greatest predictor of a person's own party identification.

    (E) the younger the voter the more likely he or she is to be conservative.

12. All of the following would need to be authorized by a constitutional amendment EXCEPT

    (A) allowing school prayer.

    (B) authorizing the line-item veto.

    (C) criminalizing the burning of the American flag.

    (D) banning abortion.

    (E) amending Social Security provisions.

13. What is the correct sequence of the steps in the lawmaking process in the House? The proposed bill

    I. is reported out to the full committee.

    II. is sent to the Rules Committee.

    III. is referred to a subcommittee.

    IV. is referred to a conference committee.

    V. is passed in the House.

    (A) I, III, II, V, IV

    (B) III, I, II, V, IV

    (C) I, II, III, V, IV

    (D) II, I, III, IV, V

    (E) IV, I, II, III, V

Questions 14 and 15 refer to the following graph.

Average Campaign Costs for Members of the House, 1988–1998
(dollars in thousands)

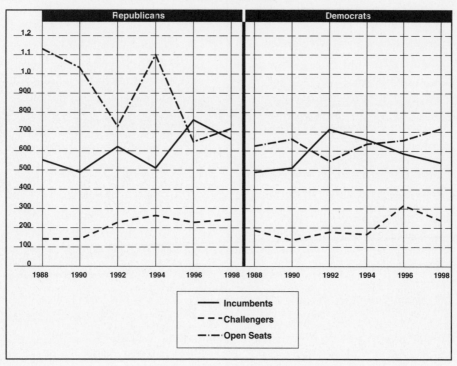

14. Which of the following statements is best supported by the data on the graphs?

(A) In general, House candidates spent more on midterm elections than races during presidential election years.

(B) The amount of money candidates spent on open seats increased and decreased in the same manner for both Democrats and Republicans.

(C) Running for an open seat was more expensive for both Democrats and Republicans than when an incumbent was in place.

(D) The most expensive contests were between Republicans running for an open seat.

(E) Incumbents spent the most money in the 1994 election.

15. The graphs point out

(A) the appeal of the Republican Party to the wealthy.

(B) one of the difficulties challengers have in trying to unseat incumbents.

(C) the intense rivalry of the 1992 Senate election.

(D) the decrease in PAC support for Democrats in 1998.

(E) the disenchantment with the Republicans after the 1994 Contract with America.

GO ON TO THE NEXT PAGE

16. The Love Canal episode provided an impetus for

    (A) the creation of the Superfund.
    (B) the passage of the Clean Air Act.
    (C) the passage of the Clean Water Act.
    (D) the passage of the bill authorizing the Environmental Protection Agency.
    (E) the deregulation of energy utilities.

17. Cloture is invoked in the Senate

    (A) to impeach a federal judge.
    (B) to censure a senator for wrongdoing.
    (C) to remove a federal judge who has been impeached.
    (D) to end debate on a bill by a three-fifths' vote of the Senate.
    (E) to return a bill to committee.

18. "Shaping the agenda" is a phrase used to describe the role of

    (A) the president in the State of the Union address.
    (B) the news media in determining which issues and personalities get attention.
    (C) the president's chief of staff.
    (D) the Supreme Court in choosing cases to hear.
    (E) the Joint Conference Committee.

19. The due process and equal protection clauses of the Fourteenth Amendment were extended by the Supreme Court to state law in

    (A) *Regents of the University of California* v. *Bakke*.
    (B) *Hopwood* v. *State of Texas*.
    (C) *Worcester* v. *Georgia*.
    (D) *Brown* v. *Board of Education*.
    (E) *Plessy* v. *Ferguson*.

20. The process through which a person acquires his or her political orientation is known as

    (A) social intelligence.
    (B) political intelligence.
    (C) political socialization.
    (D) political ideology.
    (E) social IQ.

21. Which of the following PACs most probably donated more heavily to Democrats than to Republicans?

    (A) National Rifle Association
    (B) American Medical Association
    (C) United Auto Workers
    (D) National Association of Retailers
    (E) Americans for Tax Reform

22. Judicial restraint

    (A) replaced the policy of judicial review.
    (B) refers to stricter sentencing guidelines in criminal cases.
    (C) refers to a policy of limiting due process.
    (D) underlay the Supreme Court decisions that extended the Bill of Rights.
    (E) limits the policymaking role of courts.

23. Incumbent members of the Senate tend to win reelection to Congress because

   I. often their districts have been drawn to support the incumbents' party.

   II. voters are more familiar with incumbents than with the challengers.

   III. the staff of incumbents solve problems for constituents and build up good will for their bosses that translates into support back home at election time.

   IV. incumbents are able to raise more campaign money than challengers.

   (A) I and II
   (B) III and IV
   (C) I, II, and III
   (D) II, III, and IV
   (E) I, II, III, and IV

24. The Judiciary Act of 1789

   (A) established the principle of judicial review.
   (B) designated the Supreme Court as the court to hear disputes involving federal laws.
   (C) established the office of Attorney General and the Department of Justice.
   (D) created the federal court system.
   (E) was invoked by Andrew Jackson in the dispute over enforcement of *Worcester* v. *State of Georgia*.

25. Which of the following amendments put limits on Congress's ability to enact legislation?

   (A) First
   (B) Second
   (C) Third
   (D) Fifth
   (E) Sixth

26. Bankruptcy cases are unique in that

   (A) both individuals and businesses can file for bankruptcy.
   (B) the court of original jurisdiction is U.S. district court.
   (C) although both the states and the federal government have the power to regulate bankruptcies, almost all bankruptcy cases are heard in federal court.
   (D) bankruptcy cases are criminal cases held in federal court.
   (E) the Constitution gives Congress the power to establish a uniform code of laws regulating bankruptcy.

27. Which of the following is not an example of a check on presidential power?

   (A) Only Congress can declare war.
   (B) The Senate must approve ambassadorial appointments.
   (C) The Senate recognizes foreign nations.
   (D) Presidential appointments made while Congress is in recess last only until the end of the session.
   (E) Congress passes the final annual budget.

28. All of the following are legislative tools that a president may use EXCEPT

   (A) bargaining with legislators.
   (B) having loyal members of the president's party selected as committee chairs.
   (C) exploiting the honeymoon period.
   (D) establishing priorities, thereby setting Congress's agenda before it can set its own.
   (E) making personal appeals.

GO ON TO THE NEXT PAGE

29. The group of citizens least likely to vote in an election are

(A) under 25 years of age.

(B) between 25 and 45.

(C) over 45.

(D) between 45 and 65.

(E) between 65 and 80.

30. Which of the following statements is NOT true about redistricting?

(A) State legislatures redraw Congressional districts, but a state's delegation in Congress may recommend and lobby its own ideas about how new districts should be drawn.

(B) Gerrymandering in any form is no longer a problem.

(C) State governors have the power to veto districting plans.

(D) Federal courts decide conflicts over district boundary lines.

(E) The "one man, one vote" rule refers to making sure that district boundaries are equitably drawn.

31. The most significant fact about deregulation is that

(A) it can lower costs and, therefore, what consumers pay.

(B) it marks a retreat by government from intervention in the marketplace.

(C) it was a hallmark of Ronald Reagan's presidency.

(D) cuts in the funding of regulatory agencies can cut back on regulatory oversight without changing laws.

(E) President Clinton's support for cutting regulations is unusual for a Democrat.

32. The major difference between categorical grants-in-aid and block grants are

(A) that with categorical grants-in-aid the federal government puts almost no restrictions on their use whereas block grants are restricted to certain specific uses.

(B) that block grants can be used with almost no restrictions by the recipient states and localities.

(C) that categorical grants-in-aid are based on need and block grants are given on the basis of competitive proposals.

(D) that block grants have few restrictions on how the money can be spent by state and local governments whereas categorical grants-in-aid are restricted to specific categories such as technology training for teachers.

(E) the restrictions on categorical grants-in-aid make the aid conditional.

Question 33 refers to the following table.

Voter Turnout 1996 Presidential Primaries

0 to 9 Percent	10 to 19 Percent	20 to 30 Percent	31 to 40 Percent
Alaska	Washington	California	Oregon
Hawaii	Idaho	Nebraska	Montana
Utah	Nevada	Oklahoma	West Virginia
Wyoming	Arizona	Wisconsin	New Hampshire
Kansas	Colorado	Ohio	
Minnesota	New Mexico	Vermont	
Iowa	North Dakota		
Missouri	South Dakota		
Louisiana	Texas		
Michigan	Arkansas		
Florida	Illinois		
Virginia	Indiana		
New York	Kentucky		
Delaware	Tennessee		
New Jersey	Mississippi		
Connecticut	Alabama		
Rhode Island	Georgia		
Massachusetts	South Carolina		
	North Carolina		
	Maryland		
	Pennsylvania		
	Maine		

33. Which of the following statements is best supported by the data in the table?

(A) States with the most electoral votes had the best voter turnout.

(B) As the primary season wore on, fewer voters went to the polls.

(C) Less than 20 percent of the voting-age population voted.

(D) In general, the Northeast had better voter turnout than the Sunbelt.

(E) Primary voters depend more on news stories and advertising rather than first-hand exposure to candidates to decide for whom to vote.

GO ON TO THE NEXT PAGE

34. Which of the following statements most accurately depicts the political leanings of Hispanics as a group?

(A) Most Hispanics are young, and younger voters tend not to vote.

(B) Groups with little political influence tend to be more liberal because they see government as helping them to better themselves.

(C) Fewer Hispanic women vote, so there is less of a gender gap apparent with this group.

(D) Most Hispanics are Catholic, and Roman Catholics tend to be conservative.

(E) Republican moderates are making headway with this ethnic group.

35. Passage of which of the following extended earlier laws prohibiting discrimination on the basis of sex in hiring, firing, salary, promotion, and working conditions?

(A) Affirmative action policy

(B) Equal Employment Opportunity Act

(C) Civil Rights Act of 1964

(D) Equal Credit Opportunity Act

(E) Title IX

36. Which of the following statements of comparison is correct about the differences between the Federalists and Anti-Federalists?

(A) Neither group was willing to dissolve the union over the question of counting slaves for purposes of representation.

(B) The Federalists believed a Bill of Rights was essential whereas the Anti-Federalists did not.

(C) The Federalists believed that officials should be directly elected by the people whereas the Anti-Federalists did not.

(D) The Federalists believed in national sovereignty whereas the Anti-Federalists believed in strong state governments.

(E) The Federalists did not believe in the need for a presidential cabinet whereas the Anti-Federalists did.

37. The chief initiator of foreign policy is

(A) the Senate Foreign Relations Committee.

(B) the secretary of state.

(C) the joint chiefs of staff.

(D) the president.

(E) the president in concert with the secretary of state and the national security advisor.

38. Push polling

(A) is done on the day of an election to get out the vote.

(B) is another name for random sampling.

(C) is used by candidates to determine which issues to focus on during a campaign.

(D) asks a person a loaded question about a candidate to shape the respondent's view of the opposing candidate.

(E) is a technique in which respondents are chosen whose characteristics most closely match the general population in certain demographics such as age and sex.

39. Which of the following no longer has a significant effect on Congressional elections?

(A) The coattail effect

(B) Split-ticket voting

(C) Early announcement of a candidacy

(D) Incumbency

(E) Party loyalty

40. Issuing executive orders is a useful presidential tool

I. when the opposition party controls Congress.

II. to take care of nonessential business without tying up Congress's time.

III. when Congress is in recess.

(A) I only

(B) II only

(C) III only

(D) I and II

(E) I, II, and III

41. Which of the following is not an example of the Supreme Court's incorporation doctrine extending from the federal level to the state level?

(A) The right to a hearing in front of a grand jury

(B) The exclusionary rule

(C) The right to counsel

(D) The freedom of assembly

(E) The freedom of speech

42. All of the following are criticisms of the presidential primary and caucus system EXCEPT

(A) too much attention is paid to the early primaries and caucuses.

(B) the media wields too much influence through its decisions about whom to cover and how intensively.

(C) voters who participate in the system tend not to be representative of the general voting public.

(D) the unfair advantage that regional primaries give to the region that goes first.

(E) running for president is expensive, and candidates may find it difficult to raise the required money.

43. Watergate, the Vietnam War, Iran-contra, and the economic downturn of the late 1970s have all resulted in

(A) an increased reliance on the media.

(B) a belief in the economic vulnerability of the marketplace.

(C) a decline of trust in the government.

(D) distrust of the military.

(E) a higher percentage of registered voters going to the polls.

GO ON TO THE NEXT PAGE

44. All of the following can affect the accuracy of public opinion polling EXCEPT

(A) the margin of error.
(B) the underdog effect.
(C) the wording of the questions on the survey.
(D) the interpretation of the survey results.
(E) the issues that are the subject of the survey.

45. Which of the following is a systemic reason for the foundering of President Clinton's health-care reform proposals in 1994?

(A) The number of committees and subcommittees in Congress that needed to deal with the proposals made it difficult to craft well-thought-out, consistent legislation in a timely fashion.
(B) The public did not support the potential costs of the reforms.
(C) Health-care providers strenuously lobbied Congress to defeat the measures.
(D) There was a concern that universal health care was socialist.
(E) The "Patient's Bill of Rights" stalled the measure.

46. Party affiliation in Congress is most visible on votes relating to

(A) social welfare and military policy.
(B) economic policy and deregulation.
(C) military policy and economic policy.
(D) judicial appointments.
(E) social welfare and economic policy.

47. Which of the following statements most accurately describes the pluralist theory of government?

(A) Bargaining and compromise during public policy deliberations ensures that the public interest is served.
(B) Many groups of people with shared interests attempt to influence public policy through organized efforts to present their views.
(C) James Madison would have supported the pluralist theory because he worried about domination by a majority.
(D) Pluralist government may result in confused, contradictory policies because so many groups attempt to present their views that no group is able to sway policy decisions.
(E) Pluralist theory is the opposite of the elite theory of government.

48. "In framing a government which is to be administered by men over men, the great difficulty lies in this: you must first enable the government to control the governed; and then in the next place oblige it to control itself."

James Madison wrote these words in *The Federalist,* No. 10. The Framers of the Constitution attempted to accomplish the latter goal

(A) by creating the amendment process.
(B) by establishing a system of checks and balances.
(C) through federalism itself.
(D) by limiting majority control by having senators elected by state legislatures.
(E) by establishing Congressional over-sight committees.

49. The importance of the power of recognition as wielded by the Speaker of the House and the Senate majority leader is that

   (A) it can prevent debate on a bill.
   (B) a member can be denied a seat on the committee he or she wants.
   (C) the minority party has no role in allotting time for debate on proposed legislation.
   (D) it helps whips maintain party unity.
   (E) it accelerates roll call votes.

50. All of the following are examples of government corporations EXCEPT

   (A) Amtrak.
   (B) the U.S. Postal Service.
   (C) Comsat.
   (D) the National Science Foundation.
   (E) the Tennessee Valley Authority.

51. One of the most significant problems in implementing legislation is

   (A) the fragmentation of responsibility and programs across the government.
   (B) lack of rules governing how implementation is to be carried out.
   (C) the lobbying of clientele agencies by interest groups.
   (D) lack of clear direction by Congress.
   (E) Congressional oversight.

52. "To say that a vote is worth more in one district than in another would not only run counter to our fundamental ideas of democratic government, it would cast aside the principle of a House of Representatives elected 'by the People'. . ."

   The above statement is from the Supreme Court decision in

   (A) *Miranda* v. *Arizona.*
   (B) *Gideon* v. *Wainwright.*
   (C) *Marbury* v. *Madison.*
   (D) *Wesberry* v. *Sanders.*
   (E) *Schenck* v. *United States.*

53. Which of the following is a basic tenet of the nation's attitude toward public education?

   (A) Public education is a local matter.
   (B) Charter schools endanger the future of public education.
   (C) There is a danger that national frameworks in subject areas and standardized tests will create a national curriculum.
   (D) The debate over how to improve education in the United States goes in cycles.
   (E) If vouchers can be redeemed for a parochial school education, the separation of church and state will be breached.

54. A major difference between House and Senate procedures is that

   (A) in the House there are more steps at which a proposed piece of legislation may be amended.
   (B) seniority is less important in naming committee chairs in the Senate.
   (C) bills can die either in committee or in the floor vote for the conference committee report.
   (D) the leadership of the House exerts direct control over the flow of bills to the floor whereas the Senate leadership relies on the Rules Committee.
   (E) Senate leaders do not know ahead of scheduling a vote whether a proposed bill will pass whereas in the House, the whip system ensures that the leaders are well informed.

GO ON TO THE NEXT PAGE

55. Congress could use which of the following strategies to show discontent with the federal judicial system?

   I.   Pass an amendment that, in effect, overturns a Supreme Court decision

   II. Refuse to approve nominees to federal judgeships who hold certain views of the law

  III. Pass legislation that clarifies an existing law, thus overturning a federal court's ruling

  IV. Change the size or levels of the federal judiciary

   (A) I only
   (B) II only
   (C) I and II
   (D) I, II, and III
   (E) I, II, III, and IV

56. All of the following are basic beliefs that Americans hold about their government EXCEPT

   (A) preserving the general welfare.
   (B) equality for all.
   (C) majority rule and minority rights.
   (D) the efficacy of political parties.
   (E) individual liberty.

57. Congress exercises some control over agencies in the executive branch through

   (A) oversight and committee hearings.
   (B) assisting constituents.
   (C) committee hearings and appropriations bills.
   (D) oversight and the budgeting process.
   (E) its place in appropriate iron triangles.

58. Which of the following foreign policy strategies is typically unpopular with the agricultural and business sectors of the nation?

   (A) Diplomacy
   (B) Foreign aid
   (C) Economic sanctions
   (D) Political coercion
   (E) Military intervention

59. In general, all of the following are characteristics of the federal bureaucracy EXCEPT

   (A) division of labor.
   (B) merit-based hiring.
   (C) nonpartisan workforce.
   (D) standard operating procedures to ensure consistency and efficiency in decision making.
   (E) steadily increasing growth in the number of employees.

60. Since the Reagan administration, presidents have attempted to

   (A) cut back on the size of the federal government and the reach of its programs.
   (B) promote an overall increase in funding for regulatory agencies.
   (C) lobby for an increase in funding to eliminate nonfunded mandates to the states.
   (D) break iron triangles through the combining of some agencies and the elimination of others.
   (E) clarify the responsibilities of agencies through the adoption of additional regulations.

S T O P   If you finish before time is called, you may check your work on this section only. Do not turn to any other section in the test.

SECTION II	TIME—100 MINUTES

Directions: You have 100 minutes to answer all four of the following questions. It is suggested that you take a few minutes to outline each answer. Spend approximately one fourth of your time (25 minutes) on each question. Support the ideas in your essay with substantive examples where appropriate. Make sure to number each of your responses with the number that corresponds to the question.

1.

"Do you ever have one of those days when every-thing seems unconstitutional?"

Identify the point of view of the cartoonist. Do you agree or disagree with it? Explain your position, using Supreme Court cases to illustrate your argument.

2. The relationship between the president and Congress has sometimes been characterized as close but contentious. Discuss the accuracy of this statement, emphasizing the role of constitutional checks and balances and the sources of conflict between the two branches of government since the 1960s.

3. In the twentieth century, the United States turned more and more to bureaucratic agencies to conduct the business of the federal government. Discuss the roles of the various units of the federal bureaucracy: cabinet-level departments, independent regulatory agencies, government corporations, and independent executive agencies.

4. The Second Amendment states: "A well-regulated militia, being necessary to the security of a free state, the right of the people to keep and bear arms, shall not be infringed." Opponents of gun control believe that the Constitution protects a citizen's right to bear arms under any circumstances. Write an essay that critically evaluates evidence that both supports and refutes that position.

STOP If you finish before time is called, you may check your work on this section only. Do not turn to any other section in the test.

ANSWERS AND EXPLANATIONS

Quick-Score Answers

1. C	11. E	21. C	31. B	41. A	51. A
2. B	12. E	22. E	32. D	42. D	52. D
3. B	13. B	23. D	33. C	43. C	53. A
4. D	14. D	24. D	34. B	44. B	54. A
5. D	15. B	25. A	35. B	45. A	55. E
6. D	16. A	26. C	36. D	46. E	56. D
7. A	17. D	27. C	37. D	47. B	57. D
8. B	18. B	28. B	38. D	48. B	58. C
9. E	19. D	29. A	39. A	49. A	59. E
10. A	20. C	30. B	40. A	50. D	60. A

PRACTICE TEST 2

1. **The correct answer is (C).** Choice (A) is the landmark school desegregation case of the 1950s. Choice (B) is one of the "one man, one vote" cases of the 1960s. Choice (D) is an affirmative action case relating to the use of race as an element in admissions policies in higher education. Choice (E) is a landmark interstate commerce case relating to serving African Americans.

Test-Taking Strategy

The key words are most likely *and* not. *This is a* not/except *question.*

2. **The correct answer is (B).** Typically older voters without children tend not to support additional funding for education. Choices (A), (C), and (D) may all directly affect older citizens. COLA in choice (D) refers to cost-of-living adjustments; these increase the monthly Social Security benefits on an annual basis. Choice (E) is a neutral response; some older voters may care about campaign finance reform and some may not.

3. **The correct answer is (B).** The Supreme Court has upheld the illegality of the government's use of prior restraint to forbid the publication of material; a notable case is the Vietnam War era *Pentagon Papers* case in which the *New York Times's* right to publish classified documents was upheld. That a news organization can publish material does not meant that it cannot be sued after the fact. Choices (A), (C), (D), and (E) are distracters.

4. **The correct answer is (D).** The agency provides assistance to constituents of members of the Congressional committee that is part of the iron triangle; the committee does not come to the aid of the agency. Choices (A), (B), (C), and (E) are all examples of support that an executive agency would typically receive from the other two members of the iron triangle. The interest groups may also provide information to the Congressional committee or subcommittee.

5. **The correct answer is (D).** *Roe* v. *Wade* established choice (A). *Gideon* v. *Wainwright* established choice (B). Choice (C) was the principle in *Schenck* v. *United States. Korematsu* v. *United States* is the case referred to in choice (E).

6. **The correct answer is (D).** The phrase "fact of life" is asking you for a generalization. Choices (A), (B), and (C) are specific instances of larger concepts or ideas. Campaign finance reform, choice (A), is a specific example of the kinds of issues that concern voters. Choice (B) discusses only one aspect of the voting population as does choice (C), which is also a specific and true statement about a particular campaign. Choice (E) is one method for running a campaign, but those accomplishments need to be in areas that are of interest and concern to voters. Analyses of voting trends and the demise of extremist parties demonstrate that understanding choice (D) is the way to win elections.

7. **The correct answer is (A).** The budgets for entitlements, also known as uncontrollable expenditures, are governed by the laws that authorize them, which make all people who meet certain qualifications eligible to receive benefits. Congress must fund the program to this level or change the law, which more often than not results in angry protests from beneficiaries like older voters. Choices (B) and (D) are both entitlements, but choice (A) is the more inclusive answer and, therefore, the best choice. Choices (C) and (E) are incorrect.

8. **The correct answer is (B).** Choice (A) is incorrect. The agreement of four justices, not five, is required for the Supreme Court to agree to consider a case, making choice (C) incorrect. Choice (D) refers to a writ of mandamus, so it is incorrect. Choice (E) is a distracter; often cases that the Supreme Court agrees to hear on appeal relate to civil rights and civil liberties, but there is no special process for accepting such cases.

Test-Taking Strategy

For tiered or multistep questions, determine which point(s) is correct and then find the answer choice that contains that point(s).

9. **The correct answer is (E).** Critics claim that the Federal Election Campaign Act of 1974 caused frontloading of the primary schedule not backloading, so point I is incorrect. Points II and III accurately reflect criticism of the law. The answer choice that contains both points II and III, choice (E), is correct.

10. **The correct answer is (A).** The OMB acts as a clearinghouse to which the cabinet departments and other executive agencies send proposed legislation and regulations. The OMB evaluates the costs of the proposals and their fit with the administration's goals and advises the president. Choice (B), the Council of Economic Advisors, advises the president on economic policies; its name implies the narrow focus of its work, so if you did not know the answer to the question immediately, you could eliminate this response based on its name. That is true for choice (C) as well. As its name suggests, the National Security Council advises the president on foreign and military policies. Choice (D), the chief of staff, manages the White House staff and advises the president. Choice (E), the Research Office, provides information as one of the political offices of the White House Staff.

11. **The correct answer is (E).** The younger the voter, the more likely the person is to be a liberal. One reason that the nation's politics have become more conservative in recent years is that younger voters have been staying away from the polls. Choices (A), (B), (C), and (D) are all true statements about voter behavior in general.

12. **The correct answer is (E).** Social Security is authorized by a Congressional law, so it can be amended by Congressional action. School prayer is held to be illegal under the establishment clause of the First Amendment, so making school prayer legal, choice (A), would require an amendment to the Constitution. The Supreme Court ruled that the line-item veto, choice (B), by giving the president the power to veto parts of appropriations bills, usurped the power of Congress to make laws. Therefore, an amendment to the Constitution would be required in order to restore the line-item veto. The Supreme Court has held that the First Amendment's guarantee of freedom of speech covers flag burning, choice (C). To make the act illegal, a Constitutional amendment would be required. The Supreme Court held that most abortions are legal (the state has a consideration in late-term abortions), so a constitutional amendment would be required to criminalize abortions, choice (D).

13. **The correct answer is (B).** A proposed piece of legislation is referred to a subcommittee from the committee (III). Once the subcommittee has studied the issues, held hearings, and revised the proposal, the subcommittee reports it out to the full committee (I). If the full committee votes to move the bill on, it is sent to the Rules Committee (II), which determines the length of debate and other issues for floor debate. If the bill is passed after debate in the House (V) and the Senate passed a different version of the bill, a joint conference committee meets to work out a compromise (IV). The only answer that repeats this sequence is choice (B).

14. **The correct answer is (D).** Even as a generalization, choice (A) is incorrect because less than half the data for the 1990, 1994, and 1998 elections show an increase in campaign spending over the previous election. Choice (B) is incorrect because the Republicans' expenditures for open seats decreased for the 1990, 1992, and 1996 elections and increased for the 1994 and 1998 elections while Democratic expenditures decreased for 1992 and increased for 1990, 1994, 1996, and 1998 elections. Choice (C) is incorrect because the 1992 election for incumbent Democrats was more expensive than the campaign for the open seat that year while the incumbent Republican spent more in 1996 than those running for the open seat. Choice (E) is incorrect because both the 1992 and the 1996 elections were more expensive for incumbents.

15. **The correct answer is (B).** The small amount of money that challengers were able to raise and spend in these House races illustrates choice (B) very well. Choice (A) is incorrect and also illogical; the Republican Party does not attract supporters because of the money it can raise but raises money because its policies attract wealthy supporters. Choice (C) is incorrect because the data are about House races, not Senate races. There are no data to support choice (D) nor choice (E).

16. **The correct answer is (A).** A chemical company had dumped 20,000 tons of toxic waste on a site that later became a neighborhood of homes, a school, and playing fields. The resulting medical problems that Love Canal residents experienced and the abandonment of their homes because they became uninhabitable caused pressure on Congress to pass the Comprehensive Environmental Response, Compensation, and Liability Act of 1980, establishing the Superfund to be used to clean up toxic waste sites. Choice (B), the first Clean Air Act, was passed in 1963 and dealt with efforts to control air pollution. Eliminating the discharge of pollutants into navigable waterways was the purpose of the Clear Water Act, choice (C), passed in 1972. The Superfund did not impact choice (D), the EPA, or the deregulation of energy utilities almost two decades later. Common sense would tell you that choice (E) is probably incorrect because deregulation would loosen regulations rather than tighten them.

Test-Taking Strategy

Sometimes viewing a definitional question as a vocabulary question may help you find the right answer.

17. **The correct answer is (D).** If you did not know the political function of cloture, think of the possible meaning of the word. *Cloture* looks as though it might be close to the word *closure* in meaning. In that context, choices (A), (C), and (D) all seem plausible, but choice (D), to end debate, is the closest in meaning to closure—and the correct answer. To impeach a federal judge, choice (A), is to find enough likelihood of wrongdoing to hand him or her over for trial. Choice (B), censure, means to severely reprimand and is the formal term used in both the House and the Senate for the condemnation of a member for misconduct. Choice (C) is incorrect; a federal judge is removed once he or she has been found guilty of wrongdoing. Impeachment is similar to an indictment, not a conviction. Choice (E) is incorrect. Cloture ends debate, but a vote still must be taken on the fate of the bill under discussion.

18. **The correct answer is (B).** Political activists—in and out of government, elected and appointed officials as well as interest groups—use the media to get their messages across to the public, and thus the media plays an important role in shaping the issues that the nation talks about and expects some government action to deal with. The president's annual State of the Union address, choice (A), is one example of how the president uses the media to get his message out to the people. Choice (D) is another good distracter—the Supreme Court can shape policy through the cases it chooses to hear, but it is only one actor in the larger national forum. Choices (C) and (E) are incorrect.

19. **The correct answer is (D).** Choice (A), *Bakke*, dealt with the use of quotas for college admissions. The Supreme Court declared the use of quotas was incompatible with the equal protection clause. Choice (B), *Hopwood*, is a federal court of appeals' decision that prohibited using race as a factor in determining college admissions and scholarships to state colleges and universities; it applies only to institutions of higher education in Texas, Louisiana, and Mississippi. *Worcester*, choice (C), refers to a case in which the Supreme Court recognized the Cherokees' existence as a sovereign nation, citing treaties with the U.S. government. Choice (E), *Plessy*, established the principle of "separate but equal," which the Court struck down in *Brown*.

20. **The correct answer is (C).** People acquire their political orientation through a process known as political socialization. Choices (A) and (E) are the same and refer to a theory of behavioral scientists that a person's social intelligence, his or her ability to work with others and to lead and motivate others, determines whether the person will be successful in life. Choices (B) and (D) are distracters.

Test-Taking Strategy

This question sets up a hypothetical situation that you must analyze. Look for the most typical answer choice.

21. **The correct answer is (C).** The UAW is the only labor union in the list and traditionally labor supports Democratic candidates, so choice (C) is the most likely answer. The NRA, choice (A), is a single-issue PAC that opposes Democratic efforts to pass gun control legislation, so choice (A) is illogical. Choices (B) and (D) represent professional and business interests that typically oppose the type of legislation to control fees and business practices that the Democrats propose. Choice (E), Americans for Tax Reform, is a conservative group, and, therefore, would be unlikely supporters of Democrats. If you did not know that the group was conservative, you might guess that because tax cuts and tax reform are signature issues of the Republicans, the group might be Republican leaning.

22. **The correct answer is (E).** If you did not know the answer immediately, you could eliminate choice (D) as illogical. Something that restrained or limited would not extend rights. Choice (A) is also illogical because the Supreme Court continues to review laws. While choice (C) might seem like a good choice, choice (E) is a better response because it is more inclusive. Due process would be only one area that the courts would consider. Choice (B) is incorrect.

Test-Taking Strategy

This question is a good example of why it is important to read the question and answer choices carefully. Highlight key words, in this case, Senate.

23. **The correct answer is (D).** The question asks about incumbent members of the Senate, so point I is incorrect. Senators represent entire states, not districts. If the question had asked about House incumbents, then point I would need to have been included in the answer. Points II, III, and IV are all reasons why incumbent members of the Senate tend to win reelection. Only choice (D) contains these three points.

24. **The correct answer is (D).** *Marbury* v. *Madison* established the principle of judicial review, choice (A). The Constitution established choice (B). The First Congress created the office of Attorney General, but the Justice Department was not created until 1871, choice (C). Choice (E) is incorrect; Jackson ignored the Supreme Court's ruling in this case, which is one of the problems in the system. The Supreme Court cannot of itself compel compliance.

25. **The correct answer is (A).** The First Amendment prohibits Congress from making any law that establishes a religion or from passing any law that restricts the freedoms of speech, press, assembly, and the right to petition the government. The Second Amendment, choice (B), prohibits the executive from limiting people's right to bear arms. Choice (C), the Third Amendment, places limits on the executive's ability to take private homes to house militia. The Fifth and the Sixth Amendments, choices (D) and (E), place restrictions on the courts. The Fifth Amendment prohibits self-incrimination and double jeopardy and the taking of private property by the government without just compensation. The Sixth Amendment guarantees a speedy trial and the opportunity to confront witnesses.

Test-Taking Strategy

The key word is unique.

26. **The correct answer is (C).** The federal government and the states shared the power to regulate bankruptcies until an 1898 federal law and subsequent extensions reduced the jurisdiction of the states so much that few bankruptcies are heard outside federal courts. Choice (A) is illogical; other laws relate to both individuals and businesses. Choice (B) is also illogical because U.S. district courts have original jurisdiction over any cases involving the alleged breaking of federal law. Not all bankruptcy cases are criminal cases, so choice (D) is incorrect. Choice (E) is a true statement, but it does not relate to the trying of bankruptcy cases nor does the power to regulate bankruptcies reside solely with Congress.

27. **The correct answer is (C).** The Constitution vests the power to receive ambassadors in the president, thus establishing the basis for the president's power to recognize (or withdraw diplomatic recognition from) the governments of foreign nations. Choice (C) then is not true. While the president may commit troops to a military action, Congress still retains the power to declare war, so choice (A) is true and an incorrect answer. The president nominates ambassadors with the advice and consent of the Senate, so choice (B) is incorrect. Choice (D) is an example of a check by Congress on presidential power. The president submits a budget, but Congress passes the final budget after making cuts and additions, so choice (E) is true and the wrong answer.

28. **The correct answer is (B).** The assignment of committee chairs is almost always made on the basis of seniority; presidential cajoling does not enter into selection. Choices (A), (C), (D), and (E) are all tools that the president uses to get his proposals passed in Congress. The honeymoon period, choice (C), may last for the first year or so; but the president's approval rating by the public can affect how important this is and how long it lasts.

29. **The correct answer is (A).** Younger Americans have always been the least likely to vote, but the percentage dropped from around 50 percent in 1972 to 32 percent in 1996. The decline at the other end of the age scale does not begin until after 80, and in fact there has been a slight increase in the percentage of voters after 60 years of age. Choices (B), (C), (D), and (E) then are incorrect.

30. **The correct answer is (B).** Gerrymandering to ensure racial concentrations in voting districts has been the subject of several recent cases in federal courts. Choices (A), (C), (D), and (E) are all true about the process of redistricting after the decennial U.S. Census.

31. **The correct answer is (B).** All five choices are correct, but the task here is to find the *most significant* response. You are looking for a concept. Both choices (C) and (E) refer to specific presidents, so eliminate those responses as not being general enough. Choices (A), (B), and (D) are broader, but choice (B) is the broadest statement. Choice (A) relates to one effect on consumers and choice (D) to one result of government's involvement in deregulation. Choice (B) states the cause, thus relating that response to the entire market, including consumers, the regulated industries, and Congress's various roles.

32. **The correct answer is (D).** If you did not know the answer immediately, you could eliminate choices (B) and (E) on the first reading. The question asks for the major difference and neither choice states a comparison. Choice (A) is the opposite of how the two systems are set up to administer funding. Choice (C) is incorrect.

33. **The correct answer is (C).** Choices (B) and (E) are true statements about presidential primaries, but they cannot be verified by reading the table, so they can be eliminated. Choice (A) is an incorrect statement as well as being unrelated to the table. Choice (D) is the opposite of what the table shows, so it too is incorrect. Only choice (C) can be verified based on the data in the table.

34. **The correct answer is (B).** Choice (A) may be a logical statement, but it does not deal with political ideology, the subject of the question, so it is incorrect. The same is true of choice (E); it does not talk about the ideology of Hispanics. Choices (C) and (D) are incorrect.

35. **The correct answer is (B).** The Equal Employment Opportunity Act was passed in 1972 to extend earlier laws such as choice (C), the Civil Rights Act of 1964, which banned discrimination based on race. Choice (A) is illogical because it is an implementation procedure, not a law. Choice (D) prohibited discriminatory lending practices against women and made questions about an applicant's marital status or gender illegal. Choice (E), Title IX of the Omnibus Education Act, relates to equal opportunities for girls in school sports.

36. **The correct answer is (D).** The Anti-Federalists opposed a strong national government in order to preserve states' rights. Choice (A) is incorrect because the questions asks for a comparison of differences, and this answer choice states a similarity. Choices (B) and (C) state the opposite of each side's belief. Choice (E) is incorrect information.

37. **The correct answer is (D).** While the president may consult with the secretary of state and the national security advisor, choice (E), the president is the nation's chief diplomat and shaper of foreign policy. The Senate Foreign Relations Committee, choice (A), has the function of reviewing policy and appropriations from the executive but does not initiate policy. The joint chiefs, choice (C), like the secretary of state, choice (B), have an advisory role.

38. **The correct answer is (D).** Push polling began in the 1990s and has been severely criticized for its misleading nature. Polling is used by candidates to test their messages, choice (C), but that method is not called push polling. Choice (E) is the definition of quota sampling. Choices (A) and (B) are incorrect.

39. **The correct answer is (A).** Choice (B), split-ticket voting, has made choice (A), the coattail effect, less significant in Congressional elections. Choice (D) is incorrect; incumbency is still the major factor in elections. Choice (E) is also a significant factor for voters in deciding for whom to vote. Choice (C) is incorrect.

40. **The correct answer is (A).** When faced with an unfriendly opposition party in control of Congress, a president may turn to issuing executive orders, memoranda, proclamation, and regulations to further the administration's policies (I). President Clinton found this very effective when blocked in his second term by a Republican-controlled Congress. Points II and III are incorrect, making choice (A) the correct answer.

41. **The correct answer is (A).** The incorporation, or nationalization, of the Bill of Rights to the states began with the 1925 Supreme Court decision in *Gitlow* v. *New York*, which related to freedom of speech, choice (E). However, the Supreme Court has not as yet extended the grand jury element of the Fifth Amendment, choice (A), to the states. The exclusionary rule, choice (B), found in the Fourth Amendment, was incorporated in *Mapp* v. *Ohio*. The right to counsel, choice (C), was extended through *Gideon* v. *Wainwright*. The First Amendment's guarantee of the freedom of assembly, choice (D), was extended in *DeJong* v. *Oregon*.

42. **The correct answer is (D).** Choice (D) is a criticism of a proposed regional primary system; it is not a criticism of the current system of primaries and caucuses. Choices (A), (B), (C), and (E) are all criticisms of the current system. Note that in addition to the problem of low voter turnout in primaries and caucuses, voters who do participate tend to be older, wealthier, and more committed to their party.

Test-Taking Strategy

Always read the question and all the answer choices carefully before making your choice.

43. **The correct answer is (C).** There is no reason to think that an economic downturn would encourage people to rely on the media for news, so choice (A) is illogical. Choice (B) relates to only one aspect of the question, so it is not a reasonable response. The same is also true for choice (D). Choice (E) is the opposite of the current trend.

44. **The correct answer is (B).** The question asks about causes, whereas the underdog effect, choice (B), is an effect, not a cause. The margin of error, choice (A), is typically reported along with the results to alert the reader to the presence of factors that may have influenced respondents' replies. Leading questions and ambiguously worded questions, choice (C), can affect the outcome of a survey as can biased interpretation, choice (D). The topics that are chosen can also influence survey results, choice (E). This is known as the illusion of salience, whereby topics that are not of concern to voters are listed and respondents feel compelled to respond rather than state "no opinion."

45. **The correct answer is (A).** While choices (A), (B), (C), and (D) are true statements about the health-care reform proposals that President Clinton put before Congress, only choice (A) deals with the system of Congress itself and how that system worked against passing the proposals. Choice (E) deals with a later effort to ensure the rights of patients against health-care providers.

46. **The correct answer is (E).** Democrats tend to support policies that favor government intervention in social issues and spending on social welfare policies, whereas Republicans tend to back cuts in social welfare in favor of less government and bigger tax cuts. Choice (B) is illogical because deregulation is an aspect of economic policy. While a division between the parties is often apparent on choices (C) and (D), the sharpest differences occur over social welfare and economic policy, choice (E).

47. **The correct answer is (B).** The question asks for the most accurate description of the pluralist theory of government. While choice (A) is a true statement about pluralist theory, it does not describe the theory. It describes two methods that are used in pluralist government to achieve its goals, so choice (A) is incorrect. Choice (C) may be true, but it does not describe pluralist theory, only why Madison might have supported it, making choice (C) incorrect. Choice (D) is the definition of hyperpluralism. In saying that pluralist theory is the opposite of elite theory, choice (E) does not define either theory, so it too is incorrect. Through the process of elimination, choice (B) is the correct answer.

48. **The correct answer is (B).** The separation of powers was meant to make each branch of the national government separate, but the branches could not be totally separate. They had to cooperate in order to accomplish any work, so the system of checks and balances set up a delicate tension among the branches and ensured that no one branch could take over the operation of the government. Choice (A) is illogical. Federalism, choice (C), is the system whereby the national government shares powers with state governments, thus making choice (C) illogical in this context. Choice (D) was an element of the thinking of the Framers, but it relates to the first goal—"to control the governed"—rather than the government. Choice (E) does not relate to the context of the question.

49. **The correct answer is (A).** The Speaker of the House and the Senate majority leader can deny recognition to members and thus discussion of a bill. Choice (B) is incorrect; typically, members of both chambers receive the committee assignments they wish. Choice (C) is incorrect because in both houses, the majority and minority leadership allocates debate time. Choices (D) and (E) have nothing to do with recognition.

50. **The correct answer is (D).** The NSF, choice (D), is an independent agency of the executive branch. Choice (A), Amtrak; choice (B), the U.S. Postal Service; choice (C), Comsat; and choice (E), the TVA, are all government corporations. They provide a service and charge for that service.

Test-Taking Strategy

The key words are most significant problem.

51. **The correct answer is (A).** As you evaluate the answer choices, keep in mind that the question is asking you for a big-picture answer. Choice (A) satisfies that criterion and is also true. Choice (B) is sometimes true of legislation that Congress passes; that is, writing the rules and regulations to implement the law is sometimes left to the agencies that will do the implementation, which may or may not be considered a problem. Choice (D) relates to choice (B). Choice (C) is incorrect. If one considers accountability a problem, then choice (E) might be the answer, but it is illogical.

52. **The correct answer is (D).** To answer this question correctly, you need to determine that it deals with the "one man, one vote" principle and that the only such case listed is *Wesberry* v. *Sanders.* Choice (A), *Miranda* v. *Arizona,* deals with a suspect's rights before questioning. *Gideon* v. *Wainwright,* choice (B), deals with the right of the accused to counsel regardless of how poor a person is. Choice (C), *Marbury* v. *Madison,* established the principle of judicial review. *Schenck* v. *United States,* choice (E), established the principle of a clear and present danger.

Test-Taking Strategy

The key words are basic tenet.

53. **The correct answer is (A).** The question is asking you to identify a value that has been, and is still, strongly held by most Americans. Most Americans believe that public education is a local matter for parents and communities to deal with. Choice (C) is one manifestation of this belief, but it is not a restatement of the belief, so choice (C) is incorrect. The question of charter schools, choice (B), is still open for most Americans. Choice (D) may be true, but it does not articulate a value. Choice (E) is a belief held by a number of people, but it is not the correct answer because it deals with only one aspect of public education. It is not a broad enough statement.

Test-Taking Strategy

The key words are major difference.

54. **The correct answer is (A).** In the House, a bill can amended at the following stages: (1) initial committee hearing, (2) subcommittee hearing, (3) Hearings Committee markup, (4) Rules Committee, (5) Speaker at two different points, (6) House floor debate, (7) conference committee, and (8) conference committee report vote. On the Senate side, a bill can be amended at the following stages: (1) Hearings Committee markup, (2) majority leader, (3) Senate floor debate, (4) conference committee, and (5) conference committee report vote. If the president vetoes the bill, the bill can again be amended during the floor votes in either house. Choice (B) is incorrect; seniority is still the overriding factor in who becomes a chair. Choice (C) is a correct statement, but it relates to both houses and the question asks for a contrast between procedures in the House and the Senate. Choice (D) is incorrect because the House uses the Rules Committee and the Senate leadership in consultation with the minority leadership determines the flow of bills to the floor. Choice (E) is incorrect because the whip system works in both chambers.

Test-Taking Strategy

For tiered or multistep questions, decide which of the points are correct, and then find the answer choice that corresponds to that point(s).

55. **The correct answer is (E).** All four strategies could be used by Congress to show its discontent with decisions of the federal judiciary. The Fourteenth Amendment, which overturned *Scott* v. *Sanford* is an example of point I. The Senate hearings that rejected the appointment of Ronald Reagan's nominee to the Supreme Court, Robert Bork, is an example of point II. Point III refers to the remedy in statutory construction, in which a court interprets an act of Congress as unconstitutional and Congress passes new legislation to clarify Congress's intent. According to the Constitution, Congress has the power to establish or change the federal judiciary; the creation of a level of circuit courts by the Federalists was the impetus of *Marbury* v. *Madison*.

56. **The correct answer is (D).** Choices (A), (B), (C), and (E) all relate to the principles or beliefs that Americans consider basic to the function of their government, even if at times the execution has not lived up to the principles, namely slavery and de jure segregation. Political parties, choice (D), were not considered by the Framers when writing the Constitution and in a 1998 National Election Survey, 30 percent of those surveyed agreed that we probably don't need political parties in the United States.

57. **The correct answer is (D).** Choice (A) is illogical because committee hearings are part of the oversight process. Choice (B) is also illogical because agencies help the constituents of members of Congress, not the other way around. This assistance has nothing to do with Congress's control of the agencies. Choice (C) might be correct, but choice (D) is a more complete answer because committee hearings are part of oversight. Choice (E) is illogical given the definition of iron triangles.

58. **The correct answer is (C).** Economic sanctions typically cut off markets for farmers and businesses, making it an unpopular foreign policy strategy. Choices (A), (B), (D), and (E) are all tools that the United States uses in foreign policy.

59. **The correct answer is (E).** Bureaucracies are characterized by a division of labor, choice (A); by hiring based on merit, choice (B), which is supposedly ensured by the use of civil service exams; a nonpartisan workforce, choice (C), ensured by laws protecting employees from certain practices such as being solicited to contribute to political campaigns; and choice (D), rules, or standard operating practices to take care of routine business.

60. **The correct answer is (A).** Even Bill Clinton, a Democrat, sought through his National Performance Review to decrease the rules and regulations under which the government operates. Choices (B) and (E) are the opposite of what has occurred. Rather than fund nonfunded mandates, choice (C), an attempt has been made to eliminate nonfunded mandates. Although presidents have tried to do choice (D), the resistance from the iron triangles has made it so difficult that presidents have given up on their efforts.

SUGGESTIONS FOR FREE-RESPONSE ESSAY 1

Study Strategy

Revise your essay using points from this list that will strengthen it.

You might have chosen the following points and specific cases for your essay analyzing the cartoonist's point of view and your opinion of it. Consider these points as you complete the evaluation of your essay.

Judicial Review/Activism—A Good Thing

- Safeguard for variety of peoples and interests

- Court of last resort, so cases heard are not frivolous

Test-Taking Strategy

First, decide on your interpretation of what the cartoonist is saying. Then list points to support your interpretation and whether or not you agree with the cartoonist.

Judicial Review/Activism—Not Good

- Exaggerated view of the Supreme Court to make the cartoonist's point

- Decisions made on whims, not on close reading of Constitution and/or precedents

- Need narrow interpretations

- No rhyme or reason to decisions

Cases To Illustrate Argument

- *Lemon* v. *Kurtzman*—Funds for private schools for teachers' salaries, textbooks, in nonreligious courses held unconstitutional

- *Board of Regents of California* v. *Bakke*—Using quota system to assign slots in incoming classes under affirmative action plan unconstitutional

- *Gideon* v. *Wainwright*—Overturned precedent in earlier case and ruled that every accused person must have counsel, including those too poor to pay for an attorney

Test-Taking Strategy

Remember to leave a minute or two to proofread each essay before moving on to the next essay.

- *Ohio* v. *Akron Center for Reproductive Health*—Upheld state law requiring prior parental notification for an abortion on a woman younger than eighteen

- *Plessy* v. *Ferguson*—Held that segregated facilities were not unconstitutional as long as they were equal

- *Reno* v. *American Civil Liberties Union*—Relates to part of Communications Decency Act; act stated that sending obscenity over the Internet was illegal; provision declared unconstitutional

- *Roe* v. *Wade*—Overturned all state laws criminalizing abortion

SUGGESTIONS FOR FREE-RESPONSE ESSAY 2

You might have chosen the following points about the close but contentious relationship between the president and Congress and the function of checks and balances. Consider these points as you complete the evaluation of your essay.

Study Strategy

Reading news stories about the government, political campaigns, and politicians in newspapers and news magazines will help you gather current information that you may be able to apply to your essay answers.

- The president and Congress must work closely together to make government work.

- If the president is popular, the president can dominate the national policy agenda.

- If the president is unpopular, Congress can dominate the policy agenda.

- A system of checks and balances operates

  - in the enactment of legislation.

  - in the nomination of federal judges, cabinet officials, and ambassadors.

  - in the ratification of treaties.

- Natural conflicts exist between the president and Congress because

  - they are accountable to different constituencies at different times.

  - of divided government.

  - even if the president and the majority of Congress are of the same party, conflicts over leadership and policies can arise.

- Specific areas of conflict since the 1960s

  - Reining in the budget deficit

  - Cutting taxes versus preserving social programs

  - Size and use of the military

  - Deregulation

  - Devolution of programs to the states and funding to support programs

  - Universal health care, protection of patients

  - Preserving Social Security and Medicare funding and programs

  - Role of the federal government in education

SUGGESTIONS FOR FREE-RESPONSE ESSAY 3

You might have chosen the following points for your essay that discusses the role of bureaucracy in U.S. government. Consider these points as you complete the evaluation of your essay.

Top-Level Of Bureaucracy: Cabinet-Level Departments

- Fourteen Cabinet departments

- Headed by a secretary or attorney general; assistant secretaries, undersecretaries

- Top levels of management appointed by the president with the consent of Senate

- Operate in specific policy areas

- Have own budget and staff

- Agencies and bureaus as operating units

Independent Regulatory Agencies (Agencies, Administrations, and Commissions)

- Independent of president, but in varying degrees

- Headed by single administrator or by a board of commissioners

- Top level appointed by president; confirmed by Senate; commissioners appointed for set terms of office

- Quasi-legislative and quasi-judicial in nature

- Oversees some sector of the economy for the benefit of the general good

- Implements and enforces federal regulations within industry/private sector

- Recent phenomenon; began in 1930s
    - Example: Federal Communications Commission (FCC)
        - Regulates television and radio
        - Licenses television and radio stations
    - Example: Federal Election Commission (FEC)
        - Created by the Federal Election Campaign Act of 1971
        - Responsible for monitoring campaign contributions
        - Provides matching grants to presidential candidates
    - Example: Federal Trade Commission (FTC)
        - Regulates fair trade
        - Encourages competition
        - Evaluates unfair or deceptive advertising or products that may be unsafe

- Example: Occupational Safety and Health Administration (OSHA)
  - Sets safety standards
  - Establishes health standards for the workplace
- Example: Securities and Exchange Commission (SEC)
  - Regulates sales of securities
  - Oversees stock markets

Government Corporations

- Greater degree of freedom to manage businesses

- Provide services for a fee

- Bail out troubled industries such as savings and loan (Resolution Trust Company)

- Manage business operations such as Amtrak, Comsat, Corporation for Public Broadcasting, and the U.S. Postal Service

- Headed by a board of directors

Independent executive agencies

- All agencies/bureaus not covered in one of the other categories

- Provide public services on a large scale

- Heads appointed by president; can be removed by president

  - Example: General Services Administration (GSA)
    - Manages all federal real estate and facilities
  - Example: National Aeronautics and Space Administration (NASA)
    - Responsible for space exploration by humans and space probes
  - Example: Environmental Protection Agency (EPA)
    - Implements laws such as the Clean Air Act

SUGGESTIONS FOR FREE-RESPONSE ESSAY 4

You might have chosen the following points for your essay that analyzes arguments for and against gun control. Consider these points as you complete the evaluation of your essay.

Supporting the Right to Own Guns Under Any Circumstances

- The majority of privately owned weapons are parts of collections or are for hunting.

- A high rate of ownership in an area equals a reduced burglary rate.

- People who use guns to solve family disputes have histories of violent, criminal behavior or prior arrest records.

- Convicted felons are already prohibited from owning guns

- Alcohol and drugs are factors that contribute to violence.

- There is a potential for violence or murder regardless of the type of weapon available.

- The majority of those who keep guns for protection are urban residents.

  - Not criminals or street people

  - For protection of small business

  - Feel less police protection in their areas than in wealthier suburbs

Supporting Gun Control

- Romance with handgun from the myths of the Wild West

- Uncontrolled ownership based on Second Amendment mythology

  - Militia: a military force comprised of ordinary citizens serving as part-time soldiers

  - Members subject to various requirements such as training, supplying own firearms, and engaging in military exercise

  - A form of compulsory military service under states

Test-Taking Strategy

Essays that require an examination of different positions are best organized in block style. Within each block, try organizing by order of importance.

Study Strategy

Be sure you ask a responsible person to evaluate your essays. Then include their suggestions for improvement as you continue to practice writing essays.

- Militia not simply another word for population at large

- Second Amendment written to prevent federal government from disarming state militias

- Today, Second Amendment is an anachronism; no longer have citizen militia like those of the eighteenth century

- National Guard is today's equivalent of "well-regulated militia"

  - More limited membership

  - Weapons supplied by government

  - Not subject to gun control laws; raise no serious Second Amendment issues

- Court Decisions

  - *United States* v. *Miller* (1939)—purpose of Second Amendment to "assure the continuation and render possible the effectiveness" of state militia

  - 1969: Supreme Court upheld New Jersey's strict gun control law

  - 1980: upheld federal laws banning felons from possessing guns

  - In 1965 and 1990: ruled that the term "well-regulated militia" refers to National Guard

  - In 1983: Court let stand ruling that there is no individual right to keep and bear arms under Second Amendment

- Brady Bill

- Other constitutional rights not absolute; e.g., free speech does not protect libel

- Guns bring disaster.

  - Kennedy assassinations

  - Martin Luther King Jr. assassination

  - Riots in cities

  - Snipers in schools and other public places

- Violence commonplace, result of media

- Accidents in homes

- Guns a leading cause of death among young African-American males

SELF-EVALUATION RUBRIC FOR THE ADVANCED PLACEMENT ESSAYS

	8–9	5–7	2–4	0–1
Overall Impression	Demonstrates excellent understanding of U.S. government and legal system; outstanding writing; thorough and effective; incisive	Demonstrates good understanding of U.S. government and legal system; good writing competence	Reveals simplistic thinking and/or immature understanding of U.S. government and legal system; fails to respond adequately to the question; little or no analysis	Very little or no understanding of U.S. government and legal system; unacceptably brief; fails to respond to the question; little clarity
Understanding of the U.S. Government	Scholarly; excellent understanding of the question; effective and incisive; in-depth critical analysis; includes apt, specific references; acknowledges other views	Mostly accurate use of information about U.S. government and legal system; good understanding of the question; often perceptive and clear; includes specific references and critical analysis	Some inaccuracies in information regarding U.S. government; superficial understanding and treatment of the question; lack of adequate knowledge about U.S. government; overgeneralized	Serious errors in presenting information about U.S. government and legal system; extensive misreading of the question and little supporting evidence; completely off the topic
Development	Original, unique, and/or intriguing thesis; excellent use of fundamentals and principles of U.S. government; thoroughly developed; conclusion shows applicability of thesis to other situations	Adequate thesis; satisfactory use of knowledge of U.S. government; competent development; acceptable conclusion	Inadequate, irrelevant, or illogical thesis; little use of knowledge of government; some development; unsatisfactory, inapplicable, or nonexistent conclusion	Lacking both thesis and conclusion; little or no evidence of knowledge of U.S. government
Conventions of English	Meticulously and thoroughly organized; coherent and unified; virtually error free	Reasonably organized; mostly coherent and unified; few or some errors	Somewhat organized; some incoherence and lack of unity; some major errors	Little or no organization; incoherent and void of unity; extremely flawed

Rate yourself in each of the categories below. Enter the numbers on the lines below. Be as honest as possible so you will know what areas need work. Then calculate the average of the four numbers to determine your final score. It is difficult to score yourself objectively, so you may wish to ask a respected friend or teacher to assess your essays for a more accurate reflection of their strengths and weaknesses. On the AP test itself, a reader will rate your essays on a scale of 0 to 9, with 9 being the highest.

Each category is rated 9 (high) to 0 (incompetent).

ESSAY 1
SELF-EVALUATION
Overall Impression _____
Understanding of U.S. Government _____
Development _____
Conventions of English _____

TOTAL _____
    Divide by 4 for final score. _____

ESSAY 1
OBJECTIVE EVALUATION
Overall Impression _____
Understanding of U.S. Government _____
Development _____
Conventions of English _____

TOTAL _____
    Divide by 4 for final score. _____

ESSAY 2
SELF-EVALUATION
Overall Impression _____
Understanding of U.S. Government _____
Development _____
Conventions of English _____

TOTAL _____
    Divide by 4 for final score. _____

ESSAY 2
OBJECTIVE EVALUATION
Overall Impression _____
Understanding of U.S. Government _____
Development _____
Conventions of English _____

TOTAL _____
    Divide by 4 for final score. _____

ESSAY 3
SELF-EVALUATION
Overall Impression _____
Understanding of U.S. Government _____
Development _____
Conventions of English _____

TOTAL _____
    Divide by 4 for final score. _____

ESSAY 3
OBJECTIVE EVALUATION
Overall Impression _____
Understanding of U.S. Government _____
Development _____
Conventions of English _____

TOTAL _____
    Divide by 4 for final score. _____

ESSAY 4
SELF-EVALUATION
Overall Impression _____
Understanding of U.S. Government _____
Development _____
Conventions of English _____

TOTAL _____
    Divide by 4 for final score. _____

ESSAY 4
OBJECTIVE EVALUATION
Overall Impression _____
Understanding of U.S. Government _____
Development _____
Conventions of English _____

TOTAL _____
    Divide by 4 for final score. _____

*Peterson's AP Success:
Government & Politics*

Practice Test 3

AP GOVERNMENT AND POLITICS

On the front page of the test booklet, you will find some information about the test. Because you have studied this book, none of it should be new to you, and much of it is similar to other standardized tests that you have taken.

The page will tell you that the following exam will take 2 hours and 25 minutes—45 minutes for the multiple-choice portion, Section I, and 100 minutes for the essay part, Section II. There are two booklets for the exam, one for the multiple-choice section and one for the essays.

The page in your test booklet will also say that SECTION I

- is 45 minutes.
- has 60 questions.
- counts for 50 percent of your total score.

Then you will find a sentence in capital letters telling you not to open your exam booklet until the monitor tells you to open it.

Other instructions will tell you to be careful when you fill in the ovals on the answer sheet. Fill in each oval completely. If you erase an answer, erase it completely. If you skip a question, be sure to skip the answer oval for it. You will not receive any credit for work done in the test booklet, but you may use it for making notes.

You will also find a paragraph about the guessing penalty—a deduction of one-quarter point for every wrong answer—but also words of advice about guessing if you know something about the questions and can eliminate several of the answers.

The final paragraph will remind you to work effectively and to pace yourself. You are told that not everyone will be able to answer all the questions and it is preferable to skip questions that are difficult and come back to them if you have time.

GOVERNMENT AND POLITICS

| SECTION I | TIME—45 MINUTES | 60 QUESTIONS |

Directions: Each question or incomplete sentence is followed by five suggested responses. Select the best answer and fill in the corresponding oval on the answer sheet.

1. The principle of judicial review was established in

   (A) Article III of the U.S. Constitution.
   (B) *McCulloch* v. *Maryland*.
   (C) the Judiciary Act of 1789.
   (D) the supremacy clause.
   (E) *Marbury* v. *Madison*.

2. All of the following are independent regulatory agencies EXCEPT

   (A) the Federal Reserve Board.
   (B) the Food and Drug Administration.
   (C) the National Labor Relations Board.
   (D) the Federal Communications Commission.
   (E) the Federal Trade Commission.

3. Which of the following is most probably a single-issue interest group?

   (A) Association of State/County/Municipal Employees
   (B) American Medical Association
   (C) American Bar Association
   (D) United Auto Workers
   (E) National Rifle Association

4. Which of the following groups is least likely to vote for a Democratic presidential candidate?

   (A) Women
   (B) Catholics
   (C) Protestants
   (D) Labor
   (E) Urbanites

5. The replacement of the Aid to Families with Dependent Children Act with the Responsibility and Work Opportunity Reconciliation Act is an example of

   (A) judicial review.
   (B) devolution.
   (C) realignment.
   (D) the shift from revenue sharing to block grants.
   (E) flexibility in the legislative process.

6. Primaries are governed by

   I. party rules.
   II. state law.
   III. federal law.

   (A) I only
   (B) II only
   (C) III only
   (D) I and II
   (E) I, II, and III

7. "In the extended republic of the United States, and among the great variety of interests, parties, and sects which it embraces, a condition of a majority of the whole society could seldom take place on any other principles than those of justice and the general good."

James Madison wrote these words in *The Federalist,* No. 51, about

(A) the rise of factions.
(B) the need for a system of checks and balances.
(C) the need for a system of federalism.
(D) majority rule and minority protection.
(E) why the Articles of Confederation did not work.

8. The welfare reform bill signed into law in 1996 is politically significant because it

(A) provides a time limit on benefits to recipients.
(B) is the first overhaul of welfare since the original legislation was passed in 1935.
(C) was supported by a Democratic president.
(D) provides block grants to states.
(E) extends to the food stamps program many of the welfare provisions for limiting eligibility.

9. The development of a political culture is influenced by

I. families.
II. religious organizations.
III. civic organizations.
IV. the media.
V. political activities.

(A) I
(B) I, II, and IV
(C) I, II, IV, and V
(D) II, III, IV, and IV
(E) I, II, III, IV, and V

10. The Motor Voter Act includes all of the following provisions EXCEPT

(A) people who are eligible to vote can register by checking off a box when applying for or renewing their driver's license.
(B) voter registration forms must be available in public assistance offices and in military recruitment centers.
(C) the Act has increased voter registration and voter turnout.
(D) voter registration may also be done by mail.
(E) periodically states must send questionnaires to all registered voters in order to update voting lists by removing the names of people who have died and by correcting changes of address.

11. Which of the following elections has the lowest turnout of voters?

(A) Statewide elections in odd-numbered years
(B) Presidential elections
(C) Midterm Congressional elections
(D) Local and municipal elections
(E) Presidential primary elections

12. Which of the following is not stated directly in the Constitution?

(A) Right to privacy
(B) Ban on slavery
(C) Protection of the right to vote
(D) Ban on the use of poll taxes
(E) Right to a speedy and public trial

GO ON TO THE NEXT PAGE

13. The most important reason why senators hesitate to invoke cloture is that

    (A) the Senate has a greater tradition than the House of free and unfettered debate.
    (B) censuring a fellow senator is very serious.
    (C) it is difficult to muster the two-thirds vote necessary to invoke cloture.
    (D) a senator who votes to close off another's filibuster may face retaliation in the future when he or she wishes to stage a filibuster.
    (E) the threat of cloture can kill a bill.

14. The major limiting force on how federal judges interpret the law is

    (A) senatorial courtesy.
    (B) precedent.
    (C) judicial review.
    (D) nonexistent because federal judges are appointed for life.
    (E) the Senate's advise and consent function.

15. All of the following may enter into voters' decisions about whom to vote for as president EXCEPT

    (A) party loyalty.
    (B) whether or not the choice will result in gridlock in Congress.
    (C) candidate appeal.
    (D) prospective issue voting.
    (E) how voters feel about the job the outgoing president did.

16. The Civil Rights Act of 1964 was upheld by the Supreme Court on the basis of

    (A) the supremacy clause.
    (B) concurrent powers.
    (C) extradition.
    (D) the commerce clause.
    (E) the full faith and credit clause.

17. A major problem with recent presidential primaries is that

    (A) the calendar is backloaded.
    (B) as the primary season wears on and candidates drop out, fewer voters go to the polls.
    (C) primaries attract the more ardent political party supporters, so candidates play to the extremes of the parties.
    (D) the media attention makes it difficult to assess where the candidates stand on issues.
    (E) there is a mix of open and closed primaries.

18. All of the following are indications of how pervasive the two-party system is in U.S. government EXCEPT

    (A) closed primaries.
    (B) how members are assigned to Congressional committees.
    (C) lack of effective third parties.
    (D) how the Speaker of the House is selected.
    (E) the need for the electoral college.

19. Which of the following acts was passed in response to presidential actions that Congress believed went beyond the responsible use of presidential power?

    I. Freedom of Information Act
    II. War Powers Act
    III. Budget and Impoundment Control Act

    (A) I only
    (B) II only
    (C) III only
    (D) I and II
    (E) II and III

Peterson's AP Success: Government & Politics

20. Which of the following is not an example of how political parties function as linkage institutions in the U.S. political system?

(A) Elected officials can usually count on fellow party members to support their legislative initiatives.

(B) Voters know that if they vote for a candidate from the Democratic Party, he or she will most likely support social programs and gun control.

(C) The two major political parties have clearly defined policy agendas that they promote.

(D) Few officials are elected to office without a party endorsement.

(E) The political parties determine how the media covers their policy agendas.

21. Which of the following were to be indirectly elected according to the Constitution as originally drafted?

I. President of the United States
II. U.S. senators
III. Members of the House of Representatives
IV. Justices of the Supreme Court

(A) I
(B) II
(C) I and II
(D) II and III
(E) I and IV

22. The growth in the power and influence of the presidency by the end of the twentieth century can be attributed to all the following EXCEPT

(A) the Constitution.

(B) the ability of presidents to appeal to the public through the use of the media.

(C) decisions of the Supreme Court.

(D) actions of Congress.

(E) party realignment.

GO ON TO THE NEXT PAGE

Question 23 refers to the table below.

Comparing Presidential Elections, 1860 and 1992

1860				
Party	Candidate	Popular Vote (in millions)	Percentage of Popular Vote	Electoral Vote
Republican	Abraham Lincoln	1.8	39.8	180
Democrat (N)	Stephen A. Douglas	1.3	29.5	12
Democrat (S)	John C. Breckinridge	0.8	18.0	72
Constitutional	John Bell	0.5	0.01	39

1992				
Party	Candidate	Popular Vote (in millions)	Percentage of Popular Vote	Electoral Vote
Democrat	William Clinton	44.9	43	370
Republican	George Bush	39.1	37.4	168
Independent	Ross H. Perot	19.7	18.9	0
Other		0.8	0.8	0

23. Which of the following statements is best supported by the data in the table?

(A) Both Lincoln and Clinton won their first terms in office with less than a majority of the popular vote.

(B) Third parties have the potential to throw elections into the House of Representatives.

(C) Ross Perot took more votes than any other third-party candidate before him.

(D) Ross Perot's on-again-off-again campaign on the Reform Party ticket generated enthusiasm among many nonvoters and brought out a record number of voters.

(E) The contests in 1860 and 1992 were pivotal elections that brought out more voters than participated in the next presidential election.

24. All of the following are reasons why the U.S. Supreme Court agrees to hear a case EXCEPT

 (A) that the Supreme Court disagrees with the lower court's decision.
 (B) the input of the solicitor general asking that the Supreme Court hear the case.
 (C) the broader significance of the case.
 (D) that the case involves a constitutional issue.
 (E) four justices have agreed to a writ of certiorari.

25. All of the following are examples of the jurisdiction of federal courts EXCEPT

 (A) the criminal case against Manuel Noriega, the former head of Panama, over drug smuggling.
 (B) the lawsuit between New Jersey and New York over ownership of an island.
 (C) the wrongful death lawsuit brought against U.S. law enforcement agencies and officers by relatives of the Branch Davidian cult.
 (D) a lawsuit for damages brought against New York City by an alleged victim charging violation of his civil rights during arrest.
 (E) criminal prosecution against a shipping company for polluting the coast after an oil spill.

26. Supporting one another's legislation in Congress is known as

 (A) pork-barrel legislation.
 (B) logrolling.
 (C) a rider.
 (D) senatorial courtesy.
 (E) iron triangle.

27. Although the news media greatly influences public opinion, which of the following factors limit how much any individual is influenced?

 I. Political interest
 II. Selectivity
 III. A person's understanding of the importance of a news story or political analysis
 IV. Latency

 (A) I and II
 (B) II and III
 (C) III and IV
 (D) I, II, and III
 (E) I, II, III, and IV

28. All of the following are conditions that must exist in a constitutional democracy in order for it to function effectively EXCEPT

 (A) a high level of literacy.
 (B) a relatively well-developed market economy with private ownership of property.
 (C) freedom of speech.
 (D) a variety of social institutions with which people identify.
 (E) a shared belief in certain democratic values.

GO ON TO THE NEXT PAGE

29. Which of the following responsibilities belongs to the House but not to the Senate?

    (A) Ratifying treaties with foreign countries
    (B) Approving nominees to the Supreme Court
    (C) Sending the annual budget to the Office of Management and Budget for research
    (D) Approving ambassadors
    (E) Impeaching federal judges and certain other high-level elected officials

30. The most influential committee in the House is most likely the

    (A) Budget Committee.
    (B) National Security Committee.
    (C) Rules Committee.
    (D) Conference Committee.
    (E) Judiciary Committee.

31. In the House, the selection of members to committees rests with

    (A) the Speaker.
    (B) the majority and minority leaders of the House.
    (C) the majority leader alone.
    (D) committee chairs.
    (E) two committees, one for the Republicans and one for the Democrats.

32. Since the mid-twentieth century, the regions of the nation that have consistently gained seats in the House of Representatives in reapportionment are the

    I.   Midwest.
    II. Northeast.
    III. Southeast.
    IV. Southwest.
    V.   Pacific Northwest.

    (A) I only
    (B) II and III
    (C) III only
    (D) III and IV
    (E) III, IV, and V

33. Which of the following statements about health care in the United States is NOT true?

    (A) The availability of health care depends on income level.
    (B) The interests of the working poor are seldom heard in the ongoing debate over providing health insurance.
    (C) Insurance companies have lobbied to stop efforts to establish a national health insurance system managed by the federal government.
    (D) No group represents the elderly in the debate over health care.
    (E) Health-care providers have fought efforts to limit what they can charge for their services.

34. Which of the following is not an accurate statement about public opinion polling?

    (A) A public opinion poll can gauge the intensity of people's attitudes toward a person or issue.
    (B) A public opinion poll is a picture of people's attitudes at a given point in time.
    (C) A public opinion poll can show the extent of consensus or polarization on an issue or person.
    (D) By exposing people's real wants, needs, and hopes, public opinion polling can help leaders fashion public policy to satisfy these concerns.
    (E) Public opinion polling may understate salience.

35. A major criticism of the news media's coverage of political campaigns is that

(A) the media tends to focus on where candidates are in the polls rather than where they stand on the issues.

(B) the media gives equal coverage to all candidates regardless of the seriousness of their campaigns.

(C) the media investigates candidates' campaign claims rather than reporting without comment on what candidates say.

(D) the media tends to focus on personality and character.

(E) candidates and parties manipulate news coverage with sound bites and photo opportunities.

36. Which of the following pairs of amendments places limitations on the national government?

(A) First and Second

(B) Third and Fourth

(C) Second and Third

(D) Fifth and Ninth

(E) Ninth and Tenth

37. All of the following statements explaining how the president and Congress share responsibility and control over the federal bureaucracy are true EXCEPT

(A) Congress establishes agencies, but the president may move responsibilities from agency to agency.

(B) Congress approves the appropriations to fund agencies, but the president submits the initial budget and lobbies for it.

(C) Congress provides oversight of the work of agencies, but the president has the power to set agency policy through the use of executive orders, declarations, and proclamations over which Congress has no control.

(D) the president appoints top-level non-civil service bureaucrats to oversee departments, but Congress has the power to reject political appointees.

(E) Congress passes legislation relating to federal agencies and to the civil service system, but the president has the power to veto it.

38. All of the following are examples of the various functions of Congress EXCEPT

(A) passing a law to ban assault rifles.

(B) campaigning to aid the reelection of a fellow member of Congress.

(C) holding hearings and voting on a presidential nominee to a federal district court.

(D) voting to bring a multimillion-dollar federal dam project to a region.

(E) acting as an advocate with the Veterans' Administration for a constituent who has been denied medical care.

GO ON TO THE NEXT PAGE

Question 39 refers to the following table.

Uncontrollable Federal Expenditures (in billions)

Year	Social Security and Other Retirement Benefits	Medical Benefits	Other Payments to Individuals	Net Interest on the Debt	Prior Obligations	Other Uncontrollables	Total	Percentage of Budget
1995	405.7	275.3	77.9	232.2	233.2	9.8	1.234	81.2
1996	418.1	293.6	76.9	241.1	227.9	9.2	1.266	81.2
1997	441.1	313.9	75.9	244.0	228.8	9.0	1.312	82.0
1998	453.0	324.3	77.0	243.4	228.0	12.2	1.337	81.0
1999 (est)	469.2	348.1	85.2	227.2	243.9	21.5	1.339	80.8

Source: *The Budget of the U.S. Government*

39. Based on data in the table, the percentage of the budget that is represented by uncontrollable expenditures declined in 1999 because

(A) the interest on the national debt declined.

(B) the increase in entitlements was offset by the decrease in the national debt.

(C) entitlements are based on legislation that requires a certain level of payment.

(D) using the term "uncontrollable outlays" is another way of saying entitlements.

(E) the increase in uncontrollable outlays was offset by the decrease in the interest payment on the national debt.

40. NAFTA is unlike GATT because

    (A) NAFTA seeks to eliminate barriers to trade in North America only, whereas GATT promotes free trade worldwide.

    (B) NAFTA works only with North American nations to shore up their economies, whereas GATT provides funding for programs in developing nations.

    (C) NAFTA is a mutual defense treaty organization for the North Atlantic nations, whereas GATT is a global network of defense pacts.

    (D) NAFTA is a nongovernmental organization that is interested in promoting trade, whereas GATT is a program of the IMF to promote trade.

    (E) NAFTA regulates the trade policies of multinational corporations in North America, whereas GATT regulates the trade policies of multinational corporations worldwide.

41. A major difference between the House and the Senate is

    (A) that the House uses the subcommittee to mark up a bill and the Senate uses the original committee for mark up.

    (B) that the House requires that riders be relevant to the bill to which they are attached, whereas the Senate is looser with regard to riders.

    (C) that members of the House use filibusters frequently to kill bills, whereas the Senate rarely uses filibusters.

    (D) that majority and minority leaders in the House determine the rules that will govern floor debate on a bill, whereas in the Senate, the Rules Committee determines the limits of debate.

    (E) the number of standing committees.

42. A loosely allied group of consultants, officials, activists, and interest groups with technical expertise working together to influence legislation is known as

    (A) an iron triangle.
    (B) a lobby.
    (C) an issue network.
    (D) an iron rectangle.
    (E) a constituency.

43. Which of the following statements is not true about voting behavior?

    (A) The more education a person has, the more likely the person is to vote.

    (B) More women vote than men.

    (C) With the exception of the very old and ill, the older a person is, the more likely that person is to vote.

    (D) The lower the status of a person's job, the more likely the person is to vote.

    (E) African Americans and Hispanics are less likely to vote than whites.

44. A significant effect of the proliferation of single-interest groups is

    (A) the presence of factionalism.

    (B) support for the elite, or class, theory of government.

    (C) further entrenchment by the members of iron triangles.

    (D) short-term fragmented policies that create wasteful and ineffective government.

    (E) an emphasis on fundraising by PACs.

GO ON TO THE NEXT PAGE

45. In determining its defense budget, the United States must consider all of the following EXCEPT

(A) the possibility of conventional warfare breaking out in nations of concern.
(B) nuclear proliferation among nations of concern.
(C) terrorism.
(D) WTO.
(E) germ warfare.

46. Substantive due process has been used by the Supreme Court in recent years to protect

(A) freedom of speech.
(B) freedom of assembly.
(C) the right to counsel.
(D) the right to privacy.
(E) civil rights in general.

47. The major concern voiced about independent regulatory agencies is that

(A) they are too independent of both the president, who appoints commission members, and Congress.
(B) the regulations written by these independent agencies tend to stifle competition.
(C) the federal government is too quick to set up agencies to deal with ailing industries.
(D) commission members are often chosen from the industries they are to regulate.
(E) commission members can only be dismissed for just cause.

48. Which of the following amendments to the Constitution defined U.S. citizenship?

(A) Fourteenth
(B) Fifteenth
(C) Nineteenth
(D) Twenty-Second
(E) Twenty-Sixth

49. In the last few decades of the twentieth century, the hold of the major political parties on the electorate was weakened by all of the following EXCEPT

(A) crossover voting in primaries.
(B) the substitution of direct primaries for conventions.
(C) split-ticket voting in general elections.
(D) news media coverage of campaigns.
(E) the rise of political interest groups.

50. Since the administrations of Franklin Roosevelt, which of the following functions of the presidency has increased dramatically? The president's role as

(A) chief administrator.
(B) chief legislator.
(C) chief diplomat.
(D) national morale builder.
(E) party leader.

51. Which of the following areas was exempted from the across-the-board budget cuts in the Gramm-Rudman-Hollings Act?

(A) Military pay raises
(B) Entitlements
(C) Farm subsidies
(D) Missile defense systems
(E) Federal subsidies for rail lines

52. The importance of recent Supreme Court decisions regarding parochial education and government funding is that the decisions

  (A) have distinguished between aid to the school and aid to the child.
  (B) have allowed income tax credits for parents who send their children to private schools but not to parochial schools.
  (C) have struck down practices such as student-led prayers before football games.
  (D) have begun to chip away at the wall between church and state.
  (E) have allowed the use of tax dollars to pay for textbooks and computers for student use in parochial schools.

53. The doctrine of cruel and unusual punishment has been used both to uphold decisions of lower courts and to strike down decisions in cases involving

  (A) the Fourteenth Amendment.
  (B) the Miranda rule.
  (C) the principle of clear and present danger.
  (D) the death penalty.
  (E) right to counsel.

54. Which of the following statements explains the change in voting patterns in the South since the 1960s?

  (A) Since the civil rights movement, more African Americans are registered to vote in the South and they typically vote Democratic.
  (B) The Southern economy relies less on agriculture than it once did.
  (C) Southern whites have found that the Republican Party more clearly defines issues of importance to them.
  (D) The South has experienced a large influx of Northerners in the last few decades.
  (E) In general, voters in the South and West share the same concern over family values and gun control.

55. One reason that abolishment of the electoral college meets resistance is that

  (A) critics contend that a direct election would result in a national campaign that duplicates the attention now given to primaries and caucuses in states with large populations.
  (B) some groups believe the current electoral system is more favorable to them than a direct national election would be.
  (C) critics contend that third parties cannot really affect the outcome of a presidential election.
  (D) Republicans believe that their strength in the South and West would be undercut in a direct election.
  (E) strict constructionists do not believe the original intent of the Framers of the Constitution should be abandoned.

GO ON TO THE NEXT PAGE

56. Many political scientists see the outcomes of the presidential elections of the last three decades of the twentieth century as proof of

   I. party dealignment.
  II. party realignment.
 III. divided government.
 IV. split-ticket voting.
  V. party neutrality.

(A) I
(B) II
(C) III and IV
(D) I, III, IV, and V
(E) II, III, IV, and V

57. A goal of personal and corporate income tax policy is

(A) redistribution of wealth.
(B) balancing the budget.
(C) stabilizing the economy.
(D) keeping inflation in check.
(E) balancing monetary and fiscal policies.

58. Cuts proposed by presidents to the funding of regulatory agencies, which result in a reduction in regulatory oversight,

(A) are an example of how presidents use executive management to block legislative authority.
(B) are a way to block the effectiveness of iron triangles.
(C) are not subject to a legislative check.
(D) are known as deregulation.
(E) were held to be unconstitutional by the Supreme Court on the same basis as the line-item veto.

59. "This Constitution, and the laws of the United States which shall be made in pursuance thereof, and all treaties made . . . under the authority of the United States, shall be the supreme law of the land; and judges in every state shall be bound thereby."

This excerpt is from

(A) Article I.
(B) Article III.
(C) Article IV.
(D) Article VI.
(E) Article VII.

60. All of the following are correct interpretations of the article of the Constitution quoted above EXCEPT

(A) states cannot write constitutions or laws that conflict with the provisions of the Constitution.
(B) the actions of local governments in regard to passing laws are governed by this same article.
(C) states cannot use the powers reserved to the states to interfere with the provisions of the Constitution.
(D) the Supreme Court is the final arbiter of the Constitution.
(E) state officials and judges must take an oath to uphold the Constitution.

STOP If you finish before time is called, you may check your work on this section only. Do not turn to any other section in the test.

SECTION II	**TIME—100 MINUTES**

Directions: You have 100 minutes to answer all four of the following questions. It is suggested that you take a few minutes to outline each answer. Spend approximately one fourth of your time (25 minutes) on each question. Support the ideas in your essay with substantive examples where appropriate. Make sure to number each of your responses with the number that corresponds to the question.

1. Historically, the Supreme Court developed three tests to evaluate the constitutionality of freedom of speech cases—the bad tendency doctrine, the clear and present danger doctrine, and the preferred position doctrine. Although these historic principles provide a framework for discussion, the Supreme Court is more likely to use the following doctrines to measure the limits of governmental regulation of speech. Choose one doctrine, define it, and discuss how the courts have applied it.

   - Prior restraint
   - Vagueness
   - Least drastic means
   - Content and viewpoint neutrality
   - Commercial speech

2. The development of the federal budget has long been a major area of public concern. In the latter half of the twentieth century, reform efforts by Congress were focused on giving the legislative branch greater control over the budget process. Analyze the effectiveness of Congressional budget reforms made since 1974.

GO ON TO THE NEXT PAGE

Percent of Eligible Voters Voting by Gender

Year	1980	1982	1984	1986	1988	1990	1992	1994	1996
Registered	59.2	48.5	59.9	46.0	57.4	45.0	61.3	45.0	54.2
Male	59.1	48.7	59.0	45.8	56.4	44.6	60.2	44.7	52.8
Female	59.4	48.4	60.8	46.1	58.3	45.4	62.3	45.3	55.5

3. Using the table above and your knowledge of U.S. politics, answer the following questions:

(A) What are the overall trends in voting behavior for registered voters?

(B) What similarities and differences do you find in men's and women's voting habits?

(C) What factors might account for these differences?

4. Two of the most important issues on the national agenda since the 1990s have been health care and Social Security. Evaluate the impact of public opinion on policy implementation and dollar allocation for these two issues.

Peterson's AP Success: Government & Politics

ANSWERS AND EXPLANATIONS

Quick-Score Answers

1. E	11. D	21. C	31. E	41. B	51. B
2. B	12. A	22. E	32. D	42. C	52. A
3. E	13. D	23. A	33. D	43. D	53. D
4. C	14. B	24. E	34. E	44. D	54. C
5. B	15. B	25. D	35. A	45. D	55. B
6. D	16. D	26. B	36. E	46. D	56. D
7. D	17. C	27. D	37. C	47. D	57. A
8. C	18. E	28. C	38. B	48. A	58. A
9. E	19. E	29. E	39. E	49. B	59. D
10. C	20. E	30. C	40. A	50. A	60. D

PRACTICE TEST 3

Test-Taking Strategy

For not/except questions, ask yourself if the answer is correct in the context of the question. If it is, cross it off and go on to the next answer.

1. **The correct answer is (E).** Article III of the Constitution, choice (A), established the outline of a federal judiciary system, and the Judiciary Act, choice (C), filled in the court system. The supremacy clause of Article VI, choice (D), makes the Constitution the supreme law of the land, but it does not detail the Supreme Court's duties, so choice (D) is incorrect. The decision in choice (B), *McCulloch* v. *Maryland,* established that federal law takes precedence when state and federal law conflict.

2. **The correct answer is (B).** The FDA is a regulatory agency within the Department of Health and Human Services, so choice (B) is not an independent regulatory agency and is, therefore, the correct answer. Independent regulatory agencies are run by small commissions appointed by the president. Commissioners can be removed only by the president and only for just cause, a vague term that has not been tested. The regulations written by regulatory agencies—whether independent agencies or those within departments—have the force of law and are known as administration law. Choices (A), (C), (D), and (E) are all independent regulatory agencies.

3. The correct answer is (E). A single-issue interest group is one (1) that has a limited focus, (2) that tends not be interested in compromise, (3) and whose members are new to political involvement. This definition matches the NRA, choice (E). While choices (A), (B), (C), and (D) are all dedicated to aiding their membership, each of which is admittedly limited, the range of issues that each group addresses is fairly broad. Compromise is less of an issue to these organizations and their members, many of whom are long-time supporters.

4. The correct answer is (C). As a group, Protestants tend to vote for Republican presidential candidates. Women, choice (A), tend to vote for the Democratic party because of its focus on issues of importance to them, such as gun control and education. It is worth noting that in the 1996 election, women voted for Clinton 54 to 37 percent, thereby making the gender gap significant enough to elect Clinton. In the 2000 election, Democrat Al Gore won the women's vote by 12 percent. Catholics, choice (B), have traditionally been Democrats dating back to the waves of immigrants of the late nineteenth and early twentieth centuries; the predominantly Catholic Hispanic immigrants of the late twentieth century continued in this tradition of supporting the Democratic Party. Labor unions, choice (D), have been and continue to be some of the staunchest supporters of the Democratic Party. Many urbanites, choice (E), are African American and Hispanic and thus support the national Democratic slate.

5. The correct answer is (B). Devolution is the return of functions and responsibilities from the federal government to the states. It began with the 1984 election. Choice (A) is illogical, as is choice (C). The former refers to the power of the courts to declare laws—federal or state—unconstitutional; the latter refers to a shift in power between the two major political parties. The new act provides funding to the states in the form of block grants, but the AFDC did not provide for revenue sharing, so choice (D) is incorrect. Revenue sharing was a form of passing money back to the states that began with President Nixon but which Ronald Reagan did not like. He ended it in 1982. Choice (E) is off the point.

6. **The correct answer is (D).** Both party rules (I) and state laws (II) govern primaries. Federal law (III) does not govern how primaries are run, although voters cannot be discriminated against in their attempt to vote. Only choice (D) contains the correct points.

7. **The correct answer is (D).** *The Federalist,* No. 51, is James Madison's answer to the Anti-Federalists who were concerned about the potential for a "tyranny of the majority" under the Constitution. In his essay, Madison deals with the concept of majority rule with protection for minority groups and individuals. While the reference to "the great variety of interests, parties, and sects" may lead you to believe that Madison is talking about the rise of factions, choice (A), factions are the subject of No. 10 of *The Federalist* papers. Choices (B), (C), and (D) are irrelevant to the quotation.

8. **The correct answer is (C).** Choices (A), (D), and (E) refer to provisions of the Personal Responsibility and Work Opportunity Reconciliation Act (PRA) of 1996, but they do not describe the political significance of the provisions or of the Act itself. That the bill was the first overhaul of the system since 1935 may be significant, but that a Democratic president supported welfare reform in the face of opposition from his own party and from segments of his constituency is significant politically.

9. **The correct answer is (E).** All five factors work to create a nation's political culture, the shared beliefs, values, and standards of behavior that govern the relationships of citizens with their government and with one another. Families (I), religious organizations (II), the media (IV), and schools, which are not included in this list but are likewise a factor in developing a political culture, also work together in the political socialization of people.

10. **The correct answer is (C).** While it is estimated that 12 million new voters had registered by the 1996 election as a result of the Motor Voter Act of 1993, there was not a parallel increase in voter turnout and the turnout declined precipitously for the midterm elections in 1998. Choice (C) then is untrue and, therefore, the correct answer.

11. **The correct answer is (D).** The farther down the ladder the offices are from the presidency, the lower the turnout. Even lower than local and municipal elections are the primary contests for these offices. Off-year statewide elections, choice (A), attract fewer voters than when state offices are filled at the same time as the presidency or in an election year when a race for some other federal office, such as a U.S. Congressional seat is on the ballot, choice (C). Presidential elections, choice (B), attract the most voters, but presidential primaries, choice (E), attract fewer than the election itself.

12. **The correct answer is (A).** The decisions in *Roe* v. *Wade* and *Doe* v. *Bolton* established and interpreted the right to privacy based on the Third, Fourth, and Fifth Amendments of the Constitution. The Thirteenth Amendment specifically prohibits slavery, choice (B). Article I, Section 2, Clause 1 and the Fifteenth, Nineteenth, Twenty-Third, Twenty-Fourth, and Twenty-Sixth Amendments all protect the right to vote, choice (C). The Twenty-Fourth Amendment eliminates poll taxes in federal elections, choice (D). The Sixth Amendment guarantees the right to a speedy and public trial, choice (E).

13. **The correct answer is (D).** Choices (A), (C), (D), and (E) are all true statements about cloture. While tradition, choice (A), is important in the Senate, it is not the motivating force behind the rare use of cloture. Choices (C) and (E) are not causes but results. Choice (D) is the major reason why cloture is seldom invoked. Senators have to have a very important reason to justify using cloture because few want to risk having cloture used against them. Choice (B) is a true statement, but it has nothing to do with cloture, so it is incorrect.

Test-Taking Strategy

The key word is major.

14. **The correct answer is (B).** The use of precedent, or stare decisis, is the application of previous court decisions, including the rulings of superior courts, to the case at hand. Not only federal court judges but all court judges—local and state—use precedents as the guide to their decisions. Under choice (A), senatorial courtesy, the senator from the state where a federal judge will preside is asked if there are any objections to the appointment of that judge; if there are, the judge is not confirmed. Judicial review, choice (C), is the principle by which the courts may declare actions of the legislative and executive branches unconstitutional. Choice (D) is incorrect. Choice (E) is illogical in the context of the question; it doesn't have any bearing on the issue.

Test-Taking Strategy

For not/except questions, ask yourself if the answer is true in the context of the question. If it is, cross it off and go on to the next answer.

15. **The correct answer is (B).** Choice (A), party loyalty, is still the major factor, although voters reacted to candidate appeal, choice (C), in electing Ronald Reagan and Bill Clinton. Choice (D), prospective issue voting, what candidates say they will do, may be less of a factor than retrospective issue voting, which is described by choice (E). Choice (B) is illogical and, therefore, the correct answer.

16. **The correct answer is (D).** Because of Article I, Section 8, Clause 3, Congress has the power to regulate commerce among the states. The Supreme Court used this power as the basis for finding that local discrimination in public accommodations is harmful to interstate commerce. Choice (A), the supremacy clause, establishes the Constitution as the supreme law of the land, but it does not relate to this case. Choice (B), concurrent powers, means that the federal government and state governments hold some powers jointly, such as the power to levy taxes. It is an illogical choice here, as is choice (C), extradition. Choice (E), the full faith and credit clause, refers to the civil laws of states and does not relate to this case.

17. **The correct answer is (C).** As result of choice (C), the candidates may obscure where they really stand on issues in order to play to the conservative right in the Republican Party and the left-leaning liberal wing of the Democratic Party. Candidates then spend some time during the general election trying to get back to the center in order to appeal to moderates. Choice (A) is the opposite of what has happened; the primary season has become frontloaded. While the media may tend to dwell on the personality of candidates during primary season, the candidates' own push for more televised debates even in local areas helps to get out their message on issues, making choice (D) as problematic as the answer. Choice (E) is a true statement about primaries, but the mix is not a problem.

18. **The correct answer is (E).** The electoral college was included in the Constitution before there were any political parties, so on first reading, choice (E) should be your best candidate for being the wrong completion to this statement and, therefore, the correct answer to this *not/except* question. In choice (A), a closed primary, the voter must declare his or her party affiliation, so this answer is true and the incorrect answer. Both choices (B) and (D) show how institutionalized the two-party system has become. Choice (C) is an effect of the hold that the two-party system has on the nation's politics and government.

Test-Taking Strategy

For tiered or multistep questions, decide which point(s) is correct, and then determine which answer choice contains that point(s).

19. **The correct answer is (E).** The Freedom of Information Act (I), passed in 1966, allows citizens to gain access to the files of federal agencies. Citizens may request files that relate to them personally or to agency business, the latter because the citizens want to monitor agency workings. Point I then does not relate to the presidency and can be eliminated. Point II, the War Powers Act, was passed in 1974 in response to the presidential commitment of troops in Vietnam, so point II answers the question, as does point III. The Budget and Impoundment Control Act was passed in 1974 to close the loophole that allowed presidents to refuse to spend all the money appropriated by Congress by impounding it. Only choice (E) contains both points II and III.

Test-Taking Strategy

Be sure to read questions carefully. This is a reverse, or not/except question.

20. **The correct answer is (E).** The media is another linkage institution in the political system. One of the criticisms of the news media is that it is too influential in its ability to shape the nation's policy agenda, so choice (E) is not an example of the workings of political parties, but it is the correct answer to this *not/except* question. Choice (A) is an example of political parties as coordinators of policy. Choices (B) and (C) deal with the functions of political parties as articulators of policy and identifiers of like-mindedness. Choice (D) illustrates the parties' function of candidate selection.

Test-Taking Strategy

The key words are indirectly elected.

21. **The correct answer is (C).** According to the U.S. Constitution as originally drafted, the president and U.S. senators, points I and II, were not to be elected directly by the voters. Article I, Section 3 provided for election of senators by their state legislatures; this was later changed by the Seventeenth Amendment. The president is still elected by the electoral college whose members are chosen on the basis of the popular vote. Both points III and IV are incorrect. If you weren't sure about Supreme Court justices, remember that they are appointed for life by the president with the "advice and consent" of the Senate; other federal judges are also appointed, not elected, but they serve for stipulated periods of time, which can be as much as 15 years. Since only points I and II are correct, choice (C) is the correct answer.

22. **The correct answer is (E).** Party realignment, choice (E), refers to the change in the majority party in power and is irrelevant to the question, so it is the correct answer to this *not/except* question. Choice (A) is easy to eliminate as the incorrect answer because the basic powers of the presidency are established by the Constitution. These powers have been reinforced and expanded by various Supreme Court decisions, choice (C). At times Congress has ceded power to the presidency, especially in foreign affairs—for example, the Tonkin Gulf Resolution. Choice (D) then is correct and not an answer possibility. Choice (B) is also a true statement and, therefore, not the correct answer.

Test-Taking Strategy

Don't read more into the data than is there.

23. **The correct answer is (A).** Only choice (A) is supported by the data in the table. Choice (B) is a true statement, but none of the third-party tallies shown were close to throwing either election into the House, so choice (B) can be eliminated. Choice (C) cannot be proved or disproved from the table since third parties fielded slates in more than these two elections. In fact, Theodore Roosevelt polled 23 percent of the vote when he ran on the Bull Moose Party ticket in 1912. Choice (D) may be true, but it is a hypothesis that cannot be proved or disproved by the data on the table. Choice (E) is half true. Both the 1860 and 1992 elections brought out more voters than the next elections, but that those data are not in the table, so choice (E) cannot be correct because it cannot be proved.

24. **The correct answer is (E).** Choices (A), (B), (C), and (D) state reasons why the Supreme Court agrees to hear a case. Choice (E) is the effect of the Court's decision. A minimum of four justices sign a writ of certiorari notifying the lower court to send up the case for a hearing.

25. **The correct answer is (D).** Federal courts have jurisdiction in the cases noted in choices (A), (B), (C), and (E), but not in choice (D). The latter involves a municipality, not the federal government or federal laws, and is, therefore, the correct answer to this *not/except* question. Choice (A), the drug trial of former Panamanian dictator Manuel Noriega, involved federal drug laws. Cases involving competing land claims by states come under the jurisdiction of the federal courts, so choice (B), the dispute between New Jersey and New York, is true in the context of the question and a wrong answer. Cases involving the federal government are under the jurisdiction of federal courts. Choice (C) states that the defendants are federal law enforcement agencies and their employees, so it is not the answer. Cases involving admiralty and maritime laws are also under federal court jurisdiction, so choice (E) is also true in the context of the question and a wrong answer.

26. **The correct answer is (B).** Choice (A), pork-barrel legislation, brings federal dollars into districts for projects that may not be needed but that improve the local economy and show voters that their members in Congress are working for them. A rider, choice (C), is attached to a bill to amend it in some way; often, riders have been added to appropriations bills to force passage of items that would not be approved on their own. Choice (D), senatorial courtesy, refers to the tradition by which a senator has approval rights over the nomination of a federal judge who will preside in the senator's state. Choice (E), iron triangle, refers to the combination of Congressional committees and subcommittees who initiate appropriations and legislation for a certain area, such as defense; federal agencies that are funded to implement that legislation, such as the Department of Defense; and interest groups that support and lobby for that area, such as defense contractors.

Test-Taking Strategy

For tiered or multistep questions, decide which point(s) is important and then determine which answer choice contains that point(s).

---

27. **The correct answer is (D).** How interested a person is in a particular issue, event, or candidate (I); the types and numbers of media outlets that a person uses to learn about politics and how selective that person is in the topics of interest to him or her (II); and how much the person remembers as well as understands stories and analyses (III) affect how much influence the news media has on that person. Point IV, latency, is a characteristic of public opinion, but it is not one of the factors that determines how receptive a person is to the influence of the news media. Choice (D) is the only response that includes points I, II, and III.

28. **The correct answer is (C).** Freedom of speech, choice (C), is an example of one of the shared values stated in choice (E). Freedom of speech is too specific to match what the question is asking for and is, therefore, the correct answer to this *not/ except* question. Choices (A), (B), (D), and (E) are all general conditions or underlying principles that must exist for a constitutional democracy to function well.

29. **The correct answer is (E).** According to the Constitution, the House has the responsibility of determining whether federal judges or certain other high-level federal government officials should be impeached (that is, have charges brought against him or her) based on the evidence, and the Senate then has the responsibility of trying the person on those charges. (Think of the House as a grand jury and the Senate as the trial jury.) Choices (A), (B), and (D) are responsibilities given to the Senate by the Constitution. Choice (C) is illogical; the OMB is in the executive branch.

30. **The correct answer is (C).** The Rules Committee determines the rules for floor debate on a bill, including the time allotted to debate and the amount of amendments that may be offered, thus greatly influencing the likelihood of passage of a bill. Debate may be governed under a closed rule or an open rule. The former severely limits debate and amendments and enhances the prospects of a bill's passage. Choice (D) is incorrect not because the conference committee isn't influential but because a standing conference committee does not exist. Conference committees are formed to deal with specific bills and the discrepancies between the House and Senate versions. Choices (A), (B), and (E) are not as powerful as the Rules Committee.

31. **The correct answer is (E).** The House assigns committee members based on party, so the Republicans have a Committee on Committees and the Democrats have a Steering and Policy Committee to make committee assignments. The Speaker chairs the committee of whichever party is in the majority, and the minority leader chairs the other committee. Choice (B) is partially correct in that both leaders do sit on the committees, but partially correct is partially incorrect. Choice (E) is the fullest answer choice provided. Choices (A), (C), and (D) are incorrect.

32. **The correct answer is (D).** The Southeast (III) and the Southwest (IV), also known as the Sun Belt, have consistently gained seats after the dicennial Census while the Northeast (I) and the Midwest (II) have tended to lose seats. (It isn't coincidental that these regions are also known as the Rust Belt and the Snow Belt.) The correct answer choice must contain only points III and IV, so choice (D) is correct.

Test-Taking Strategy

Beware of answer choices that state absolutes, such as no group.

33. **The correct answer is (D).** The elderly are among the most vocal lobbies in the health-care debate, so choice (D) is incorrect, but it is the right answer to this *not/except* question. The elderly are ably represented by the American Association of Retired Persons. Also, older people tend to vote, so their support of a candidate can be an important factor in a race. Choice (A) is true, as is choice (B). Both of these facts could be used to support an opinion that the United States has an elite form of government. Choices (C) and (E) are also true and, therefore, incorrect.

34. **The correct answer is (E).** Salience, or the extent to which people believe an issue is relevant to them, is one of the factors that public opinion polling can show. There is no evidence to indicate that choice (E) is true; therefore, in this *not/except* question, it is the correct answer. Choices (A), (B), (C), and (D) are all true statements about public opinion polling. Choice (D) refers to the factor known as latency.

Test-Taking Strategy

The key word is major. *Be sure to read the question carefully in order to know what it is asking.*

35. **The correct answer is (A).** Choice (B) is the opposite of what tends to occur. The news media tends to choose candidates to follow in primaries who make interesting news stories, who give them access, and who are ahead in the polls, which the news media can influence by their coverage. Choice (C) is not considered a concern by many, but it is a legitimate function of reporting. Some people consider personality and character appropriate topics for consideration when choosing a person for president, so choice (D) is incorrect. Choice (E) may be a true statement, but it does not answer the question, which asks for the major criticism of how news media cover presidential primaries.

Test-Taking Strategy

Be sure all parts of an answer choice are correct. A partially correct answer is a partially incorrect answer— and a quarter-point deduction.

36. **The correct answer is (E).** The Ninth Amendment deals with unenumerated rights, and the Tenth Amendment is concerned with powers reserved to the states or to the people of the states. Choice (A) is incorrect because the First Amendment places limits on Congress and the Second Amendment on the executive. The First Amendment ensures that Congress may not establish a state religion and that it may not curtail the freedoms of speech, press, assembly, or petition. According to the Second Amendment, the executive may not interfere with the right to bear arms. Choice (B) is incorrect because the Third and Fourth Amendments place limits on the executive. The executive may not take over homes to lodge the militia, and it must have a warrant to undertake a search and seizure of evidence. Choice (C) is incorrect because the Second and Third Amendments deal with the executive as stated above. The Fifth Amendment deals with limits on the courts and the Ninth Amendment deals with limits on the federal government, so part of the answer is correct, but overall choice (D) is wrong. The Fifth Amendment sets provisions for the use of grand juries, protection against self-incrimination, and compensation for the taking of private property for public use.

37. **The correct answer is (C).** Answering this question is difficult because all five statements are true. However, the question asks for the ways in which Congress and the president share power and responsibilities. The first part of choice (C) deals with how Congress makes the bureaucracy accountable to Congress, whereas the second half of the statement deals with how the president blocks this accountability. The two parts do not show a sharing of power and responsibility, so choice (C) is incorrect but the correct answer for this *not/except* question. Choice (A) is true, but Congress must agree to any changes that the president makes. Choices (B), (D), and (E) are all correct statements, and, therefore, the wrong answers.

38. **The correct answer is (B).** Helping a fellow representative or senator in his or her reelection bid is not a function of Congress, that is, it does not relate to the business of Congress. Passing laws, regardless of the content, choices (A) and (D), is mandated in the Constitution as a function of both the House and the Senate. Choice (C), confirming presidential nominees to the bench, is a Constitutional duty assigned to the Senate. Choice (E), serving the people by acting as an advocate, comes under the function of representing the people, a duty under the Constitution.

39. **The correct answer is (E).** Both choices (A) and (E) are true, but choice (E) is a more complete response and is therefore the better answer. Choice (B) is incorrect because the table does not show the size of the national debt, only the interest payment on the national debt. Also, more than entitlements increased in 1999; "Outlays from Prior Obligations," which are not defined, and "Other Uncontrollables" also increased. Choice (C) is a true statement but irrelevant to the data and the question. Choice (D) is incorrect and irrelevant. According to the table, uncontrollable outlays include more than entitlements because the interest payment on the national debt is included.

40. **The correct answer is (A).** NAFTA, or the North American Free Trade Association, is a joint effort of the United States, Canada, and Mexico to eliminate trade barriers over time. Signatories to GATT, or the General Agreement on Tariffs and Trade, agree to remove trade barriers against one another over time; it is a worldwide agreement that gave birth to the World Trade Organization in 1995, which had 129 members by the end of the century. Using these identifications as your basis for analysis, choice (A) is correct. Choice (B) is incorrect, but the erroneous description of GATT could be applied to the World Bank. Choice (C) is incorrect, but the erroneous description of NAFTA is a correct description of the North Atlantic Treaty Organization (NATO). Choice (D) is incorrect; the International Monetary Fund (IMF), an affiliate of the United Nations, acts as a facilitator to stabilize the international financial markets. Choice (E) is incorrect; both NAFTA and GATT operate through national governments, not directly with multinational corporations, and not all tariffs apply only to multinational corporations.

41. **The correct answer is (B).** The use of riders is a major difference in the legislative processes in the two houses. Choice (A) is incorrect because in both chambers subcommittees mark up bills. Choice (C) is the opposite of the use of filibusters. Filibusters are rarely used in the House, where debate is more closely regulated than in the Senate. Choice (D) states the opposite of what occurs. The Rules Committee operates in the House, not the Senate. The number of standing committees, choice (E), is approximately the same.

42. **The correct answer is (C).** Neither choices (A) nor (D) can be the correct answer because one point of an iron triangle or an iron rectangle is bureaucrats, and the question does not mention them. Choice (B) might seem like a good answer, but lobbies don't include officials. This fact also rules out choice (E), constituency.

43. **The correct answer is (D).** If you are not sure about the answer to this question, try comparing statements and eliminating those that seem contradictory. Either choice (A) or choice (D) must be incorrect because higher education would typically mean higher status jobs. Because of historical discrimination, many African Americans and Hispanics have less or inferior education and, therefore, lower status jobs. African Americans were also among the groups who were politically disenfranchised, which means they may register and vote less because they have less of a tradition of voting than whites. Choice (E) seems to contradict choice (D), which is the incorrect statement and the correct answer for this *not/except* question. While women, choice (B), were also a disenfranchised group, in recent elections they have voted more than men. Some political scientists reason that this is because of increased educational levels and income. Choice (C) is also true; the younger the voter the less likely the person is to vote, while the over-60 voter has increased in numbers.

44. **The correct answer is (D).** Choices (B), (C), (D), and (E) are all true statements about the effects of single-interest groups, but choice (D) states the most *significant* effect. Single-interest groups are used by some theoreticians to prove that the United States has an elite form of government, choice (B), but it is a theory that is not accepted by everyone. It would be safe to eliminate it provisionally on your first reading. Choices (C) and (E) fall into the category of very specific effects. Choice (D) is the most general statement, having the greatest implications for how the government operates. Choice (A) is meaningless. Factionalism existed before PACs and before the great increase in their numbers.

45. **The correct answer is (D).** Choice (D) stands for the World Trade Organization, an international organization working to reduce trade barriers. How nations deal with U.S. exports may involve U.S. foreign or economic policy, but it does not usually involve the military as it did in the later nineteenth and early twentieth centuries. Preparedness to meet choices (A), (B), (C), and (E) all impact U.S. defense spending.

46. **The correct answer is (D).** Procedural due process deals with how a law is administered and substantive due process with how reasonable or fair the law is. Once used mainly to decide contract cases, the principle is used now to uphold the right to privacy, choice (D), including the right to an abortion. Procedural due process guarantees choice (E), civil rights in general.

47. **The correct answer is (D).** Choices (A), (B), and (D) are all concerns voiced by various critics of independent regulatory agencies, but choice (D) is the most significant because it has the most potentially harmful consequences. Not only do commission members come from regulated industries, but they often go back to work in them when their terms are over. Choice (C) is incorrect. Choice (E) is a true statement but irrelevant since commission members can be removed.

48. **The correct answer is (A).** The Fourteenth Amendment states: "All persons born or naturalized in the United States, and subject to the jurisdiction thereof, are citizens of the United States and of the state wherein they reside." (The amendment went on to replace the three-fifths compromise for counting slaves for purposes of apportionment, forbade former Confederate officers and officials to serve in reconstructed governments, and invalidated the Confederate debt.) Choice (B), the Fifteenth Amendment, guaranteed the right to vote regardless of race, color, or "previous condition of servitude." The Nineteenth Amendment, choice (C), gave women the franchise. The Twenty-second Amendment, choice (D), deals with presidential tenure, and the Twenty-sixth, choice (E), gave 18-year-olds the right to vote.

Test-Taking Strategy

Be sure to highlight the important words in questions. It's especially important in not/except *questions so that you know what you are looking for.*

49. **The correct answer is (B).** Substituting primaries for nominating conventions spread the choice among more voters, not fewer, so it is the correct answer to this *not/except* question. In addition, the move to primaries occurred in the beginning of the twentieth century, not at the end. Crossover voting in a primary, choice (A), means that voters may vote for candidates in the opposition party rather than in their own party. It weakens party discipline, as does choice (C), split-ticket voting, which means that a person votes outside his or her party for some or all of the candidates on the ballot. When the news media provides constant coverage, choice (D), voters no longer have to rely on their party for information on candidates and the issues. People have limited interests, so an interest group with a specific focus would appeal to people of like ideas better than a political party, which usually houses many differing interests, choice (E).

50.   **The correct answer is (A).** The administrative duties of the presidency grew in the twentieth century as the size and influence of the federal government grew, beginning with the first administration of Franklin Roosevelt. All the other functions listed, chief legislator, choice (B); chief diplomat, choice (C); booster of the nation's morale, choice (D); and party leader, choice (E) are all accurately stated as roles of the presidency, but the single greatest change has been in the executive or administrative role of the president.

51.   **The correct answer is (B).** One of the reasons that the Gramm-Rudman-Hollings Act did not achieve its goal of balancing the budget was because entitlements were omitted. Together, entitlements (Old Age, Survivors, and Disability Insurance; Medicare; Medicaid; food stamps; unemployment compensation; student loans; and veterans' benefits) make up about two thirds of the national budget. Budget cuts could be made in discretionary spending only, such as hypothetical spending for choice (A), federal pay raises; farm subsidies, choice (C); defense spending, choice (D); and rail subsidies, choice (E).

52.   **The correct answer is (A).** Choices (A), (C), and (E) are all true statements about recent Supreme Court decisions in regard to aid for parochial school students. A decision in the 1999–2000 court session added computers to the items that can be bought with tax dollars for use by parochial school students, choice (E), and the Supreme Court in the same session overruled the practice of student-led prayers at football games, choice (C). Choice (B) is a misstatement of the Supreme Court ruling; the Court held that parents of all children, including those attending parochial and private nonsectarian schools, could be allowed tax deductions for tuition and related expenses. The correctly stated decision and choices (C) and (E) point to choice (A) as the correct answer. It is the most inclusive choice, stating a general principle. These rulings do not support choice (D).

53. **The correct answer is (D).** The Eighth Amendment's guarantee against cruel and unusual punishment has been used both to uphold the use of the death penalty and to strike down decisions involving the death penalty. The Supreme Court has ruled that adequate guidelines must be established in order to use the death penalty. Subsequent rulings have struck down mandatory imposition of the death penalty and upheld a staged process that includes a trial to determine guilt or innocence and then a sentencing phase to consider circumstances, including the effect of the crime on the victim's family. The Fourteenth Amendment, choice (A), extends due process to the states. Choice (B), the Miranda ruling, provides for procedural due process. Choice (C), the principle of clear and present danger as applied in *Schenck* v. *United States,* trumps freedom of speech in certain circumstances. Choice (E), the right to counsel, is illogical in the context of the question.

54. **The correct answer is (C).** To answer this question, you first must know what shift occurred in the voting patterns of the South since the 1960s. The answer is the end of the Democratic "solid South" in presidential elections and the emergence of the Republican Party as a viable competitor for public offices in general in the South. If you know this fact, then you can eliminate choice (A) quickly because it deals with Democratic voters in the South. Choices (B) and (D) are both true statements about the South in recent decades but have little to do with an impact on voting. You might consider that more Northerners might mean more Republicans, but choice (C) implies more clearly that Southern whites are more likely to support the Republican Party. Choice (E) does not relate to voting or to political parties.

55. **The correct answer is (B).** Choices (B) and (D) are both true statements about resistance to changes to or abandonment of the electoral college. Choice (D) names one group that opposes changes, Republicans, whereas choice (B) states the fact that there are some number of groups that oppose the change for reasons of self-interest, making choice (B) a broader answer. Choice (A) is incorrect because the earliest attention of the primary season is on two smaller states, Iowa and New Hampshire. Choice (C) is incorrect because it looked at times that both the candidacies of George Wallace in 1968 (who ran on the American Independent Party ticket) and Ross Perot in 1992 (as the Reform Party presidential candidate) could have thrown the election into the House. Choice (E) is a distracter because it seems to make sense, but it is not an argument that is used to support the current system.

56. **The correct answer is (D).** Party dealignment (I) results in divided government (III), and split-ticket voting (IV) contributes to divided government. Party neutrality (V) also results from party dealignment. Party realignment, point II, would be characterized by more control of state governments by Republicans than has occurred; for example, in 1999, twenty-five states had divided control, fourteen states were controlled by Republicans, and ten had Democrats in control. Therefore, point II is incorrect and should not be part of the answer choice. Only choice (D) has the correct points, I, III, IV, and V.

57. **The correct answer is (A).** Choice (B), balancing the budget through the use of personal and corporate income taxes, would be impossible, so it is an illogical answer and can be eliminated. Choice (C) is also illogical; the Federal Reserve's monetary policy attempts to do this. Choices (D) and (E) are also illogical.

58. **The correct answer is (A).** This method was used by President Reagan to cut back on enforcement of government regulations. Choice (B) is incorrect; it is not the purpose of the strategy. Choice (C) is incorrect because Congress must approve appropriations. The indirect outcome of the strategy may have been similar to deregulation because regulations were less vigorously enforced, but the regulations still existed, so choice (D) is incorrect. Choice (E) is not true; the funding appropriations still have to be voted on by Congress.

59. **The correct answer is (D).** This excerpt from Article VI is known as the supremacy clause. Choice (A) established Congress and its powers. Choice (B) established the judicial branch. Article IV, choice (C), dealt with relations among the states, and Article VII, choice (E), with the ratification process for the Constitution.

Test-Taking Strategy

For not/except *questions, ask yourself if the answer is correct in the context of the question. If it is, cross it off and go on to the next answer.*

60. **The correct answer is (D).** Article III sets out the federal court system's duties and its judicial power, but the decision in *Marbury* v. *Madison* established the principle of judicial review. Choices (A), (B), (C), and (E) are all true statements about Article VI and are, therefore, incorrect answers.

SUGGESTIONS FOR FREE-RESPONSE ESSAY 1

Study Strategy

Revise your essay using points from this list that will strengthen it.

You might have chosen the following points for your essay discussing the government regulation of free speech. Consider these points as you complete the evaluation of your essay.

Prior Restraint

- Restraint—censorship—imposed before a speech is given or an article is published

- Includes governmental review of speeches, movies, and publications

- Usually unconstitutional: "prior restraint on expression comes to this court with a 'heavy presumption' against its constitutionality"

- Circumstances involving approval of prior restraint

    - Military matters

    - Security situations

    - School authorities exercising control over style and content of school newspapers

Vagueness

- Rigid standards regarding vagueness

    - Unconstitutional if administrators of laws have discretion in interpreting the laws

    - Unconstitutional if vagueness causes people to fear exercising right to free speech

- Concern that standard could be used to discriminate against opposing or unpopular views

- Court has struck down:

    - Laws forbidding sacrilegious movies

    - Laws against publications that present violent criminal acts feared to incite crime

Least Drastic Means

- Principle that a law infringing on First Amendment freedoms may not be passed if there are other means are available to handle problem

- Example: State wants to protect citizens from unscrupulous lawyers

  - May not pass a law by forbidding advertisement of fees—interferes with First Amendment

  - May provide disbarment for unethical attorneys

Content and Viewpoint Neutrality

- Laws that apply to all views and all kinds of speech more likely to be constitutional

- Content-neutral

- Viewpoint-neutral

- Laws tending to be unconstitutional

  - Laws restricting time, place, manner of speech for some people but not others

  - Laws regulating speech or publication of some views but not others

- Example: Ordinance prohibiting the display of a symbol that arouses anger on basis of race, color, creed, religion, or gender

  - Unconstitutional: Not viewpoint-neutral; did not forbid display that aroused anger for other reasons, such as political affiliation or sexual orientation

Commercial Speech

- Commercial speech protected but more subject to regulation

  - Advertising something that is illegal can be forbidden

  - False or misleading advertising is illegal

- Example: Law forbidding false and misleading political speech or political advertising

  - Unconstitutional: Government does not have right to forbid expression of ideas even if considered false or misleading

SUGGESTIONS FOR FREE-RESPONSE ESSAY 2

1974 Budget Reform Act

- Congress given a more effective role in budget process

- President must include in the budget proposal:

  - Proposed changes in tax laws

  - Estimates of amounts of revenue lost through current tax system

  - Five-year estimates of costs of new and continuing federal programs

- President to seek authorization for new federal programs one year previous to funding

- Created Congressional Budget Office (CBO)

  - Gives Congress own independent agency to prepare budget data

  - Analyzes budgetary issues and presidential recommendations for Congress

  - Furnishes biennial forecasts of the economy

  - Analyzes alternative fiscal policies

  - Prepares five-year estimates of costs for proposed legislation

  - Studies requests made by Congressional committees

  - Monitors results of Congressional action on appropriations and revenues as related to targets or limits established by law

The Gramm-Rudman-Hollings Act (1985)

- Automatic across-the-board cuts in defense and domestic programs

  - Entitlement programs exempt

- Modified by 1990 Budget Enforcement Act

- Adoption of concurrent resolution for next fiscal year by April 15

- Set levels of new budget authority and spending

- Limits became ceiling for appropriations committees

- Adopt resolution later to revise or reaffirm decisions

- Recently, reconciliation

  - Budget resolution setting ceilings on what appropriations subcommittees can appropriate

  - How to achieve goal is up to committees

- Established procedure to reduce federal deficit to zero

Effects

- Set limits on president's role

- Increased effectiveness of Congressional role in budget process

- Established discipline and frame of mind that helped move toward balanced budget

- Tax revenues from economic boom of 1980s and 1990s also assisted in balancing budgets of late 1990s

- End of century, budget surplus

    - Extensive debate on what to be done with surplus

    - General Republican approach: tax cuts

    - General Democratic approach: tax cuts only after funding of Social Security

    - Some: pay down national debt and build up surplus

SUGGESTIONS FOR FREE-RESPONSE ESSAY 3.

Test-Taking Strategy

Quote from the statistics you are given to strengthen your arguments.

You might have chosen the following points for your essay analyzing voting trends. Consider these points as you complete the evaluation of your essay.

Overall Trends
- The percent of registered voters participating in elections has declined over time. (based on table and outside knowledge)
- More registered voters participate in presidential year elections than in off-year elections. (based on table and outside knowledge)

Voting Differences Between Men and Women
- A higher percentage of women vote than men.
- A higher percentage of registered female voters participate in presidential-year elections than registered male voters.
- The difference in percentage of voters in presidential and non-presidential years is greater for women than men.
- More women than men have some years of college, and a higher level of education means a greater likelihood of voting.

Voting Similarities Between Men and Women
- Both vote more in presidential election years.
- The percentage of those voting has declined over the years.

Reasons for the Trends
- People feel that their individual votes don't count.
- Party identification is at an all-time low.
- More money is spent during presidential election years.
- There is more media attention on politics during presidential election years.
- Women care more about social issues, so campaigns that address these as major issues will draw more women voters.

SUGGESTIONS FOR FREE-RESPONSE ESSAY 4

You might have chosen the following points for your essay evaluating the impact of public opinion on health care and Social Security policies. Consider these points as you complete the evaluation of your essay.

Presidential Position

- Polls to find what position appeals to most voters

- Campaign promises

- Backroom deals

- Interparty deals

- Reelection concerns

- Efficacy of PACs, lobbyists

Congressional Makeup

- Congress dominated by Republicans

- Fiscal conservatives versus social liberals

- Influence and clout of older Americans

- Constituencies of socioeconomic groups

- Efficacy of PACs, lobbyists

Voting Patterns

- Political dealignment

- Older Americans more likely to vote

- Gender of voters

  - Women more concerned with social issues

  - Men interested in economic and military issues

- Poor less likely to vote and less likely to organize to push agenda

- Media coverage

- Money behind viewpoints

- Efficacy of PACs, lobbyists

Test-Taking Strategy

No matter how much you practice, if you find yourself running short of time, use an outline form or bullets to communicate your ideas. Abbreviations can also speed up your writing, but use them only in an emergency.

SELF-EVALUATION RUBRIC FOR THE ADVANCED PLACEMENT ESSAYS

	8–9	5–7	2–4	0–1
Overall Impression	Demonstrates excellent understanding of U.S. government and legal system; outstanding writing; thorough and effective; incisive	Demonstrates good understanding of U.S. government and legal system; good writing competence	Reveals simplistic thinking and/or immature understanding of U.S. government and legal system; fails to respond adequately to the question; little or no analysis	Very little or no understanding of U.S. government and legal system; unacceptably brief; fails to respond to the question; little clarity
Understanding of the U.S. Government	Scholarly; excellent understanding of the question; effective and incisive; in-depth critical analysis; includes apt, specific references; acknowledges other views	Mostly accurate use of information about U.S. government and legal system; good understanding of the question; often perceptive and clear; includes specific references and critical analysis	Some inaccuracies in information regarding U.S. government; superficial understanding and treatment of the question; lack of adequate knowledge about U.S. government; overgeneralized	Serious errors in presenting information about U.S. government and legal system; extensive misreading of the question and little supporting evidence; completely off the topic
Development	Original, unique, and/or intriguing thesis; excellent use of fundamentals and principles of U.S. government; thoroughly developed; conclusion shows applicability of thesis to other situations	Adequate thesis; satisfactory use of knowledge of U.S. government; competent development; acceptable conclusion	Inadequate, irrelevant, or illogical thesis; little use of knowledge of government; some development; unsatisfactory, inapplicable, or nonexistent conclusion	Lacking both thesis and conclusion; little or no evidence of knowledge of U.S. government
Conventions of English	Meticulously and thoroughly organized; coherent and unified; virtually error free	Reasonably organized; mostly coherent and unified; few or some errors	Somewhat organized; some incoherence and lack of unity; some major errors	Little or no organization; incoherent and void of unity; extremely flawed

Rate yourself in each of the categories below. Enter the numbers on the lines below. Be as honest as possible so you will know what areas need work. Then calculate the average of the four numbers to determine your final score. It is difficult to score yourself objectively, so you may wish to ask a respected friend or teacher to assess your essays for a more accurate reflection of their strengths and weaknesses. On the AP test itself, a reader will rate your essays on a scale of 0 to 9, with 9 being the highest.

Each category is rated 9 (high) to 0 (incompetent).

ESSAY 1
SELF-EVALUATION
   Overall Impression _____
   Understanding of U.S. Government _____
   Development _____
   Conventions of English _____

   TOTAL _____
     Divide by 4 for final score. _____

ESSAY 1
OBJECTIVE EVALUATION
   Overall Impression _____
   Understanding of U.S. Government _____
   Development _____
   Conventions of English _____

   TOTAL _____
     Divide by 4 for final score. _____

ESSAY 2
SELF-EVALUATION
   Overall Impression _____
   Understanding of U.S. Government _____
   Development _____
   Conventions of English _____

   TOTAL _____
     Divide by 4 for final score. _____

ESSAY 2
OBJECTIVE EVALUATION
   Overall Impression _____
   Understanding of U.S. Government _____
   Development _____
   Conventions of English _____

   TOTAL _____
     Divide by 4 for final score. _____

ESSAY 3
SELF-EVALUATION
   Overall Impression _____
   Understanding of U.S. Government _____
   Development _____
   Conventions of English _____

   TOTAL _____
     Divide by 4 for final score. _____

ESSAY 3
OBJECTIVE EVALUATION
   Overall Impression _____
   Understanding of U.S. Government _____
   Development _____
   Conventions of English _____

   TOTAL _____
     Divide by 4 for final score. _____

ESSAY 4
SELF-EVALUATION
   Overall Impression _____
   Understanding of U.S. Government _____
   Development _____
   Conventions of English _____

   TOTAL _____
     Divide by 4 for final score. _____

ESSAY 4
OBJECTIVE EVALUATION
   Overall Impression _____
   Understanding of U.S. Government _____
   Development _____
   Conventions of English _____

   TOTAL _____
     Divide by 4 for final score. _____

ANSWER SHEETS

DIAGNOSTIC TEST

1	A B C D E	16	A B C D E	31	A B C D E	46	A B C D E
2	A B C D E	17	A B C D E	32	A B C D E	47	A B C D E
3	A B C D E	18	A B C D E	33	A B C D E	48	A B C D E
4	A B C D E	19	A B C D E	34	A B C D E	49	A B C D E
5	A B C D E	20	A B C D E	35	A B C D E	50	A B C D E
6	A B C D E	21	A B C D E	36	A B C D E	51	A B C D E
7	A B C D E	22	A B C D E	37	A B C D E	52	A B C D E
8	A B C D E	23	A B C D E	38	A B C D E	53	A B C D E
9	A B C D E	24	A B C D E	39	A B C D E	54	A B C D E
10	A B C D E	25	A B C D E	40	A B C D E	55	A B C D E
11	A B C D E	26	A B C D E	41	A B C D E	56	A B C D E
12	A B C D E	27	A B C D E	42	A B C D E	57	A B C D E
13	A B C D E	28	A B C D E	43	A B C D E	58	A B C D E
14	A B C D E	29	A B C D E	44	A B C D E	59	A B C D E
15	A B C D E	30	A B C D E	45	A B C D E	60	A B C D E

PRACTICE TEST 1

1	A B C D E	16	A B C D E	31	A B C D E	46	A B C D E
2	A B C D E	17	A B C D E	32	A B C D E	47	A B C D E
3	A B C D E	18	A B C D E	33	A B C D E	48	A B C D E
4	A B C D E	19	A B C D E	34	A B C D E	49	A B C D E
5	A B C D E	20	A B C D E	35	A B C D E	50	A B C D E
6	A B C D E	21	A B C D E	36	A B C D E	51	A B C D E
7	A B C D E	22	A B C D E	37	A B C D E	52	A B C D E
8	A B C D E	23	A B C D E	38	A B C D E	53	A B C D E
9	A B C D E	24	A B C D E	39	A B C D E	54	A B C D E
10	A B C D E	25	A B C D E	40	A B C D E	55	A B C D E
11	A B C D E	26	A B C D E	41	A B C D E	56	A B C D E
12	A B C D E	27	A B C D E	42	A B C D E	57	A B C D E
13	A B C D E	28	A B C D E	43	A B C D E	58	A B C D E
14	A B C D E	29	A B C D E	44	A B C D E	59	A B C D E
15	A B C D E	30	A B C D E	45	A B C D E	60	A B C D E

PRACTICE TEST 2

1 Ⓐ Ⓑ Ⓒ Ⓓ Ⓔ 16 Ⓐ Ⓑ Ⓒ Ⓓ Ⓔ 31 Ⓐ Ⓑ Ⓒ Ⓓ Ⓔ 46 Ⓐ Ⓑ Ⓒ Ⓓ Ⓔ
2 Ⓐ Ⓑ Ⓒ Ⓓ Ⓔ 17 Ⓐ Ⓑ Ⓒ Ⓓ Ⓔ 32 Ⓐ Ⓑ Ⓒ Ⓓ Ⓔ 47 Ⓐ Ⓑ Ⓒ Ⓓ Ⓔ
3 Ⓐ Ⓑ Ⓒ Ⓓ Ⓔ 18 Ⓐ Ⓑ Ⓒ Ⓓ Ⓔ 33 Ⓐ Ⓑ Ⓒ Ⓓ Ⓔ 48 Ⓐ Ⓑ Ⓒ Ⓓ Ⓔ
4 Ⓐ Ⓑ Ⓒ Ⓓ Ⓔ 19 Ⓐ Ⓑ Ⓒ Ⓓ Ⓔ 34 Ⓐ Ⓑ Ⓒ Ⓓ Ⓔ 49 Ⓐ Ⓑ Ⓒ Ⓓ Ⓔ
5 Ⓐ Ⓑ Ⓒ Ⓓ Ⓔ 20 Ⓐ Ⓑ Ⓒ Ⓓ Ⓔ 35 Ⓐ Ⓑ Ⓒ Ⓓ Ⓔ 50 Ⓐ Ⓑ Ⓒ Ⓓ Ⓔ
6 Ⓐ Ⓑ Ⓒ Ⓓ Ⓔ 21 Ⓐ Ⓑ Ⓒ Ⓓ Ⓔ 36 Ⓐ Ⓑ Ⓒ Ⓓ Ⓔ 51 Ⓐ Ⓑ Ⓒ Ⓓ Ⓔ
7 Ⓐ Ⓑ Ⓒ Ⓓ Ⓔ 22 Ⓐ Ⓑ Ⓒ Ⓓ Ⓔ 37 Ⓐ Ⓑ Ⓒ Ⓓ Ⓔ 52 Ⓐ Ⓑ Ⓒ Ⓓ Ⓔ
8 Ⓐ Ⓑ Ⓒ Ⓓ Ⓔ 23 Ⓐ Ⓑ Ⓒ Ⓓ Ⓔ 38 Ⓐ Ⓑ Ⓒ Ⓓ Ⓔ 53 Ⓐ Ⓑ Ⓒ Ⓓ Ⓔ
9 Ⓐ Ⓑ Ⓒ Ⓓ Ⓔ 24 Ⓐ Ⓑ Ⓒ Ⓓ Ⓔ 39 Ⓐ Ⓑ Ⓒ Ⓓ Ⓔ 54 Ⓐ Ⓑ Ⓒ Ⓓ Ⓔ
10 Ⓐ Ⓑ Ⓒ Ⓓ Ⓔ 25 Ⓐ Ⓑ Ⓒ Ⓓ Ⓔ 40 Ⓐ Ⓑ Ⓒ Ⓓ Ⓔ 55 Ⓐ Ⓑ Ⓒ Ⓓ Ⓔ
11 Ⓐ Ⓑ Ⓒ Ⓓ Ⓔ 26 Ⓐ Ⓑ Ⓒ Ⓓ Ⓔ 41 Ⓐ Ⓑ Ⓒ Ⓓ Ⓔ 56 Ⓐ Ⓑ Ⓒ Ⓓ Ⓔ
12 Ⓐ Ⓑ Ⓒ Ⓓ Ⓔ 27 Ⓐ Ⓑ Ⓒ Ⓓ Ⓔ 42 Ⓐ Ⓑ Ⓒ Ⓓ Ⓔ 57 Ⓐ Ⓑ Ⓒ Ⓓ Ⓔ
13 Ⓐ Ⓑ Ⓒ Ⓓ Ⓔ 28 Ⓐ Ⓑ Ⓒ Ⓓ Ⓔ 43 Ⓐ Ⓑ Ⓒ Ⓓ Ⓔ 58 Ⓐ Ⓑ Ⓒ Ⓓ Ⓔ
14 Ⓐ Ⓑ Ⓒ Ⓓ Ⓔ 29 Ⓐ Ⓑ Ⓒ Ⓓ Ⓔ 44 Ⓐ Ⓑ Ⓒ Ⓓ Ⓔ 59 Ⓐ Ⓑ Ⓒ Ⓓ Ⓔ
15 Ⓐ Ⓑ Ⓒ Ⓓ Ⓔ 30 Ⓐ Ⓑ Ⓒ Ⓓ Ⓔ 45 Ⓐ Ⓑ Ⓒ Ⓓ Ⓔ 60 Ⓐ Ⓑ Ⓒ Ⓓ Ⓔ

PRACTICE TEST 3

1 Ⓐ Ⓑ Ⓒ Ⓓ Ⓔ 16 Ⓐ Ⓑ Ⓒ Ⓓ Ⓔ 31 Ⓐ Ⓑ Ⓒ Ⓓ Ⓔ 46 Ⓐ Ⓑ Ⓒ Ⓓ Ⓔ
2 Ⓐ Ⓑ Ⓒ Ⓓ Ⓔ 17 Ⓐ Ⓑ Ⓒ Ⓓ Ⓔ 32 Ⓐ Ⓑ Ⓒ Ⓓ Ⓔ 47 Ⓐ Ⓑ Ⓒ Ⓓ Ⓔ
3 Ⓐ Ⓑ Ⓒ Ⓓ Ⓔ 18 Ⓐ Ⓑ Ⓒ Ⓓ Ⓔ 33 Ⓐ Ⓑ Ⓒ Ⓓ Ⓔ 48 Ⓐ Ⓑ Ⓒ Ⓓ Ⓔ
4 Ⓐ Ⓑ Ⓒ Ⓓ Ⓔ 19 Ⓐ Ⓑ Ⓒ Ⓓ Ⓔ 34 Ⓐ Ⓑ Ⓒ Ⓓ Ⓔ 49 Ⓐ Ⓑ Ⓒ Ⓓ Ⓔ
5 Ⓐ Ⓑ Ⓒ Ⓓ Ⓔ 20 Ⓐ Ⓑ Ⓒ Ⓓ Ⓔ 35 Ⓐ Ⓑ Ⓒ Ⓓ Ⓔ 50 Ⓐ Ⓑ Ⓒ Ⓓ Ⓔ
6 Ⓐ Ⓑ Ⓒ Ⓓ Ⓔ 21 Ⓐ Ⓑ Ⓒ Ⓓ Ⓔ 36 Ⓐ Ⓑ Ⓒ Ⓓ Ⓔ 51 Ⓐ Ⓑ Ⓒ Ⓓ Ⓔ
7 Ⓐ Ⓑ Ⓒ Ⓓ Ⓔ 22 Ⓐ Ⓑ Ⓒ Ⓓ Ⓔ 37 Ⓐ Ⓑ Ⓒ Ⓓ Ⓔ 52 Ⓐ Ⓑ Ⓒ Ⓓ Ⓔ
8 Ⓐ Ⓑ Ⓒ Ⓓ Ⓔ 23 Ⓐ Ⓑ Ⓒ Ⓓ Ⓔ 38 Ⓐ Ⓑ Ⓒ Ⓓ Ⓔ 53 Ⓐ Ⓑ Ⓒ Ⓓ Ⓔ
9 Ⓐ Ⓑ Ⓒ Ⓓ Ⓔ 24 Ⓐ Ⓑ Ⓒ Ⓓ Ⓔ 39 Ⓐ Ⓑ Ⓒ Ⓓ Ⓔ 54 Ⓐ Ⓑ Ⓒ Ⓓ Ⓔ
10 Ⓐ Ⓑ Ⓒ Ⓓ Ⓔ 25 Ⓐ Ⓑ Ⓒ Ⓓ Ⓔ 40 Ⓐ Ⓑ Ⓒ Ⓓ Ⓔ 55 Ⓐ Ⓑ Ⓒ Ⓓ Ⓔ
11 Ⓐ Ⓑ Ⓒ Ⓓ Ⓔ 26 Ⓐ Ⓑ Ⓒ Ⓓ Ⓔ 41 Ⓐ Ⓑ Ⓒ Ⓓ Ⓔ 56 Ⓐ Ⓑ Ⓒ Ⓓ Ⓔ
12 Ⓐ Ⓑ Ⓒ Ⓓ Ⓔ 27 Ⓐ Ⓑ Ⓒ Ⓓ Ⓔ 42 Ⓐ Ⓑ Ⓒ Ⓓ Ⓔ 57 Ⓐ Ⓑ Ⓒ Ⓓ Ⓔ
13 Ⓐ Ⓑ Ⓒ Ⓓ Ⓔ 28 Ⓐ Ⓑ Ⓒ Ⓓ Ⓔ 43 Ⓐ Ⓑ Ⓒ Ⓓ Ⓔ 58 Ⓐ Ⓑ Ⓒ Ⓓ Ⓔ
14 Ⓐ Ⓑ Ⓒ Ⓓ Ⓔ 29 Ⓐ Ⓑ Ⓒ Ⓓ Ⓔ 44 Ⓐ Ⓑ Ⓒ Ⓓ Ⓔ 59 Ⓐ Ⓑ Ⓒ Ⓓ Ⓔ
15 Ⓐ Ⓑ Ⓒ Ⓓ Ⓔ 30 Ⓐ Ⓑ Ⓒ Ⓓ Ⓔ 45 Ⓐ Ⓑ Ⓒ Ⓓ Ⓔ 60 Ⓐ Ⓑ Ⓒ Ⓓ Ⓔ

WITHDRAWN